*Lion in the
Garden*

Lion in the Garden:

Interviews with
William Faulkner
⋇ 1926-1962 ⋇

*Edited by James B. Meriwether
and Michael Millgate*

University of Nebraska Press
Lincoln and London

Publishers on the Plains

UNP

First Bison Book printing: 1980
Most recent printing indicated by the first digit below:
1   2   3   4   5   6   7   8   9   10

Library of Congress Cataloging in Publication Data

Meriwether, James B   comp.
  Lion in the garden.

    Reprint of the ed. published by Random House, New York.
    Includes index.
    1. Faulkner,   William,   1897–1962—Interviews. 2. Authors,
American—20th century—Interviews.   I.   Millgate, Michael.   II.
Title.
[PS3511.A86Z892   1980]   813'.52   80–17080
ISBN 0–8032–3068–0
ISBN 0–8032–8108–0 (pbk.)

Published by arrangement with James B. Meriwether and
Michael Millgate
Manufactured in the United States of America

Acknowledgments

The editors wish to acknowledge the generous assistance of Professor Robert A. Jelliffe, of Professor Donald A. Pizer, of Professor Carvel Collins, and of the several interviewers—most notably Miss Beale, Mlle. Chapsal, Mr. Allen, Mr. Claxton, Mr. Howe and Professor Smith—who supplied information about the circumstances in which the interviews took place.

Introduction

WILLIAM FAULKNER's love of privacy and hatred of publicity lasted from the beginning of his career as a writer until his death nearly forty years later. He was a man of profound courtesy, who tended to treat strangers with an easygoing if reserved informality. But as a writer he early learned to meet the public with an imperviousness to contact, an unyielding formality, which discouraged some—though it often angered the more persistent—of those who sought to invade his privacy. In the right mood and with the right audience, Faulkner was always capable of interviews in which he made extraordinarily illuminating, if deceptively simple-seeming, comments upon his works and working methods, upon art and upon other artists. But such occasions were exceptional. More usual was the situation described by Madeleine Chapsal in the perceptive essay which supplies the title for this volume. At a publisher's garden party in Paris in 1955, she noted the wall of "the most exquisite but the most obdurate politeness" behind which he withdrew, and also his reasons for doing so.

> There is no use looking at Faulkner. You must read him. To someone who has read him, Faulkner has given all that he has, and he knows it. Then one can understand that when he keeps saying "I am a farmer," or "I wrote that book so that I could buy a good horse," it is only another way of putting first things first—what Faulkner wants one to be interested in are his books.

By 1931, when the publication of his sixth novel, *Sanctuary*, resulted in wide publicity for its author, Faulkner had already developed various defenses against invasions of his privacy. He assumed a tone of deadpan, hostile irony in an interview published in a New York newspaper in the fall of that year

—recommending, among other cures for America's troubles, a return to slavery for the Negro. (This tone, one which he permitted himself less frequently later on, is close to that he chose for the introduction he wrote for the Modern Library reissue of *Sanctuary* early in 1932.) And in a lighter vein, the previous summer he made fun of his own evasiveness concerning biographical questions in an interview with the Memphis reporter Marshall Smith:

> I was born male and single at an early age in Mississippi. I am still alive but not single. I was born of a Negro slave and an alligator, both named Gladys Rock. I had two brothers, one Dr. Walter E. Traprock and the other Eagle Rock, an airplane.

When Smith published the interview he commented that this pose "was Faulkner's barrier, the hazard he places about the sensitive part of him that can create such novels as *Soldiers' Pay, Mosquitoes, Sartoris,* and *As I Lay Dying.*" A great deal of misunderstanding would have been avoided if all Faulkner's interviewers had been as perceptive as Mlle. Chapsal and Mr. Smith.

Faulkner's attitude toward the world of literary publicity and advertising came naturally to him, and had been established long before *Sanctuary* made him newsworthy. To his friend Phil Stone he relinquished most of the responsibility for seeing to the publication of his first book, a volume of poetry. (Stone also wrote the preface and paid for the printing costs.) A telegram Stone sent the publisher in September 1924 reveals Faulkner's attitude, one that remained unaltered for the rest of his life. Faulkner, Stone cabled, "TELLS ME TO AUTHORIZE YOU TO USE ANY FACTS REAL OR IMAGINARY THAT YOU DESIRE TO USE IN THE BOOK OR ADVERTISING MATTER."[1] Though he supplied accurate data about himself for early editions of *Who's Who,* Faulkner remained consistently indifferent to the errors which marred nearly all accounts of his career, including some by people like Stone who knew him, or thought they did, fairly well. The interviews, capsule biographies for the dust jackets of his books, and articles about him which were submitted to Faulkner for correction contain as much misinformation as those which were not. He held to the old-fashioned view that it was his duty to write books, someone else's to publicize them, and as a writer he refused to participate in the standard processes of publicity and advertising. So he got his books written; and so he often had a bad press.

But indifference and a need to save time were not the only elements in Faulkner's attitude toward the proliferation of errors in accounts of his life and career. Presumably there was a certain amount of enjoyment too, since the extent of error could be a measure of how well privacy had been preserved. And a number of wildly untrue (or, as he might have put it himself, unfactual) legends about Faulkner obviously derive, at least in part, from the subject's own love for yarn-spinning. A number of anecdotes about his Hollywood experiences are cases in point; or, perhaps best-known, some of the stories about his having flown with the RAF in France in World War I. For most of his life William Faulkner obviously regarded his own experiences as something to be shared with the public only in the form of fiction.

As his fame grew, so did the number of unwelcome encroachments upon Faulkner's privacy, his energy, and his time. Normally he restrained his feelings but in 1946 he revealed them in a letter to Malcolm Cowley, who had informed him that the Russian writer Ilya Ehrenburg was planning to visit him in Mississippi.

> Thank you for warning me [Faulkner wrote]. What the hell can I do? Goddam it I've spent almost fifty years trying to cure myself of the curse of human speech, all for nothing. Last month two damned swedes, two days ago a confounded Chicago reporter, and now this one that cant even speak english. As if anything he or I either know, or both of us together know, is worth being said once, let alone twice through an interpreter. . . . I can even put up with mankind when I have time to adjust. But I do like to have the chance to invite people to come to look at me and see where I keep my tail or my other head or whatever the hell it is strangers want to come here for. . . . Maybe

the b hasn't realised he's in America now; I still own my home.[2]

But though he did all he could to discourage them, such encroachments became more frequent and more serious during the latter part of Faulkner's career. In 1953 he made a strong but quite unsuccessful attempt to prevent a writer from a weekly pictorial magazine from doing a profile of him. Two years later, in one of his most angry and bitter essays, "On Privacy," Faulkner told the story of that violation—a violation, among other things, of his belief "that only a writer's works were in the public domain, to be discussed and investigated and written about . . . that, until a writer committed a crime or ran for public office, his private life was his own."[3] However, he made it clear that ultimately he blamed not so much the individual magazine and reporter as the entire monstrous American system of publicity and advertising which despised individual privacy and pandered to bad taste.

Even after this episode, which was in some ways a crisis, a turning point in his dealings with the press, Faulkner nearly always managed to restrain his anger and display only indifference or icy politeness to reporters who intruded upon him, unbidden. In 1954, when another such attempt was made, Faulkner again refused, in no uncertain terms, to cooperate. The reporter sought an introduction through Phil Mullen, a Faulkner friend who was a newspaperman himself. "Thank you for calling and giving me that much warning," Faulkner wrote Mullen after refusing to see the reporter. "I can't stop this one coming here and asking questions . . . but tell him he must not worry my mother . . . [If he does], I will help this one make some news indeed . . ." Nevertheless, the reporter attempted to see Faulkner at his home. His own report of the subsequent encounter deserves a place in any collection of Faulkner's interviews.

Mrs. Faulkner greeted me graciously, and while I was talking to her Faulkner came into the room. Unshaven and bare-chested, he had the cold confidence and elemental courtesy of an aristocrat. Absolutely composed, he asked me if Mr. Mullen had told me that he would not see me.

I said he had, but that I felt obliged to get the answer face to face.

Faulkner impressed me as a man who does not like to have the initiative taken away from him. Sincerely wrathful about any interference in his private life, he would not talk about his work or about himself. Nevertheless, my reception at his home was most courteous.[4]

"On Privacy," which Faulkner subtitled "The American Dream: What Happened to It?", is ultimately a profoundly pessimistic document, for its author apparently saw no reasonable hope of curing the evil he described. ("On Fear," the other essay to which Faulkner gave that subtitle, is an equally scathing indictment of an evil, racial injustice in the deep South; to that problem, however, he could see an eventual, if gradual, solution.) But his pessimism about America's treatment of her public figures did not prevent him, during the last years of his life, from repeatedly taking stands, as a public figure and as an American, that paradoxically involved the sacrifice of his privacy.

For during those years, beginning with his acceptance of the Nobel Prize, Faulkner emerged frequently from behind that barrier he had labored so long to maintain between himself and the world. He made speeches at public functions. He organized and headed a committee of writers at the request of the President. He made trips abroad for the Department of State, including the full-scale publicity enterprise of the Nagano Seminars in 1955. He spent several semesters as Writer-in-Residence at the University of Virginia, and consented to the publication in 1959 of a volume of his classroom question-and-answer sessions, *Faulkner in the University*. He made brief appearances at Princeton and at the U.S. Military Academy. He wrote formal articles on public issues and permitted his informal remarks to be tape-recorded and published.

"I have a great deal of work which I want to get done in my lifetime," Faulkner told his audience at Nagano, "and I get more work done if I stay at home and do it than by travelling around." But Faulkner had clearly accepted, along with the Nobel Prize, a measure of responsibility as a public figure, and clearly he had decided to include among his professional duties, as a part of his last years of work as a writer, the speeches and public appearances he made, here and abroad, the teaching he did at Nagano and Virginia, even when they diminished the time he could otherwise have spent writing novels. In November 1955 he could note, in an address to the Southern Historical Association, that in the preceding two years he had seen something ("a little of some, a good deal of others") of Japan, the Philippines, Thailand, India, Egypt, Italy, Germany, England, and Iceland;[5] he could have added Greece, France, and several South American countries to the list. The change in his life and working habits that such a record of travel represented was very great, and, although he published five novels between 1950 and 1962, may have been partially the result of a slowing of his creative energies. But it also represents Faulkner's fidelity to that principle of individual responsibility which he made the subject of a speech in 1952 to the Delta Council of his native Mississippi.

"That's what I am talking about: responsibility," he told his Delta audience. "Not just the right, but the duty of man to be responsible, the necessity of man to be responsible if he wishes to remain free. . . ." Americans, he warned, "true heirs of the old tough durable fathers . . . still capable of responsibility and self-respect," must recall that the right to freedom is a right that must be earned, "that, to be free, a man must assume and maintain and defend his right to be responsible for his freedom."[6]

All his years, as a man and as an artist Faulkner adhered to a remarkably high conception of duty and honor. In his personal life this was apparent again and again in his immense generosity to a variety of people—friends, relatives, servants, younger artists, students. As a writer he was ruthlessly professional, dedicated to his art and capable of making very great sacrifices for it. But the public appearances he made, the public responsibilities he accepted in his last years, do not represent a weakening, as some have supposed, but only a change in Faulkner's conception of his duty as an artist.

Two collections already published in this country have preserved the texts of the tape-recorded interviews and class-room sessions which Faulkner gave at the University of Virginia in 1957-1958 and at West Point in 1962. The intent of the present volume is to collect and make available the texts of his other significant interviews, here and abroad, from the beginning of his career to its end. In addition the texts of the Nagano Seminars, which were edited and published in Japan in 1956, are made available again here.

The contents of this volume are here printed in chronological order according to the date when the interview took place, not by date of original publication. For all except the Nagano interviews, a standard form, Q and FAULKNER, has been substituted for the various forms in the original texts which were used to distinguish between questions and answers, interviewers and Faulkner. Obvious printers' and typists' errors have been silently corrected, and titles and sub-headings supplied by the editorial staffs of newspapers and magazines have been omitted. For consistency's sake, all book and periodical titles have been italicized, and titles of stories, poems, and parts of books have been put in quotation marks.

Editorial annotation has been kept to a minimum, and a good many errors of fact, in both questions and answers, have been left uncorrected. Comprehensive annotation would have been highly repetitious and would have involved the impertinence of attempting to distinguish between intentional and accidental error. Faulkner's interviews, like most others, abound in misstatements and exaggerations. Some of the factual errors in his remarks—his handling of most dates, for instance—were probably unintentional. Others—the reader may supply his own examples—may have been deliberate, the result of his good manners, his sense of humor, his desire for privacy, or all three. Therefore relatively few explanatory notes have been provided, and those only where the editors felt that errors on Faulkner's part were clearly demonstrable

and seemed likely to mislead the reader about significant
matters of fact. These corrections have been supplied in
the headnotes, or in footnotes; all parenthetical or bracketed
editorial interpolations in the texts of the interviews were
supplied by the interviewers themselves, or by their original
editors.

Notes

1. Telegram in the Faulkner Collection of the Humanities Research
   Center, University of Texas.
2. Quoted from the original typescript in the Yale University Library.
   The letter was published in *The Faulkner-Cowley File,* ed. Malcolm
   Cowley, New York, 1966, p. 96.
3. *Essays, Speeches, & Public Letters,* by William Faulkner, New York,
   1966, p. 66.
4. *Newsweek,* August 30, 1954, p. 7.
5. *Essays, Speeches, & Public Letters,* p. 146.
6. *Essays, Speeches, & Public Letters,* pp. 129, 133, 131.

Lion in the

Garden

--**◄ 1926 ►**--

Interview with
a Reporter for the
NEW ORLEANS *ITEM*

In his introduction to the collection of Faulkner's New Orleans
Sketches which he edited (Rutgers University Press, 1958),
Carvel Collins quoted from the earliest published interview
with Faulkner—it obviously dates from the early fall of 1926—
which has yet turned up. According to Professor Collins, his
text was taken from a clipping which was identified only as
having been published in the New Orleans Item, *but a search*
of the files of the Item *has failed to discover the interview, and*
the text printed here therefore consists of the excerpts included
in New Orleans Sketches.

WILLIAM FAULKNER, native of Oxford, Mississippi, who wrote
Soldiers' Pay . . . returned to the Vieux Carre Sunday to plan
a winter's work. Incidentally, he announced the publication
of *Mosquitoes*, another novel.

. . . Mr. Faulkner, sun-tanned from working as a fisherman
on a Pascagoula schooner, and sucking an inscribed pipe, won
last Spring when he shot a hole in one while acting as professional at the Oxford golf club, sat in an apartment in the old
town and watched the rain-splashed roofs. . . .

He told of a summer spent working in a lumber mill, until
a finger was injured, and then on the fishing boats of the

Mississippi coast. At nights, after working hours, he wrote his new book.

Monday, he will return to Oxford for a short stay and at the end of September he will return to this city for the winter.

‒‒◄{ 1931 }►‒‒

Interview with

MARSHALL J. SMITH

During the summer of 1931 Faulkner was interviewed at his home in Oxford by Marshall J. Smith, a reporter for the Memphis Press-Scimitar. A report of the interview appeared in that paper on July 10, 1931, and a much fuller account, accompanied by excellent photographs, was published in the Bookman that December under the title "Faulkner of Mississippi." Both versions of the interview are included here.

The two versions, close enough in some ways, are by no means identical. The longer, later one was obviously worked up carefully from the original notes, but something may have been lost in the process: compare, for example, the two accounts of the writing of Sanctuary and As I Lay Dying. The confusion about Faulkner's wartime service here makes an early appearance, but it is possible that Smith had drawn to some extent upon such published sources as the biographical sketch that had appeared in the February 1930 Wilson Library Bulletin. And he obviously took over directly the account Faulkner had given of himself to Forum when that magazine published "A Rose for Emily" in April 1930, quoting it almost exactly in both versions of his "interview."

PRESS-SCIMITAR *version*

A GREAT VOICE CRYING in the wilderness—the literary wilderness of Mississippi—that is William Faulkner.

This author who has shot from obscurity into fame in the last few months—the man who wrote *Sanctuary*—is living at Oxford, Miss., in Bilboland.

Not only is William Faulkner living, but he is farming, dirt farming with a hoe and a plow. Seventy-five miles south of Memphis lives the man whose praises the New York critics cannot sing too loudly.

Faulkner is author of *Soldiers' Pay, Mosquitoes, Sartoris, Sound and Fury, As I Lay Dying* and *Sanctuary*.

Now he is working on a book of 13 short stories. Many of them have been published before in *Scribner's, Mercury* and *Harper's* magazines. Faulkner's book of short stories will be on the market in November.

The man who wrote of Memphis' "hell holes" in *Sanctuary*, is 33. He is dark, small, keenly alive, virile and as he might term it—touched with a little sadness and a mild sense of frustration.

In the uniform of a British Tommy this Mississippian fought during the World War. He scrubbed decks on a British freight boat in return for passage to Europe. He starved in Paris. He was fired as a postmaster in Oxford, Miss., and climaxed a career of failures with the brilliant achievement —*Sanctuary*.

But the man himself—there are no velvet curtains to be ripped aside, no secretaries or watchdogs set up as barriers. He is at home. Faulkner lives in a house that was showing its age when Gen. Bedford Forrest was "skeerin" the Yankees in 1863.

The Faulkner home on the outskirts of Oxford is a frame building. Simple wooden columns lend gentle dignity. It was built in 1830[1] and surrounded with cedars. An architect from the Old World laid out a garden of magnolias and crepe myrtles.

Today Faulkner sits beneath these cedars. With the sky for a canopy he talks, talks in the cool of the evening—not of books and criticism—but of men, of the fishing in the Tallahatchie, of the corn in the bottoms and all the time cat squirrels chase thru the oaks on the side of the hill.

"The squirrels? Why, yes, they sleep in the attic. See those holes up there where they go in and out."

Serious? Not Faulkner.

He is laughing to himself when he says quite seriously:

"I was born in 1826 of a negro slave and an alligator—both named Gladys Rock. I have two brothers. One is Dr. Walter E. Traprock and the other is Eaglerock—an airplane."

Traprock is a mythical character invented by the humorist, Dr. George Chappell.

"Born male and single at early age in Mississippi. Quit school after five years in seventh grade. Got job in grandfather's bank and learned medicinal value of his liquor.

"Grandfather thought the janitor did it. Hard on janitor. War came. Liked British uniform. Got commission R.F.C. pilot. Crashed. Cost British government 2000 pounds, ($10,000).

"Was still pilot. Crashed. Cost British Government 2000 pounds. Quit. Cost British Government $84.30. King said, 'Well done.'"

Faulkner is married. This modern writer of tragedy had none of the earmarks of a successful novelist when he said "I do" at the proper time in 1928.[2] His account of events leading up to this adventure into matrimony sheds a different light on this Mississippian.

"After working 18 months on my novel *Sound and Fury*, my publishers, Harcourt, (Harcourt, Brace Publishing Co.) refused it.

"Harrison Smith was at that time connected with Harcourt. He left the firm and set up for himself. He obtained from Harcourt the manuscript of *Sound and Fury* and published it.

"We both believed we wouldn't sell a copy. The next year—1928—wrote *Sanctuary*.

"Hal Smith said this was too tough. He wouldn't publish it then.

"Got married that summer. Needed $500. Wrote Smith if he would let me have $500 I would give him a book by the first of March.

"Spent the $500.

"Got a job rolling coal in a power plant. Found the sound of the dynamo very conducive to literature.

"Wrote *As I Lay Dying* in a coal bunker beside the dynamo between working spells on the night shift.

"Finished it in six weeks. Never changed a word. If I ever get rich I am going to buy a dynamo and put it in my house. I think that would make writing easier."

Faulkner says this book *As I Lay Dying* is his best novel. This frank admission and this story of how literature is created comes from the man of whom the late Arnold Bennett said "He writes like an angel."

Today, Faulkner is loafing. He says the luxury and calm, the quiet and solitude of his home so apart from the rest of the world is "conducive to doing nothing."

Notes

1. The house was built in the 1840's by Robert Shegog. Faulkner acquired it in April 1930.
2. The marriage actually took place on June 20, 1929. Smith was consistent in misdating it; his interview later in the same year (see pp. 25–27) with Mrs. Faulkner also assigns the marriage to 1928, as it does the writing of *Sanctuary*, which actually took place early in 1929.

BOOKMAN *version*

SUNDAY MORNING down in Oxford, Mississippi, I found William Faulkner bottling beer in the kitchen. I had come to see the author who had impressed the critics with *The Sound and the Fury*, had been discovered by the intelligent public in *Sanctuary,* and had been surrounded by a chorus of praise as his stories appeared in magazines and his earlier books were reissued—a new luminary in the South, in the very darkest part of the South. It was Faulkner, but not the man I expected. I was looking for an author whose interest was in idiocy, rape, suicide and a lost gentility. Instead I found another William Faulkner. He was squatting on the floor beside a cracked churn siphoning scummy homebrew out through a piece of hose into second-hand ginger ale bottles. Sam, his neighbour, was helping him.

Nick Pappas in the café at Oxford had told me about this Bill Faulkner. He was Murry Faulkner's oldest boy. He went fishing and liked to hunt. He was the man the corner garage owner said was "farmin' an old place an' doin' some moh of that smart writin.' " But surely this was not the author of *Sanctuary.* The man who wrote that masterpiece of realism could not be this unshaven, amateur beer-maker.

Sam went on with the beer. Faulkner lighted his pipe and considered the first question I asked after an introductory explanation.

"Born?" He restated the query to get set for his smart-crack. "Yes. I was born male and single at an early age in Mississippi. I am still alive but not single. I was born of a Negro slave and an alligator, both named Gladys Rock. I had two brothers, one Dr. Walter E. Traprock and the other Eagle Rock, an airplane."

This was Faulkner's barrier, the hazard he places about the sensitive part of him that can create such novels as *Soldiers' Pay, Mosquitoes, Sartoris,* and *As I Lay Dying.* On the surface he was a young Mississippi farmer who didn't mind bottling beer in his kitchen on Sunday. I had to turn elsewhere to learn that he had been born in Ripley, Mississippi, in October, 1897, and that several years afterward the family moved to Oxford where stood the University supported by the state. When he entered the University, of which his father was treasurer, he was enrolled as a special student, but after two years he quit to join the Canadian Flying Corps.

I watched the last of the muddy homebrew drain into a bottle while on the back porch a barefooted nigger stared at fuzzy young cats as he mumbled something to Faulkner about "two bits" being needed "foh cawn meal." The man shuffled off in the dew spinning a quarter in the air. Carrying several pitchers of the new brew we walked out under the shade of cedars that were planted for the admiration of a plantation mistress in 1830. There at a table made from young willows we found rough chairs and conversation.

As Faulkner stood for a moment before sitting down in front of the old house, now gray and rotting but once a white mansion, I recalled the description of Bayard Sartoris who lived "where the dusk was peopled with ghosts of glamorous and old things. And if they were just glamorous enough . . . then they were sure to be disastrous." The phrase "glamorous fatality" seems at times to cloak Faulkner.

But Faulkner is not walking about in a veil of heavy tragedy with the poison cup of Socrates in his hand. While to the critics Faulkner is a figure to be compared with the Russians and is termed a "genius" and one who "writes like an angel," he gives the impression that he is much more interested in where the catfish are biting and how to keep rabbits out of his field peas.

We talked and smoked. We talked of Mississippi politics and of mutual friends in Memphis, where the chief action of *Sanctuary* takes place. The iced pitcher moved about. Gradually the man who created the idiot Benjy in *The Sound and the Fury*, Miss Jenny in *Sartoris* and the sensational Popeye in *Sanctuary* came to sit at the table. Faulkner, the artist, emerged from behind the mask of a Mississippi gentleman.

I asked him about his motive—why it was so hard to understand portions of his books—just what was he trying to convey?

Faulkner relighted his stained cob pipe and sighed at such questions. "Folks try too hard to understand. The public expects too much of present-day novelists. Read a book and let it go at that. You can read it in two days. It takes months to write one. If you can't understand it after reading it, then forget it. Your time and the author's time have been wasted. If a story is in you, it has got to come out. If you have something to say—you can write it—in fact, you have got to write it."

This inner compulsion to give himself to writing may ex-

plain why a novelist of the first rank today prefers to live in
the small Mississippi town of Oxford—the original of Jefferson
of his novels—and why he has no intention of living elsewhere.
"I haven't written a real novel yet," Faulkner confessed.
"I'm too young in experience. It hasn't crystallized enough
for me to build a book upon one of the few fundamental
truths which mankind has learned. Perhaps in five years I can
put it over. Perhaps write a *Tom Jones* or a *Clarissa Harlowe.*"

Two generations ago his grandfather, also William Faulkner, wrote a sentimental novel, *The White Rose of Memphis,*
in which sweetness and virtue triumphed over the powers
of evil.[1] The grandfather pictured the magnolias and myrtle
flowers of the Victorian era but the present William Faulkner
sees and writes of a tragic decadence. His characters come
from among the people with whom he lives.

But there is one character that did not come from Oxford.
He was one of Roark Bradford's boys. Do you remember the
Negro who was hanged in *Sanctuary* and who protested that
his execution would mean the end of the "best baritone singer
in Mississippi"?

"Oh, yes, I stole that character from Roark Bradford,"
Faulkner admitted. "He told me that story one night while
we were just talking. I waited two years for him to use it,
but he never did."

The inspiration—Faulkner would scoff at the word—for
his first novel, *Soldiers' Pay,* came from Sherwood Anderson.
He met Anderson after being fired as postmaster at the
University of Mississippi—according to one version, postal
inspectors complained he was throwing away incoming mail,
particularly newspapers, and unanimously agreed on his re-
moval; another story is that the students beat in vain upon
the doors of the office, crying for their mail while the postmaster sat in the back office with his feet on a table, reading
poetry; while a third and still more libellous version has it
that the future novelist was caught studying life as it is
revealed in private mail.

"I took the rest of the money I had saved as postmaster
and went to New Orleans," Faulkner went on. He rarely
uses the personal pronoun, or slurs it so that you cannot

hear it. "Planned to go to Europe. Met Sherwood Anderson for the first time, although had known his wife in New York. Lived at Anderson's house in New Orleans.

"He suggested to me that I write a novel. As I did not show any inclination to go to work, that might be a good way to avoid it—turn writer.

"In six weeks told Anderson had finished the novel. He offered to write a letter to his publisher, Liveright. He did so without having read a line of the book. He told Liveright it was a fine book and he shouldn't miss it. Liveright accepted the manuscript. For the next three years I was Liveright's bondslave."

Anderson had been feeding and rooming Faulkner for weeks and was willing to pass on the task of providing for a genius. The book had been written in a side street in New Orleans where cheap music accompanied cheaper drinks. Faulkner also wrote poems and sketches for the New Orleans *Double Dealer* and lush stories for the Sunday magazine section of the *Times-Picayune*.

That was in 1925. In the summer of that year the freighter *West Ivis*, carrying a cargo from New Orleans to Genoa, numbered among its crew two rough-bearded young men both bearing the name of William. The one surnamed Spratling was an artist who later exiled himself in Mexico and became a commentator with pen and crayon on Mexican art and folklife. Before the *West Ivis* had landed there had been thrown overboard along with its garbage some dozens of sonnets written by the other William between his duties in the engine room and on deck. It made him feel clean, Faulkner said.

The European jaunt lasted six or eight months, most of it in Italy. Then during his stop of a few weeks in New York Faulkner arranged with Liveright for a second novel and went back to Mississippi to write it, *Mosquitoes*. The writing was not done in Oxford but in a little town down on the Gulf of Mexico, Pascagoula, near Biloxi.

Three of Faulkner's novels have been refused, though today they are highly esteemed. Liveright wouldn't take *Sartoris*. Harcourt, Brace accepted it but balked at *The Sound and the Fury*. Harrison Smith took the manuscript and published it.

Neither Faulkner nor Smith expected the book to sell. "The next year—1928—I wrote *Sanctuary* but Hal Smith said this was too tough and he held it up until I had written *As I Lay Dying.*"

The novel which Faulkner considers his best—*As I Lay Dying*—was written in a coal bunker at Oxford, Mississippi when he was working on the night shift of a power plant. The hum of the dynamo fascinated Faulkner and his book seemed to fairly build itself; it was completed in six weeks. He says he never rewrote a line. "Some day I'm going to buy a dynamo and put it in my work-room."

When I saw him Faulkner was working on a new book, a collection of short stories. He believes that a book of short stories should be linked together by characters or chronology. This collection was to be called *These Thirteen,* the stories dealing with the war, the imaginary town of Jefferson, and a few in other settings.

But away with literature. Sam was bored. He went to the garden where another churn had been "making" for three days and returned with a pitcher of beer. He said something about the corn "needin' rain."

"Then something will have to be done about it," Faulkner said. "I don't mind buying corn to feed my stock but I'd hate to have to buy corn to piece out the fall run with."

We laughed. Then I asked Faulkner what he thought about education. He replied he had spent five years in the seventh grade and the smart-cracking Faulkner, the one that had first greeted me, appeared again:

"Quit school and went to work in grandfather's bank. Learned the medicinal value of his liquor. Grandfather thought it was the janitor. Hard on the janitor. War came. Liked British uniform. Got commission R.F.C. pilot. Crashed. Cost British government 2000 pounds. Was still pilot. Crashed. Cost British government 2000 pounds. Quit. Cost British government $84.30. King said, 'Well done.' Returned to Mississippi."

The war hurt Faulkner. It took him time to recover. He painted roofs at the University of Mississippi at Oxford while he tried to regain what the conflict had taken away. Stark

Young was in Mississippi at that time. He was absorbing material in Oxford that later resulted in *Heaven Trees*.

"Met Stark Young on the street one day," Faulkner said. He laid aside his pipe and smiled as he recalled his adventure. "Young said I should go to New York. He said that was the place to be. Well, that was an idea. I had one hundred dollars. I had been painting, you know. So with sixty dollars of my stake spent for railroad fare I went to New York. Went to see Stark Young—he had said to be sure and come to see him.

"Young wasn't at home. He wasn't at home for a week. Lived on my forty dollars till he got to town. Then I moved in on Young. He had just one bedroom so I slept on an antique Italian sofa in his front room. It was too short. I didn't learn until three years later that Young lived in mortal terror that I would push the arm off that antique sofa while I slept.

"Stayed with Young until he suggested I better get something to do. He helped me to get a place at Lord and Taylor's. I worked in the book department until I got fired. Think I was a little careless about making change or something. Then I came on home."

The success business has never worried Faulkner. He has been fired or quit every job he has ever held. Yet he says:

"We are here to work. It is either sweat or die." Faulkner leaned further back in his chair and put his feet on the table. "Where is there a law requiring we should be happy? A man can be happy doing a tough job well or failing in a tough job. But contentment and happiness come only to vegetables when they sit still, never to man himself because he is the victim of his own thinking and his own sweat.

"Now about education. A man cannot be educated into happiness. The best education can do for him is to enable him to learn something about the history of mankind—that is, the printed word—and the printed word that lasts over centuries has for its skeleton tragedy or despair.

"So when a man learns to read, he learns of the tragedy and despair of his own kind which he himself may suffer. It is better for him not to know this since he may escape it, but once he reads it, it is part of his life—a part of his own experience.

"Let a man fill his days with hard work, then he will fill his nights with sleep. If he does this, he will not have time to outrage moral law. He will lead a pure life in spite of himself."

Note

1. It was Faulkner's great-grandfather, not his grandfather, who wrote *The White Rose of Memphis*. The description of it here is inaccurate, but may have been what Faulkner believed and said.

Interview in
UNIVERSITY OF VIRGINIA
COLLEGE TOPICS

This interview appeared in the University of Virginia under-graduate weekly, College Topics, *on November 2, 1931. The preceding week Faulkner had visited Charlottesville to attend a Southern Writers' Conference and to see his publisher, Harri-son Smith, who was there. After a brief visit to Chapel Hill and the University of North Carolina with Paul Green, he returned to Charlottesville, where he paid his youthful inter-viewer the compliment of what appear to have been some serious answers to questions on the novel, though there is a suspicious recurrence of the tale about his service in France in World War I.*

AS MIDNIGHT STRUCK from a nearby steeple, I knocked at a door on the top floor of the Monticello Hotel. From within came only a faint snoring. Again I knocked, more vigorously. Someone got out of bed and, timorously cracking the door, peeped out at me. I explained who I was and was admitted by Mr. William Faulkner, with many apologies for giving me such an ungodly interview appointment, but he had just returned from Chapel Hill with Mr. Paul Green. Mr. Faulkner offered me a chair and himself reclined on the bed as we talked. A small, very thin, insignificant-looking man with greying black hair cropped close, he seemed almost shy and far from talkative as he answered my questions slowly, deliberately, in few words.

As for biographical details, Mr. Faulkner was afraid his had been a "most ordinary childhood" in rural Mississippi. He quit school at seven, though he admitted he did "right smart reading," he guessed. His favorite books? Ah yes, Conrad's *Nigger of the Narcissus* and Melville's *Moby Dick*. Also, as a child, he and his grandfather read together the whole of a paper bound set of Dumas every year. (On the bureau I noticed a worn paper bound copy of one of Dumas' less important works: at any rate I had never heard of it. Later Mr. Faulkner showed it to me: it was yellowed and smelled of old, cheap paper.) There were no more details interesting enough to cite, he said, till he entered the War with the British and went into action in France.

After that he began to write, though he has "never yet started to write a novel." The plot for a novel? It's "anything that moves you enough to keep working on it. A story usually makes its own plot, works itself out as you go." No, he had nothing definite to say in his work—no special program. He usually begins with a character and just starts writing.

The novel form as we know it, Mr. Faulkner is certain, will break down completely; there are too many written these days. But there will always be a market for stories. Most people are just finding out about this thing, reading. And as to the why of writing novels, it's "usually the money question," and the demand of one's publishers, who not only set the dead line, but suggest the topic and length of your story.

The merit of these books is another question. Asked about the most significant literature being produced in the world today, Mr. Faulkner said very decidedly that there is none being produced. He once thought, he said, that Russia was producing work of lasting merit, but he has outgrown that delusion. The South? Nothing of any real value is likely to come out of it in the next twenty-five years at least. The outstanding Southern authors of today are only the pioneers:

their own work is setting the pace, but not very significant in itself.

Modern American life? Well, throwing by the board all discussion of the era of leisure and the triumph of man over his machines, "life," Mr. Faulkner said, "is more an itch than anything else." It is not a thing we plan out and systematize. To him, the most outstanding feature of modern America is its idle women, supported by our way of life. Ordinarily they would have to take in washing or do scrub work, but not in this land of opportunity.

Returning to the subject of the novel and its inevitable breakdown, Mr. Faulkner had a very interesting idea, centering about the thesis that Dostoevski could have written the *Brothers* in one third the space had he let the characters tell their own stories instead of filling page after page with exposition. In the future novel, or fiction—Mr. Faulkner contends —there will be no straight exposition, but instead, objective presentation, by means of soliloquies or speeches of the characters, those of each character printed in a different colored ink. Something of the play technique will thus eliminate much of the author from the story. And the consequent loss of personality? Is not all writing interesting and important only insofar as it expresses the personality of the author? All exclusive of the story, Mr. Faulkner says, is dead weight. What is interesting in Dickens is not the way he takes things, but "those people he wrote about and what they did."

Movie technique and current cynicism? Mr. Faulkner knows nothing about them.

Interview in
NEW YORK HERALD TRIBUNE

*After leaving Charlottesville, Virginia, at the end of October
1931, Faulkner went on to New York, where he spent several
weeks before returning to Oxford in time for Christmas. This
interview in the* Herald Tribune *for November 14, 1931, was
originally headlined "Slavery Better for the Negro, Says Faulkner"; Faulkner and the reporter had clearly been out of sympathy with each other, and Faulkner obviously allowed his
irritation with the questioning to emerge in his comments on
racial problems, politics, and book reviews.*

WILLIAM FAULKNER, the Mississippi novelist, who has been
called the Dostoievsky of the South, revealed himself yesterday
in an interview as a curious mixture of the modern and the
conservative, a Southern sage who reads scarcely at all, thinks
the Negroes were better off under slavery, and votes Democratic to protect his property.

Arnold Bennett said of him, "He writes like an angel."
But Mr. Faulkner hates interviews, hates being asked questions,
and "Ah don't care much about talkin'," he says. He is a
pleasant, somewhat embarrassed young man, until he gets
interested in something he is saying, when he speaks with
assurance. He answers questions slowly, almost reluctantly,
in a Southern drawl so low that he is a little difficult to
understand.

Mr. Faulkner is a writer, and has been one since he was

a boy, but it is only in the last year or two that he has had any public recognition. "I never sold a short story until about a year ago. For about six years I didn't average more than $100 a year from my writing. I finished one novel and pretty near finished another one before I sold the first."

But he is not the kind of author to whom market difficulties offer a real obstacle. "That didn't have anything to do with it. I'd have gone on writing just the same. Anybody would, that had anything to say."

He met his first literary opposition early, when he was a student at the University of Mississippi, where he contributed poetry to the college magazine. "I was the only man I ever heard of that was black-balled from the literary society down there."

The people down in Oxford, Miss., where he lives, do not think he is a great man. Mr. Faulkner says most of them think he is merely lazy. "A lot of them don't know I write books, and they think I don't do anything at all. The bookstore in Oxford only sells school-books. The drug store down there has some of my books—some times."

Mr. Faulkner thinks the Southern Negroes would be better off under the conditions of slavery than they are today. He pictures a kind of "benevolent autocracy" as the ideal condition for the Negroes, though he admits such a system would not be sound theoretically. "Facts don't fit theories very often," he says, "but I never heard or read about a lynching in the slave days."

"The Negroes would be better off because they'd have some one to look after them. I don't think it would be as good for the white peoples as for the Negroes to have slavery come back—theoretically, anyhow."

But when asked if he thought slavery would soften the white slave owners, he said, "Most white men wouldn't need very much softening."

He believes that Negroes are like children in many of their reactions, and when asked to explain Negro artists, he simply said, "Well, most artists are children, too."

He refused to take any stock in the notion prevalent in

certain circles of literary New York, that all Negroes are born artists of one kind or another, any more than he would believe that the Southern "poor whites" had a deep-rooted fear of the Negro, based on the latter's physical or mental superiority. He said he had never been to a party where there were Negroes, but said that if he went to one he would shake hands and in general behave like a sophisticated New Yorker.

It is unlikely that he will find himself in this position, however, as he admits he dislikes literary parties, and he finds New York's liquor "just like tea" after the moonshine of Mississippi. "They've been making corn liquor down there ninety years and it's pretty good now."

The author grew almost perversely vague when he was asked questions about books. He was definite, however, about reviews. "I never read them," he said. "Maybe my friends have some influence with me about my books," he responded to another question. "I don't know. I like to think nobody's got any influence, but you can't tell."

He refused, with some justification, to name his favorite author. "The two books I like best are *Moby Dick* and *The Nigger of the Narcissus*," he said, "but I wouldn't say Melville or Conrad was 'my favorite author.' I'd just like to have written those two books more than any others I can think of." He admires the work of Ernest Hemingway, whom he has never met. "I think he's the best we've got," he said.

Asked about the stories in *These 13*, one or two of which have been mentioned by literary critics as showing signs of Hemingway's influence, he said they had been written four or five years ago. Mr. Faulkner never read any of Hemingway's work until two years ago. The possibility of his having influenced Hemingway is ruled out by the fact that the stories in question had never been published in any form until *These 13* was issued last month.

Mr. Faulkner is interested in politics, but not national politics. He is aware that the Democrats will probably control the House of Representatives in the next Congress, but it seems to affect him like the election of a very distant relative to office. He votes mostly for town and county officers down in Mississippi. "I vote Democratic because I'm a property owner. Self-protection," he says.

The author of *Sanctuary, As I Lay Dying* and *The Sound and the Fury* arrived in New York on November 4, and will be here for a month longer.

1931

Interview in

THE NEW YORKER

This little piece—perhaps better described as a treatment than as an interview—was published in the "Talk of the Town" section on November 28, 1931, under the heading "Oxford Man": it contains, considering its brevity, more than its share of biographical errors. A comparison with the piece which The New Yorker *did on Faulkner in 1953 suggests how consistent the magazine's style has remained over the years.*

WILLIAM FAULKNER, whose violent novels about the darker reaches of the soul have been attracting increasing interest latterly, is now occupying an apartment in Tudor City and will be there until the middle of December. He spends most of his days alone, working on his next novel, which is to be called *Light in August*. It's about a quarter done. Invitations have poured in on him, but he's been to only one literary party, one given by his publishers. The usual crowd was there. Faulkner is very Southern, his "a"s very broad. This is his second visit. He was here four years ago while still obscure. He was born in Oxford, Mississippi, thirty-four years ago and that has been his home ever since. He owns a small cotton plantation and lives on it, with his wife and two children, in a fine old house built in 1818. In 1915 he enlisted in the Canadian air force and went to France. He crashed behind his own lines. He was hanging upside down in his plane with both legs broken when an ambulance got to him.

He heard one of the men say: "He's dead all right," but had strength enough to deny this. After he recovered he transferred to the American air force. He has a pilot's license now[1] and sometimes flies a rather wobbly plane owned by a friend in Oxford. After the war he studied about five months in the University of Mississippi, which is at Oxford, and of which his father is secretary. That is the extent of his higher education. In Oxford he spends much time writing. "Ah write when the spirit moves me," he says, "and the spirit moves me every day." For relief he fishes, hunts, and bosses the plantation. Only a few of the townspeople know he writes at all; most of them think he's lazy. The local drugstore ordered several copies of his last novel but didn't do very well with them. His mother reads every line he writes, but his father doesn't bother and suspects his son is wasting his time.

Note

---

1. It is unlikely that Faulkner held a pilot's license earlier than 1933.

Mrs. William Faulkner
Interviewed by
MARSHALL J. SMITH

As the opening paragraphs of the interview make clear, Mrs. Faulkner was on her way to New York to join her husband toward the end of his 1931 visit there. Smith, whom she may already have met when he interviewed Faulkner the previous summer, apparently saw Mrs. Faulkner in Memphis on Monday, November 30, the day before the interview was published in the Memphis Press-Scimitar.

WILLIAM FAULKNER, the solemn-faced novelist of Oxford, Miss., is going "Hollywood."

This news about the sad-eyed author of *Sanctuary* and five other as startlingly different novels was revealed by Mrs. Estelle Faulkner, his wife, before she left Memphis Monday night for New York.

"Billy is working on a manuscript for a movie now," Mrs. Faulkner said, referring to her husband as "Billy." "You know, Tallulah Bankhead is to use the story. It seems strange, perhaps, but I went to school with Tallulah in Virginia."

Mrs. Faulkner was enthusiastic about her trip East. She is young, has reddish-brown hair and friendly eyes. She is slender; an animated, vivid person. Besides being the wife of the now famous author, she is the mother of two children.[1]

A concocter of foreign dishes, Mrs. Faulkner prides herself in catering to her husband's peculiar relish for rare foods.

Her curries and dishes she learned while living in Shanghai are the particular delight of the Mississippi author.

Besides *Sanctuary*, Faulkner has written *As I Lay Dying*, *The Sound and the Fury*, *Sartoris*, *Mosquitoes* and *Soldiers' Pay*. His latest book is a collection of short stories entitled *These 13*. Eastern critics have been applauding Faulkner's writings for more than year. He usually employs Mississippi settings.

"I don't think Billy writes such good short stories," Mrs. Faulkner said. "I don't think he understands them. Novels? Now that is different. I think his best work is *As I Lay Dying* —that is his best work so far. I believe his greatest novel is yet to come.

"Did I understand *Sanctuary* the first time I read it? Well, that's hardly fair. No, I didn't. When we were married in 1928, he began what he termed my education. He gave me James Joyce's *Ulysses* to read. I didn't understand it. He told me to read it again. I did and understood what Mr. Joyce was writing about.

"Then I tried to read *Sanctuary* in manuscript form. I couldn't get the meaning. But the second time, with *Ulysses* for a background, it wasn't difficult. I've read it a third time but I don't think it is his best at all."

But the life of an author's wife is not all roses, according to Mrs. Faulkner.

"There are times when Billy will go into his workroom and stay for hours. He hasn't any key, so he takes the door knob off and carries it inside with him. No one can get in and he is quite secure.

"He is difficult to get along with when he is working hard on something. He does most of his work in the morning. He never writes at night. There are no lights in that room."

According to Mrs. Faulkner, the noise and confusion of a city do not go well with her husband's writings. He prefers the old two-story house on the outskirts of Oxford.

"The reason I'm going to New York is to keep people away from him. He has an apartment on the 28th floor of a building and his last letter said that he liked it better, for he could forget the noise and see the sun and sky.

"When I said Billy liked rare dishes, don't think there is anything the matter with his appetite. He eats tremendous breakfasts of fruits, eggs, broiled steak and coffee. He drinks unlimited quantities of coffee."

While in New York, Faulkner has been working on his movie manuscript. The couple expect to return to Oxford for Christmas and will probably go to California in the spring if the material for the picture develops.

Note

1. The son and daughter of her first marriage, with Cornell Franklin.

Interview with

HENRY NASH SMITH

Smith, who was then teaching at Southern Methodist University, saw Faulkner in Oxford shortly before this interview was published in the Dallas Morning News, *February 14, 1932. It is the best of the early interviews, and much of its excellence obviously derives from Smith's sympathetic familiarity with Faulkner's work and from the trouble he had taken to read book reviews and earlier interviews, notably that with Marshall J. Smith.*

Smith has recently recalled (in an interview with one of the editors, January 29, 1966) that he was working part-time for the Dallas Morning News *and had been sent to cover the initiation of an air route between Dallas and Jackson, Mississippi. When he got to Jackson he took the train to Oxford, primarily to consult with Faulkner about the forthcoming publication of* Miss Zilphia Gant *by the Book Club of Texas, for which Smith was to write a sympathetic introduction. Although it might seem that Faulkner sought deliberately to mislead his interviewer on such matters as his wartime service and his reading of* Ulysses, *Smith's impression is that this was rather the result of Faulkner's natural reserve: he simply preferred not to talk about his private life or about the technical aspects of his work.*

GOING TO SEE WILLIAM FAULKNER, author of *The Sound and the Fury*, *As I Lay Dying*, and *Sanctuary*, was not an undertaking to be entered upon lightly. One had heard all sorts

of wild, preposterous legends—that he went habitually bare-
foot; that he ran a distillery at his Oxford, Mississippi, home
for which he raised the corn himself; that he was peremptory
with casual callers. And though Arnold Bennett had said that
Faulkner "writes like an angel," Henry Canby had put him
at the head of the "School of Cruelty" in contemporary
American fiction.

But the pretext of a slight matter of business which I might
logically discuss with him was too good an opportunity to be
lost. I got into an American Airways plane and went to Mississippi to see him.

I found him, a small man in a blue shirt and carpet slippers,
standing before a coal fire in a front room of his delightful
old house on the outskirts of Oxford, built before the Civil
War, and now in the process of a gentle renovation to prepare
it as the residence of Faulkner and his wife.

From the window could be seen two rows of magnificent
cedars leading to a small formal garden laid out in circular
beds outlined in brick around a prodigious magnolia tree.
The sky was gray, the fire hissed quietly, the setting was subdued, but it had a hint of somberness which made it seem
eminently appropriate for the workings of the imagination
which had conceived Quentin Compson, though it was a little
too tranquil for Popeye of *Sanctuary*. One must go to the
sullen red of the clay hillsides of the country around Oxford,
perhaps, to find a hint of the tensions of such a character.

And as Faulkner spoke—later—of how hard it was to get
any work out of a colored boy and girl employed about the
place because they would stand for hours, one holding a mop
and the other a broom, gazing into one another's eyes, I could
see also the source of much of the limpid comedy of his negro
characters.

But for the present there was the annoyance of a self-intro-
duction and the first few difficult minutes necessary for the
tentative establishment of any acquaintance. We talked first
of Oxford. Faulkner had loved the Mississippi town as it was
in his boyhood, before billboards and electric signs invaded
the quiet, when a two-story gallery had surrounded the square.
The lawyers had their offices upstairs overlooking the court-

house and in the afternoons used to sit with their feet on
the railing. Sometimes they chewed tobacco. Faulkner, his
feet resting comfortably on a table, declared for these second-
story galleries. "The most comfortable place to sit I've ever
found," he said, "is a hickory chair and a post."

Bit, a small smoke-colored kitten, nuzzled into his lap.
He stroked her gently as he talked. "I raised this cat from a
kitten," he said. "Her mother went off and left her and I fed
her with a rag soaked in milk." He was reminded to send
Jack, the negro boy, into town for some meat.

Like many writers, Faulkner is disinclined to talk about
his books, but he is Mississippian enough to be polite about
questions. He showed me his work table—a small typewriter
table with curving legs, on which rested a sort of metal rack
holding a completed page of manuscript. There were also
several sheets of typewriter paper ruled in pencil about two
inches from the top and, vertically, two inches from the left
side. He writes with a fountain pen in a beautiful and almost
illegible hand, leaving the generous margins at the top and
side for revision. When he has finished a book he copies it
himself on the typewriter.

He put the cat down and walked across the room to a pile
of papers on the floor. "I bind my own manuscripts," he said,
showing me a carbon copy of *As I Lay Dying*, which he had
bound in cardboard with librarian's tape.

Then it was time to build up the fire again, and when he
had settled himself I tried to find out something about his
sources. Almost every critic who has commented on *The Sound
and the Fury* has thought that Mr. Faulkner must have derived
his method from Joyce. But no. "I have never read *Ulysses*,"
he said, reaching over to his table to hand me a 1924 edition
of the book. "Until recently I had never seen a copy."

I took it that a friend had lent the book to him during
his recent visit to New York.

"But surely you had some idea of modern experimentation
with the technique of the novel," I insisted, perhaps a little
too vigorously.

"You know," he smiled, "sometimes I think there must be
a sort of pollen of ideas floating in the air, which fertilizes

similarly minds here and there which have not had direct
contact. I had heard of Joyce, of course," he went on. "Some
one told me about what he was doing, and it is possible that
I was influenced by what I heard. When I started to write
The Sound and the Fury, however, I had no idea of writing
the book it finally became. It simply grew from day to day,
and it was not until the book was finished that I realized I
had in it the anecdote of the girl who ran away with the man
from the traveling show."

Perhaps the most striking incident in Faulkner's last book,
These 13, deals with an Indian chieftain in Northern Mississippi back in the early 1800's who found a grounded steam-
boat and made his slaves transport it overland with rollers
to make him a house. I asked Faulkner where he ran on this
incident.

"I just invented it," he said, smiling again. "It just seemed
to me an awfully good story, that chief making the slaves
move that boat, and hunting them through the woods with
dogs when they tried to escape."

But for the most part he draws upon his intimate knowledge of the townspeople and the inarticulate, tense tenant
farmers of the countryside, characters like those in *As I Lay
Dying*. Faulkner knows these people. "There is no violent
contrast between hill country and bottom land in this section,"
he said, "but I can tell hill folks from bottom folks by seeing
them on the street. The hill women hold their heads high
and stride out from the hips. The women from the bottom
look like dried-up cows that don't earn their keep. These
people are of the same stock as the Tennessee mountaineers,
but they are slower. They'd shoot you if you offended them,
but they wouldn't shoot you before breakfast."

I tried to get him to talk about his experiences with the
British air forces in France. I had heard that during the war
he had been pulled out, more dead that alive, from under
a couple of wrecked planes. But he didn't have much to say
about that. "I just smashed them up," he said. He was interested, however, in the fact that I had come from Dallas
to Jackson in a trimotored cabin plane. "I've never ridden
in a cabin plane," he said. "I'd like to have a chance to

fly one. I was looking at the inside of one some time ago. They don't have the old stick—a steering wheel instead. I guess the plane couldn't be steered by one man's strength—they need a wheel with gears."

But he still refused to say much about the war.

I asked him if he enjoyed writing. "It's right smart fun," he said, reflectively, as if the idea had never occurred to him to wonder whether he liked it or not. "I usually get to work pretty early in the morning, and by 10:30 or 11 I'm through. But I can sit down and write almost any time. The stories seem to shape themselves as they go along. I'm working on two novels now, and it may take me two years to finish one of them."

Of his own books, he tends to like *As I Lay Dying* best, although he seems to think it is hardly worth while classifying them as better or worse. He is somewhat apologetic about his earlier work; but in general he has a very objective attitude toward his writings, and seems to take them as facts of nature, like the rain, about which one does not feel impelled to pass judgment, good or bad. He has no theory of fiction, but he does feel that he has passed through three stages in his attitude toward people and thus in his attitude toward his own characters. "There is the first stage," he said, "when you believe everything and everybody is good. Then there is the second, cynical stage when you believe that no one is good. Then at last you come to realize that everyone is capable of almost anything—heroism or cowardice, tenderness or cruelty." I think that is his attitude now.

And so I left. Faulkner, at the end of our conversation as at the beginning, was a quiet, courteous man, unobtrusive and not very much impressed with himself, a little amused at the sudden enthusiasm of Eastern cities for books a good deal like his earlier ones, which they did not even bother to read or dismissed without comment. He is much interested in the new draperies which Mrs. Faulkner is planning for the living room of their very fine old house, and he seemed prouder of the hand-hammered locks on the doors than of anything he has written.

·◄{ 1 9 3 7 }►·

Interview in

MEMPHIS COMMERCIAL
APPEAL

This brief interview, dated from Oxford the previous day, was published on November 18, 1937. Faulkner had left Hollywood the preceding August, not to return until the summer of 1942. Probably the novel he was working on was The Wild Palms, *published in January 1939.*

———

WILLIAM FAULKNER[1] thinks Hollywood is an over-grown country town, hasn't read *Gone With the Wind* and believes his best novel has yet to be written.

The author of *Sanctuary* and other best-sellers of recent years, home following a stay of several months in New York and Hollywood, also announced the publication of a new book, *Unvanquished,* a collection of short stories, to appear in February.

"My general impression of Hollywood," he said, "is that of a very wealthy, over-grown country town. In fact, it reminds me very much of a town that has sprung up as the result of an oil boom. I know very few actors, but the ones with whom I did come in contact were normal, hard-working people, leading much saner lives than we are led to believe."

While in Hollywood, Mr. Faulkner wrote scripts for several successful pictures, but he said he prefers novels and doesn't plan to return to the movie capital.

"I don't like scenario writing," he explained, "because

I don't know enough about it. I feel as though I can't do myself justice in that type of work, and I don't contemplate any more of it in the near future."

His reason for not having read *Gone With the Wind* is that it is "entirely too long for any story." Nor has he read *Anthony Adverse* for the same reason: That no story takes 1000 pages to tell.

Mr. Faulkner is at present working on a novel that he expects to complete by next Summer, although he said it may take longer. "I have turned out books in as short a time as six weeks," he explained, "but sometimes it takes as long as a year and a half, time depending on the amount of concentration necessary."

In describing the actual writing of a novel, Mr. Faulkner said he always makes his first draft in longhand, then makes revisions and rewrites when he types out his manuscript for the publisher.

Mr. Faulkner quickly admitted he hasn't written his "best novel," that it is yet to come. He didn't care to discuss possibilities of his book now in progress.

He announced his intentions of remaining at his picturesque Oxford home for some time, or until he completes his book at least.

Note

1. The name was spelled "Falkner" throughout in the original text.

Interview in
NEW ORLEANS *ITEM*

This interview was published in the "Carrier Edition" of the New Orleans Item *on April 5, 1939, over the initials "M. A."— probably those of Mike Amrine, who was doing interviews for the* Item *at this period and who had published an interview with Bertrand Russell a few days earlier, signing his full name. Particularly interesting are Faulkner's comments on* The Wild Palms, *which should be compared with the rather different accounts he gave in the* Paris Review *and* Nagano *interviews, and the indication that while he was working on* The Hamlet *he had the subsequent volumes of the Snopes trilogy already in mind.*

WILLIAM FAULKNER, the writer whose books about Southern poor whites and more poor Negroes have pictured Southern decay, degeneration and doom, passed through New Orleans this morning and said quite a few good words for the South.

"The South seems to be the only place in the country that is interested in art these days," he said at the home of friends who were preparing to take him on a three-day fishing trip. "Maybe it's because the North is more industrialized than we are. Maybe in 80 years we'll be as highly industrialized and we'll quit turning out art."

Faulkner, who's lived most of his life in the little town of Oxford, Miss., and who still lives there with his wife and 6-year-old daughter, has a picture in his mind of "maybe a

Keats coming out of the backwoods, a hardshell Baptist with a celluloid collar and a short tie, who writes good poetry." He thinks maybe this backwoods Keats will show up one of these days.

Faulkner doesn't have any hopes for the scores of would-be writers who are living down in the French Quarter, sitting around in cafes and bars nightly talking about what they're going to write. Faulkner lived in the Quarter himself around 1925, wrote his first published book, *Soldiers' Pay,* down there. "But the fellows who are going places are too busy working to sit around and talk about it."

Faulkner is a short, delicately built man, with a slender face, medium-sized mustache, and a rather high-pitched voice. His dark black eyes are his strongest feature, and they're more impressive for their brilliance than their expressiveness. He's not expressive, demonstrative, or really sociable, and he doesn't like to talk about writing.

His novels are acute and keen studies of Southern characters, generally drawn from the lower economic levels. They contain a good many horrible and gruesome incidents. *The Wild Palms,* his latest book, is really two books. He wrote one story and thought it was good but not enough. So he wrote another and slipped the chapters of the two in between each other like shuffling a deck of cards, only not so haphazardly. "I played them against each other," he said. "Contrapuntally."

It's interesting to note that he, himself, can't read his writings sometimes. But that's only when they're in manuscript. He writes in an extremely pinched hand which goes back to the days when he had to economize on writing paper. It is even and fine, but to any one else not only looks like, but is as unreadable as Greek. He says he can't read it if he leaves it for a time.

The days when he was a struggling and unknown writer have left a slight touch of bitterness in him. The writing business, "which is a job," would be all right "if you didn't have to stop and boil the pot now and then." He doesn't consider any of his books pot-boilers, but was alluding to other work he couldn't bring himself to mention.

On the other hand, when he was making fabulous sums in Hollywood he wasn't happy, either. "It isn't money you make out there. It comes and goes. It's just tokens."

He's now working on a three-volume novel he began in New Orleans 15 years ago. He'd have finished it sooner, but for boiling the pot.

It's about a poor white who comes to a little Southern town and teaches the populace corruption in government and. . . .

Interview with
MICHEL MOK

First published in the New York Post, *October 17, 1939, this is one of the few interviews in which Faulkner spoke at all freely of work in progress—although the episode involving Montgomery Ward Snopes did not appear in* The Hamlet *the following year but in* The Town *(not published until 1957), and then in a much revised version which omitted Senator Clarence Snopes. The interview also contains the fullest elaboration until the 1956* Paris Review *interview of the Louisiana shrimp-fishing background of some of Faulkner's early movie-making experiences.*

WILLIAM FAULKNER, the beardless Dostoievsky of the cane-brakes, was having lunch at the Plaza Hotel. That the specialist in the more harrowing phases of life among the white trash should take his meals at New York's sturdiest citadel of elegance was incongruous enough in itself, but it wasn't the only thing that amazed this reporter, who was the novelist's guest.

You could have knocked The Post man over with the Sherman statue when he discovered that Mr. Faulkner, whom he had imagined as a light-shy, morose and misanthropic creature, was a jolly little man who likes nothing better than telling droll yarns between puffs of a well-seasoned pipe.

The author of *Sanctuary, Pylon, Absalom, Absalom!* and

The Wild Palms, who is forty-two, looks like a country squire, and there's reason why he should. When he isn't putting nasty people on paper he bosses his cotton plantation near Oxford, Miss., where he lives with his family in a fine 120-year-old house.

He has iron-gray hair, sly, dark-brown eyes, aquiline features, a ruddy complexion and a bristly little black mustache. In his rough herringbone tweeds there is about him something of the outdoor Englishman—until he talks. Then he drawls in an accent so heavily Southern that one suspects he may have some difficulty in understanding himself.

Mr. Faulkner talked of the Snopes family, ruling clan of Jefferson, Miss., a mythical community of misfits familiar to the readers of his work, and of his now almost legendary adventures as a film-script writer in Hollywood and elsewhere.

If you have dipped into his books you must be acquainted with at least some of the members of the Snopes tribe, who pop in and out of the Faulkner novels much in the manner of some of the characters in Balzac's "Comédie Humaine."

There is, for instance, young Virgil Snopes (in *Sanctuary*), who rented a room in a Memphis bordello without being aware of the nature of the establishment. So sure was he that he was living in a respectable rooming house that, when setting forth on an occasional spree of his own, he sneaked out the back door to avoid questioning and possible chiding by his "landlady."

Your reporter enjoyed the privilege of hearing an as yet unpublished Snopes tale, dealing with Montgomery Ward Snopes, named for the mail-order catalogue. This estimable citizen will figure prominently in a book about the family to be brought out by Random House.

"The Snopeses," said Mr. Faulkner, "are a family who, by petty chicanery and unscrupulous politics, take possession of the county town of Jefferson, Miss. They creep over it lahk mold over cheese and destroy its traditions and whatever lav'liness there was in the place.

"Ah've often written about them in mah other books and stories, but foh fifteen years Ah've also been puttin' them

into a novel of their own. It's goin' to be a big book, three
or foh volumes. The fust volume is finished now. Ah've come
to N'Yawk to see about its publication.

"It's a humorous book—Ah mean it's a tribe of rascals who
live by skullduggery and practice it twenty-foh hours a day.
Take Montgomery Ward Snopes. In the World War he was
a Y.M.C.A. secretary. When he came back to the old home
town he had a wad of money, earned, he said, by buyin' left-
over stocks of cigarettes and candy and sellin' them cheap
to the soldiers.

"Putty soon the boys of the town discovered that Montgomery Ward had brought back a collection of French post-
cards, which he showed, for a fee, in a shack behind his house.
His cousin, a State Senator in Jacksonville,[1] heard about the
pictures and demanded to see them. As he was the most
pahful member of the family, Montgomery Ward obliged.

"When the cousin had seen enough, he sent the cards back.
A political enemy, who long had been plannin' the Senator's
undoin' brought him up on charges of sendin' obscene matter
through the mails. The Senator was arrested. Other influ-
ential members of the tribe almost got him off on a tech-
nicality but the Senator insisted on makin' a long speech in
cote. Even the jedge tried to stop him but his forensic impulse
got the better of him and he talked himself raht into jail."

By this time, almost everybody knows the famous Faulkner
Hollywood anecdote—how he signed a contract that didn't
specify a definite story assignment; how the producers told
him to go home until he was called, and how they found
him—in Oxford, Miss.—when they next needed him on a
dialogue job.

But there are few who know what happened when his
Hollywood employers finally located him by long-distance
phone. They told him to proceed at once to New Orleans,
there join a director, and work with the megaphone man on
a story with a shrimp-fishing background.

"A few days after Ah got to N'Orlee-ans," said Mr. Faulkner, "specially chartered planes began to arrive loaded with
technicians, carpenters and cameramen. They started buildin'
a complete fishin' village. When they'd been at it a week or

so, the cull-ed people would come in parties, with their children and their lunch baskets, to see the white folks workin' and that wonderful village goin' up.

"Meanwhile, Ah'd asked the continuity writer to give me the script so Ah could begin writin' the dialogue. He refused. He told me to write the dialogue fust and look at the story afterward. Ah wrangled with him foh putty near three weeks. Then a letter came by airmail—Faulkner was fired. Ah was jest walkin' off the lot when a second letter was delivered. The director was fired."

Note

1. Faulkner presumably said "Jackson."

---❈ 1940 ❈---

Interview with

DAN BRENNAN

This piece, originally published under the title "Journey South," is not strictly speaking an interview, and it was first published in the University of Kansas City Review, XXII *(Autumn 1955), more than fifteen years after the meeting between Brennan and Faulkner took place in 1940. Brennan, who himself published novels in the years between 1940 and 1955, wrote up the original incident in a fairly elaborate manner, but "Journey South" seems nonetheless to demand a place in this particular volume because of the picture it offers of Faulkner at work and, more specifically, because of its preservation of some characteristic Faulknerian "interview" comments. See also Russell Roth, "The Brennan Papers,"* Perspective, II *(Summer 1949); this is the article which Brennan mentions on p. 47.*

IN MAY, 1940, a young man in faded blue jeans, with his head full of glory and war names: Spitfire, Hurricane, Messerschmitt, the British retreat in France—and readings of Faulkner's World War I flying stories, together with a pocket full of impressionistic poetry about the Mississippi countryside —got down from a cotton truck on which he had hitchhiked a ride into Oxford, Mississippi.

"Do you know where Faulkner lives?" the young man in cotton tennis shirt asked the truck driver.

The driver looked down, puzzled, from his perch high in

the truck cab. Sunlight hammered down heat on the stone head of the Confederate soldier in the town square. Mules passed, heads bobbing drowsily in the windless bright afternoon.

"Faulkner?" said the man in the truck cab. "Don' he own a farm out south a piece?"

"No," the young man said. "He's a writer."

The driver shook his head.

"Don' know him. Man named Faulkner got a farm out a piece." He pointed across the square.

"Okay—thanks," said the young man. He looked about nineteen as he crossed the street and entered a drug store. He carried a battered leather suitcase.

Setting the suitcase down in front of the telephone booth, he found the name in the book. When he called, a woman answered. Her voice was soft, quite pleasant.

"Mr. William Faulkner live there?" the young man asked.

There was no sound for an instant on the wire.

Then the woman's voice, different now, careful, guarded: "Who's calling, please?"

"I'm just a college student from up north," said the young man. "I've always liked Mr. Faulkner's books, and I'd like to meet him. I'm passing through." He hoped he had sounded simple and direct.

"Will you hold the line, please?"

Again only the wire hum. She's going to come back with some excuse, thought the young man. He waited. For a moment he thought the line was dead, cut off. Then he heard the voice, a man's voice, at once slow and measured: "Yes?"

"Mr. Faulkner?"

"Yes." The same patient, slow measured tone. Later, the young man thought that even then he could feel those black, motionless eyes over the telephone wire. He explained the purpose of his call.

There was a brief pause, then Faulkner's voice, different now, careful, still slow, but more friendly: "Why don't you come out in the morning? About nine."

The morning sunlight came in thin yellow shafts through the pole-like cedar trees that lined the drive as the young

man walked up to the house that MGM might have built
or bought or borrowed for a film set—a house built in 1856
and slept in by Sherman's troops. It still bore traces of a
ruined arbor in the high grass below the house where southern
women had strolled in the afternoon heat of the dead years
of Mosby and Early and Lee. He must have bought the house
to put in a book, the young man thought, seeing the white
portico, the red-brick unwalled porch joining it—the high
white, august-looking southern mansion taking the July heat
looking like something out of a novel by Stark Young.

It was then that he saw the figure of a man coming around
the corner of the building, leading a pony. Upon the pony
sat a little girl, perhaps eight or nine years old. Her hair
was long, an aura of gold light in the morning air—a pink
and white face made for a cameo brooch. The face was like
the older faces the young man saw a year later in Bucking-
hamshire, when he was sitting in a punt on the Thames below
Abingdon, thinking "I never should have read those damn
flying stories by Faulkner"—knowing tomorrow he was going
out in a two-engine bomber again to raid Milan wearing a
uniform that was not that of his own country.

But in the summer of 1940, the older man looked as if
he might have fitted easily into the cockpit of a 1917 S. E. 5
or Sopwith Camel, only he would need a pillow under
him to see the Aldis machine-gun-sight mounted just ahead
of the wind screen. For this man he had sought out was
short, spare, black-eyed, hawk-nosed. Change that nose, the
young man thought, and you'd have Ronald Coleman. The
same stature, the same intact air of abstraction and restrained
energy.

The little girl on the pony wore a velvet riding cap, fawn-
colored twill jodhpurs, and one of those soft blue sweaters
she was to wear fifteen years later when the old fighter pilot
with the Nobel Prize came to her graduation at Pine Manor.[1]

The hawk-nosed man now wore white duck trousers, tennis
shoes, and a white shirt with the sleeves rolled to the elbows.
His hands looked small, fragile, finely wrought. He stood
there with an aristocratic air, head faintly lifted. Yet there

was something professional, academic in his attitude. His hair was black then, black as his small, motionless eyes.

"I called you last night," the young man said awkwardly.

"Oh, yes," said Faulkner, but already, even before he finished speaking, his eyes and face seemed fixed upon something invisible, with rapt inattention to the voice of his visitor.

Then the young man saw the pipe in the older man's hand. He watched the man lift the pipe. It was unlit. The man's hand was slow and measured in lifting the pipe. Then he clamped the pipe, bowl down, between his teeth.

"Jill, this is Mr. Brennan."

"How do you do, sir," said the little girl, bobbing her head as if in half-curtsy from the saddled pony. Her voice was bell-like, light, airy, a fairy-tale voice.

The father jerked the pony's bridle. They went on along the drive, Faulkner leading the pony. The drive curved among the cedar trees. Beyond lay the tarred smooth-surface street of modern Oxford. The silence went on, too long.

The silence troubled the young man. "Has she been riding long?" he asked. He felt like an intruder. After all, he had invited himself to this meeting.

Faulkner did not answer immediately. He walked slowly, his gaze unfocused, one hand touching the bowl of the pipe.

After another long minute he said, "Three years." Then, without turning his head, and still looking down the drive with its cedar shadows thin and black, he said, "You know, a woman should know only how to do three things—" He paused, moving the pipe to the other corner of his small lips. His eyes were remote, and he spoke again as if thinking aloud —"tell the truth, ride a horse and sign a check."

The young man smiled. He did not want to be rude but he could not stop. "Can she sign a check yet?" he asked.

Faulkner still did not turn his head, nor change the quiet expression on his face.

"That's the last thing you want to teach a woman," he said. Then, "Jill, you go ahead. We're going back to the house." He handed the reins to the little girl.

The two men turned toward the house.

"What part of the North are you from?" Faulkner asked.

"Minnesota."

"Good hunting up there?"

"Everything—pheasants, ducks, partridge, deer."

"Ever hunt possum?" Faulkner asked.

"Raccoon."

Again Faulkner was silent. They went on toward the house. A tall woman appeared on the porch. She looked about forty. Her face was oval-shaped, with pleasant blue eyes—the face of the little girl on the pony.

"Hello, Mr. Brennan," she said, her voice light, cheery. "Did you find a place to stay in town all right?"

"This is my wife," Faulkner said. "Mr. Brennan."

Mrs. Faulkner smiled, extended her hand. She spoke again in her easy, warm, welcoming voice: "Come in. It's getting hot already. Bill, there's more beer missing. Six bottles."

"Damn that boy," Faulkner said. "Drinks all my beer if I don't watch him. Damn house boy."

The young man followed Faulkner into the house. The hall was wide, high, ante-bellum, straight back through the length of the house. To the left the young man saw a high-ceilinged library with book-lined walls. In the center of the room was a knee-hole desk with a portable typewriter on it. A glass break-front cabinet stood at one end of the room. Inside, colored jackets bore the French, Italian, and German titles of Faulkner's novels. Near the desk stood a brown smoothly polished table, and upon the table lay an oblong volume bound in maroon-colored velvet-like material. The young man opened the volume upon the black large print:

THE CASE OF TEMPLE DRAKE
Starring
Miriam Hopkins

He remembered when the movie had played in his home town with the theater-marquee advertising:

NO CHILDREN ADMITTED.

Here was Faulkner's first movie script, the film adaptation of *Sanctuary*.[2]

The young man turned upon the sound of a chattering typewriter. Faulkner sat at the knee-hole desk now, his fingers suddenly idle on the keys of the machine, his gaze thoughtful, contemplative. Then he looked at his sheet of paper, and after a long moment drew it out, crumpled it in a ball and dropped it in a wastebasket beside the desk.

"Is it okay if I stay in here while you work?" the young man asked.

Faulkner did not answer—only nodded his head. Already he was typing again. The visitor looked around the room. At the far end stood a metal filing cabinet and beside it a high old fashioned phonograph. Upon the phonograph a stack of records was topped by "Rhapsody in Blue." A manuscript, untitled and dedicated to Phil Stone, lay on the filing cabinet.[3]

After a while the young man walked over to Faulkner and asked if he had any objection to his taking the discarded story sheets out of the wastebasket. Faulkner did not answer—only nodded his head again.

Almost fifteen years later, after the possum hunter came home from Stockholm with the Nobel Prize and the scholars and literary critics were feeding themselves upon his novels and short stories, the scholars and literary critics decided from reading the fifteen pages of retrieved manuscript the Minnesota pilgrim salvaged that, to quote only one—"Contrary to the prevailing conception, Faulkner is neither possessed nor divinely inspired in his literary practice, but an extremely conscious craftsman."

The pilgrim found nothing unusual in the craftsman's method, having seen it practiced by writers of high school themes and police reporters. He had never worked on two stories at the same time, however, and the discarded sheets in the wastebasket indicated Faulkner was working on two stories that day. On the sheets he wrote with pencil: "To Dan Brennan, William Faulkner, July 19, 1940, Oxford, Mississippi."[4]

Years later scholars and syntax explorers compared the

discarded sheets with the published stories and found changes in narration, polishing of diction, and complete altering of characters. Illuminatingly, they decided that Faulkner "was not an enemy of revision."

But that day Faulkner looked more interested in direct carpentry than in any metaphysical ideas concerning writing techniques.

Or as Faulkner later expressed it to New York reporters when they asked how he wrote his stories: "I just try to drive the nails straight so the cabinet comes out right."

So the young man sat in the library and listened to Faulkner type that day. He also read some of the books in the cases along the walls. He found a large number of little known German experimental novels, published in the early twenties, and a single blue-paper bound collection of Faulkner's poems on typed sheets. They were written when Faulkner was young, possibly just after the First World War. None of them have been published. Swinburnian, they contained even then powerful seeds of Faulkner's later rhetorical magic.

About three o'clock that afternoon, Faulkner unrolled the last sheet of the story from the machine. Then he sat for another half hour, making changes in the manuscript with a pen.

"What're you going to call it?" asked the young man as Faulkner arranged the manuscript into a neat pile.

" 'Go Down, Moses,' " said Faulkner. "Do you like the title?" In his voice there was something almost like a boyish desire for acceptance.

"What's it about?"

"A Negro funeral."

"Where'd you get the idea for it?" asked the young man.

"I was down to the station last week and a coffin came in off the train."

"How many story ideas do you keep in mind?"

"I'm usually about four or five behind."

"Do you read much?"

"Not any modern novels. Not for several years. I'm reading *Moby Dick* now to Jill."

"She's pretty young for it, isn't she?"

Faulkner chuckled. "She still wants to know what's going to happen to the whale."

"What do you consider the greatest novel of this century?" the young man asked.

Faulkner answered without a pause: "*Buddenbrooks* by Thomas Mann."

"What books might a young writer read with profit?"

"Well," said Faulkner, "there are Shakespeare's sonnets and *Henry the Fifth*—some Dickens, and Conrad's *Lord Jim* and *Nostromo* . . . ."

"Do you feel your work is getting better?"

Faulkner smiled. "Ten years ago I was much better. Used to take more chances. Maybe I'm tired. I've had insomnia lately."

Faulkner rose. "Let's eat," he said, "then go fishing."

The walls in the dining room looked ten or twelve feet high. Mrs. Faulkner was seated at the table. She served blackeyed peas, corn bread, fried chicken, and a green salad.

As he ate, the young man again had the feeling that Faulkner could sit there forever without saying anything.

"Are there any actual places near here on which the Old Frenchman's place in *Sanctuary* is modeled?" the young man asked.

Faulkner did not look up from his plate. His voice was soft, polite. "No—no actual places." But had the young man noticed some of the Negro shacks with big red brick chimneys set back in the fields? They were ruins of Civil War plantation houses.

What did Faulkner think about women novelists? Were there any good ones?

"Evelyn Scott is pretty good," he said, "for a woman."

After lunch they went fishing beside a small pool encircled by trees deep in a woods. The little girl sat with a cane pole while her Pappy, as she called him, threaded the worms onto her hook. Sunlight was dying through the trees. It was almost dusk when the little girl caught a little fish.

On the way back to the house in Oxford, Faulkner stopped

at his farm. The young man sat in the 1937 Ford phaeton
and listened to Faulkner and a big Negro tenant farmer
discuss the care of a brood sow.

On the way back to town Faulkner explained "If the next
book goes I'll buy some more land."

The next book, untitled on top the filing cabinet, was
published later as *The Hamlet.*

In the dark they drove past the red brick school buildings.
Faulkner stopped the car briefly. From the darkness came
the piping of young frogs. His Civil War-haunted voice spoke.
"The wounded were brought in here from a battle up at
Holly Springs. You can see the shell marks in the wall in
day time." The moon stood overhead now. The car ground
into gear.

"Come back again," Faulkner said. "Stay with us next
time." The young man descended from the car onto a street
off the Oxford town-square.

But he never came back. He was twenty-one then—full of
thoughts of splendid war deeds and the spirit of romantic
courage, his head still full of those Royal Flying Corps stories
by Faulkner. That was the summer of 1940. The next year
was 1941, and after that 1942, and then he was no longer
young. He had gone over to England in 1940 and discovered
courage and honor and love and death were easier in thought
and in books. "Damn you, Faulkner," he thought, lying in
a hospital in Norfolk with a cannon shell wound in his leg.
"Damn you, and your war stories." But when the librarian
came around four days later the young man who had stopped
being young the night the Junkers 88 shot him down asked
for a book of Faulkner's short stories. Because lying there
he had started thinking again about Faulkner, and he knew
he himself would never write any as good as "All the Dead
Pilots" and "Ad Astra." And he knew when he read them,
and thought about them, they were more real long after than
the night with the Junkers 88 blinking threads of fire in the
dark. He knew they were more real than that because moments of horror and fear and courage had been preserved
on paper by the old possum hunter stronger than reality
itself. You better not get me into the next war, damn you,

Faulkner, the young man thought, opening the book, beginning to read, feeling peaceful now, knowing he was in two
worlds again, the words stronger than memory, a Mississippi
afternoon, the recklessness of war, and youth.

Notes

1. Faulkner's daughter Jill graduated from Pine Manor College, Wellesley,
   Massachusetts, in June 1953. Faulkner's commencement address was
   subsequently published in the *Atlantic Monthly* under the title, "Faith
   or Fear."
2. Faulkner had no hand in the film adaptation of *Sanctuary*.
3. This was the manuscript of *The Hamlet* (mentioned again on p. 50)
   which had actually been published already, in April 1940.
4. This, rather than the "May 1940" of the opening paragraph, was presumably the date of the original interview.

--≪ 1947 ≫--

Classroom
Statements at the
UNIVERSITY OF
MISSISSIPPI

In the spring of 1947 Faulkner, at the request of the University of Mississippi English Department, met several classes, in which he talked informally and answered questions on literature. One of the students, R. M. Allen, took notes which were later copied and used by other students and by the English Department in preparing an account, for publicity purposes, of the Faulkner class sessions.

After one of the other students published, in the Western Review, *XV (Summer 1951), as "An Interview with William Faulkner," a series of questions and answers from those class sessions, Mr. Allen mimeographed and distributed copies of his original notes, taken in longhand during the class. He prefaced the mimeographed notes with the statement that a graduate student, Miss Peggy Parker, who was present at the same class meeting, recalled at least one of the statements by Faulkner as differing from his notes, and obviously it is quite possible that there are errors in Mr. Allen's record of both questions and answers. Further, there is evidence that Faulkner went over the notes with Miss Parker, not long after the class meetings, and he may have made suggestions and changes which were incorporated in the text printed in the* Western Review. *However, the most reliable version of what Faulkner actually said at that occasion still appears to be what Mr. Allen originally set down, and it is this text which is reprinted here. Mr. Allen's notes, in paraphrased form, were used in the preparation of A. Wigfall Green's "First Lectures at a University" in James W.*

Webb and A. Wigfall Green, eds., William Faulkner of Oxford *(Baton Rouge, Louisiana, 1965); the piece also contains additional material not recorded by Mr. Allen.*

The interview is especially notable for Faulkner's famous listing of his contemporaries in order of excellence. This list, as reported in the Western Review *version, aroused a good deal of misunderstanding, which Faulkner later endeavored to correct; see, for instance, the interview with Harvey Breit (p. 81 below) and the letter to Richard Walser printed in Walser, ed.,* The Enigma of Thomas Wolfe *(Cambridge, Mass., 1953). In his preface to the interview, Mr. Allen noted Miss Parker's belief that Faulkner either said or intended to say "Caldwell" instead of "Cather," and Faulkner certainly spoke of Caldwell in the 1955 interview with Harvey Breit. Mr. Allen also commented: "I wish I could clearly convey the complete humility with which Mr. Faulkner placed himself second to Thomas Wolfe. The papers carried it as the work of a supreme egotist without stating the amount of insistence which was necessary before he did it. Throughout the class, Mr. Faulkner was retiring to the point of shyness and much impressed me by his sincerely cooperative spirit. The class ended at noon but he offered to stay on to answer further questions."*

Q: Did Popeye (in *Sanctuary*) have any human prototype?

FAULKNER: No. He was merely symbolical of evil. I just gave him two eyes, a nose, a mouth and a black suit. It was all allegory. That isn't a very good book. I was probably wrong in my portrayal because it was impossible for me to use anything like a scientific approach.

Q: Did you attempt to read into Popeye characteristics similar to those of Milton's Satan?

FAULKNER: No. That is assuming that a trait is good or evil in its own right. You must study the result. Anything that brings misery is bad. Consistency is good only in its result. You have to stretch a character out to make him last the length of the book.

Q: Which do you consider your best work?

FAULKNER: Well, *As I Lay Dying* was easier and most enjoyable. *The Sound and the Fury* still continues to move me. *Go Down, Moses*—I started this out as a collection of short stories. After reworking it became seven different facets of one field. It is simply a collection of short stories.

Q: How do you choose your words?

FAULKNER: In the heat of getting it down, you might put in some extra words. If you go back over and rework it and the words still ring true, leave them in.

Q: In *The Wild Palms* was your technique mechanical? If so, why?

FAULKNER: I used that technique simply as a mechanical device to bring out the story I was telling which was the contrast between two types of love. One man gave up everything for love of a woman, the other gave everything up to get away from love.

Q: How much do you know about how a book will turn out before you start writing?

FAULKNER: Very little. I just start writing. The character develops with the book and the book with the writing of it.

Q: Why do you present the picture you do of our area?

FAULKNER: I have seen no other. I just try to tell the truth of man. I use exaggeration when I have to, and cruelty as a last resort. The area itself is incidental. It's just all I know.

Q: Since you do present this picture, don't you think it gives a wrong or distorted view?

FAULKNER: Yes, and I'm sorry. I feel I'm written out. I don't think I'll write much more. You have only so much steam and if you don't use it up in writing, it'll get off by itself.

Q: Did you write *Sanctuary* as a boiler just to draw attention to yourself or was it a serious endeavor?

FAULKNER (Apologetically): The basic reason was that I needed money. I had already written two or three books that had not sold. I wrote *Sanctuary* to sell. After I sent it off, the publisher told me, "Good God! We can't print this. We would both be put in jail!" The blood and guts period hadn't arrived yet. After the first ones began to sell, they wanted to publish *Sanctuary*. I got the galleys back but said, "No." I was indebted to my publisher by contract and financially and finally upon his continued insistence I finally agreed. I then completely re-wrote the entire book. I had to have a complete new set of galleys made. For these reasons, I didn't like the book and don't now.

Q: How do you find time to get in a certain environment and mood conducive to writing?

FAULKNER: You can *always* find time to write. Anybody that says they haven't time are living under false pretenses. To that extent depend on inspiration. Don't wait. When you have an inspiration jot it down. The sooner you put it down the stronger the picture will be. Don't wait till later and then try to recapture the mood and color.

Q: How long does it take for you to write a book?

FAULKNER: A hack writer can tell. The time varies. I wrote *As I Lay Dying* in six weeks, *The Sound and the Fury* in six months, *Absalom, Absalom!* in three years.

Q: It's rumored that you keep two books going at one time. Is that advisable?

FAULKNER: It's O.K. but don't write for a deadline. Write just as long as you have something to say.

Q: What is the best training for writing? Courses, experience, or what?

FAULKNER: Read, read, read. Read everything—trash, classics, good and bad, and see how they do it. Just like a carpenter who works as an apprentice and studies the master. Read! You'll absorb it. Then write. If it is good, you'll find out. If it's not, throw it out the window.

Q: Is it good to copy a style?

FAULKNER: No. If you have something to say, use your own style. The story will choose its own type of telling, own style. What you have liked will show through in style.

Q: Are you aware of your following in England?

FAULKNER: I know I have a better reputation abroad than here. I don't read any reviews. The only people with time to read are women and rich people. More Europeans read than Americans.

Q: Why do so many people prefer, for example, *Sanctuary* to *As I Lay Dying*?

FAULKNER: That's another phase of our American nature. The former just has more commercial color.

Q: Are we degenerating? (literary standpoint)

FAULKNER: No. Reading is something that is in a way necessary like Heaven or a clean collar but is not important. We want culture but don't want to go to any trouble to get it.

Q: That sounds like a slam on our way of life.

FAULKNER: It needs slamming. Everybody's aim is to help people, turn them to Heaven. You write to help people. The existence of this class in Creative Writing is good in that you take time off to learn to write at a period in your life when time is your most valuable possession.

Q: What is the best age for writing?

FAULKNER: 35-45 is the best age for writing novels, fire not used up, author knows more. This type of writing is slower, the fire lasts longer. 17-26 is the best age for writing poetry. Writing poetry is like a sky rocket—all the fire condensed in one rocket. Most outstanding poetry is written by young men.

Q: How about Shakespeare?

FAULKNER: There *are* exceptions. He wrote much in his youth *and* later years.

Q: Why did you quit poetry?

FAULKNER: When I found my poetry not good, I changed my medium. At 21 I thought my poetry very good. I continued to write it when 22 but at 23 I quit it. I found my best medium to be fiction. My prose is really poetry.

Q: Do you read a good bit?

FAULKNER: Up to 15 years ago I read everything I could get (my hands on) hold of. I don't even know fiction writers' names now. I have a few favorites I read over and over again.

Q: Has "The Great American Novel" been written?

FAULKNER: People will read *Huck Finn* for a long time. Twain has never really written a novel, however. His work is too loose. We'll assume that a novel has set rules. His work is a mass of stuff—just a series of events.

Q: I understand you use a minimum of restrictions.

FAULKNER: I let the novel write itself—no length or style compunctions.

Q: What do you think of script writing?

FAULKNER: It is a good medium but you can never do anything in it, too much commercialism. Pictures made 30 years ago made 'em rich. They don't want to change. I would like to get about 2,000 feet of film and the accessories. I could film a good short story. After I made it, what could I do with it? Show it to my friends? It's a good medium, though. Books will remain the cheapest medium of getting your work to the public.

Q: How does collaboration on a script work out? For example, you and two others collaborated on "The Big Sleep."

FAULKNER: A person is rehired the next year on the basis of the number of times his name was on the screen this year. This causes much bribery. Back in the old days, if one could get 300# of sugar for the producer, more than likely his name would find a place on the screen. If you can get the producer to put your name in, O.K. They fight about it and for it.

Q: To what extent did you write the script for "Slave Ship"?

FAULKNER: I'm a motion picture doctor. When they run into a section they don't like, I rework it and continue to rework it until they do like it. In "Slave Ship," I reworked sections. I don't write scripts. I don't know enough about it.

Q: How do you like Hollywood?

FAULKNER: I don't like the climate, the people, their way of life. Nothing ever happens and one morning you wake up and find yourself sixty five years old. I like Florida better.

Q: Is travel necessary for preparation to write?

FAULKER: No, it's not. Homer did O.K. without it. Just talk to people.

Q: Did your perspective change after travel to Europe and around?

FAULKNER: No. When you are young, you are sensitive but don't know it. Later you seem to know it more. Wider view is not caused by what you have seen but by war itself. Some people can survive anything and get some good out of it. The masses got no good from war. War is a dreadful price to pay for experience. The only good I know of that comes from a war is that it allows men to be free of their womenfolks without being blacklisted by it.

Q: What effect did the RCAF have on you?

FAULKNER: I still like to believe I was tough enough that it didn't hurt me too much. It didn't help much. I hope I have lived down the harm.

Q: Which was tougher? World War I or II?

FAULKNER: Last war, we didn't have any parachutes. We prayed that the plane wouldn't catch fire. Not much difference. The pilots of this war had a lot of instruments to watch. I guess this war must have been tougher.

Q: Is association (such as living in a boarding house) good or bad?

FAULKNER: Neither, but you may be able to store facts in mind for future use. You might want to write about a boarding house some time.

Q: Which novels (nationality standpoint) were greatest or best of the 19th century?

FAULKNER: Probably Russian—I remember more Russian names than any others.

Q: How much attention should be paid to a printed criticism?

FAULKNER: Such criticisms are tools of a trade. They work for money. It is best not to pay too much attention to printed criticisms. A few are sound and worth reading but not many.

Q: Who do you consider the five most important contemporaries?

FAULKNER: 1. Thomas Wolfe; 2. Dos Passos; 3. Hemingway; 4. Cather; 5. Steinbeck. (To the above questioner, a teacher auditing the class turned and added after the above listing, "I am afraid you are taxing Mr. Faulkner's modesty." Mr. Faulkner then listed them this way:)

1. Thomas Wolfe—he had much courage, wrote as if he didn't have long to live. 2. William Faulkner. 3. Dos Passos. 4. Hemingway—he has no courage, has never climbed out on a limb. He has never used a word where the reader might check his usage by a dictionary. 5. Steinbeck—I had great hopes for him at one time. Now I don't know.

Interview with

JOHN K. HUTCHENS

These few paragraphs from the "On the Books" section of the New York Herald Tribune Weekly Book Review *for October 31, 1948, are interesting for their indication of Faulkner's political views at the time of the publication of* Intruder in the Dust, *which appeared shortly before the 1948 presidential election.*

UP FROM OXFORD, MISS., on his first visit in ten years to New York, William Faulkner preferred—as on other visits—not to talk about his writing. Small, graying, still very shy, he sat the other day in the mansion of his publisher, Random House, and said: "I think of myself as a farmer, not a writer." But finally he did say something about his writing. He said that for several years he has been at work on a "big book" that will need five or six years more, the longest single effort of his career thus far. "I call it," said Mr. Faulkner, "a fable based on the story of the Crucifixion and the Resurrection," and that would be all for the moment, please, about that.

In the eight years between his last novel and his current one, *Intruder in the Dust,* he hasn't done much writing, he said—only the fable-in-progress and his new book. Not many short stories, because "I never wrote a short story I liked." He didn't like "The Bear"? Yes, but he didn't call that a short story. A short story is 3,000 words or less. Anything more is, well, a piece of writing.

Not much reading, either, except of "the old books," to

which he goes back regularly: *Don Quixote, Moby Dick, The Nigger of the Narcissus* and Dickens; and he carries a one-volume Shakespeare wherever he goes, though he doesn't travel much. ("Too many people," he said.) In the last fifteen years he has not read a book by a contemporary.

He would rather talk of the life around him in Oxford, though "this is a bad time." He guesses the Dixiecrats will carry Mississippi this Tuesday, and "I'd be a Dixiecrat myself if they hadn't hollered 'nigger.' I'm a States' Rights man. Hodding Carter's a good man, and he's right when he says the solution of the Negro problem belongs to the South." He paused a moment and added, with mild irony: "There isn't a Southerner alive who doesn't curse the day the first Northern ship captain landed a Negro slave in this country."

He once avoided reviews of his books, but now he reads them, and he appreciates the high estimate most critics have of him. He especially liked the *Portable Faulkner* which Malcolm Cowley edited, though he regretted it, in a way.

"I planned to get out a book like that myself some day, when I was all written out," he said.

⊶ 1948 ⊷

Interview with

RALPH THOMPSON

In this brief interview—published in the New York Times *on November 7, 1948—Faulkner commented on a number of topics about which he usually remained silent, notably his relationships with Oxford, Mississippi, and with the official literary world. Particularly interesting and appealing are his nostalgic remarks about the early days in New Orleans when he was "a free man."*

THERE ARE, according to a recent issue of a literary quarterly, "images of linear discreteness" in William Faulkner's fiction. Also "images of curve."[1]

Mr. Faulkner is a shy man. This sort of lingo makes him shyer still. In town the other day from his home in Oxford, Miss., he did his best to be accommodating, but clearly preferred to talk about almost anything except curves and linear discreteness. No, he hadn't seen the piece in the quarterly. No, he didn't much care about reading such pieces. Long silence. "Look," he said at last, "I'm just a writer. Not a literary man."

Small, sharp-nosed, gray-haired, he shifted uncomfortably in his chair. "I write about people. Maybe all sorts of symbols and images get in—I don't know. When a good carpenter builds something, he puts the nails where they belong. Maybe they make a fancy pattern when he's through, but that's not why he put them in that way.

"I'm just a writer. I wrote about the Civil War because I'd heard about it all my life. I knew where every battle was fought. As a boy I saw General Longstreet once. I marched up to him and said, 'General, what happened to you at Gettysburg?' The old man about blew his top.[2]

"I write about the people around Oxford. I know them, and they know me. They don't much care what I write. 'Why, look here,' they'll say. 'Bill Faulkner's gone and got his picture in the New York paper. It says here he's written a book.' So they come around and try to borrow money, figuring I've made a million dollars. Or else they look twice and figure I couldn't make a thousand.

"I got to be a writer pretty much by chance. After the first war I was down in New Orleans, bumming around. Met Sherwood Anderson. I thought he led a good life—worked a few hours during the day, and sat around evenings talking and drinking. So I went off and wrote a novel myself: *Soldiers' Pay.* When it was done, Sherwood said, 'Bill, if you promise you won't make me read it, I'll tell Horace Liveright to bring it out.'

"Sure enough, Liveright did. In those days I was a free man. Had one pair of pants, one pair of shoes, and an old trenchcoat with a pocket big enough for a whisky bottle. Now I get stacks of letters asking what I eat for breakfast and what about curves and linear discreteness. Suppose I ought to answer them, but I don't. Got my own work to do, and haven't got a secretary."

Notes

1. The allusion is to Richard Chase's article, "The Stone and the Cruci-fixion: Faulkner's *Light in August*," published in the *Kenyon Review,* Autumn 1948.
2. According to Faulkner's old friend Phil Stone (in an interview with one of the editors in Oxford, Miss., in July 1956), this episode actually happened to Stone, not to Faulkner.

⊶⊱ 1951 ⊰⊷

Interview with

EDWARD KIMBROUGH

On Friday, October 26, 1951, Faulkner was made an Officer of the Legion of Honor by the French Consul-General in New Orleans. The following morning two reporters for the New Orleans Item *went together to interview Mr. and Mrs. Faulkner at their hotel; the two interviews appeared side by side in the* Item *on Monday, October 29. Faulkner appears to have been in quite a genial mood on this occasion, although Mrs. Faulkner is reported as saying beforehand that Mr. Faulkner would throw her out of the window if she so much as mentioned the possibility of an interview.*

"IF I HAD MY LIFE to live over again?"

The great man holds his bourbon up, studies its color.

"Why, youngster, I reckon I'd be a woman or a tramp. They don't have to work so hard."

The quick smile flits over the dark, clean-cut face.

"Or maybe a rich orphan—with a trust company instead of kinfolks."

The smiler is William Faulkner.

To the world at large he is the most famous living writer, winner of the Nobel Prize. Friday evening he was decorated here as a Knight of the Chevalier of the French Legion of Honor.

To 18-year-old daughter Jill, he is "Pappy"—and the best blamed horseback rider in and around Oxford, Mississippi.

To wife Estelle he is "Billy"—the childhood sweetheart she married when only a few Mississippians knew his name.

It took work and long struggling years for the name to be known everywhere people read.

But it's known now, and Bill Faulkner doesn't like work any more than he ever did. But:

"What else are you going to do?" he says. "You can't drink eight hours a day. Or make love. Work's about the only thing a fellow has to do to keep from being bored."

So Faulkner works—at writing often, but more often he's occupied with supervision, not chores, on his stock farm.

"I'm a farmer," he says. It's the only moment when pride touches the thoughtful, sensitive face. He slips into Mississippi dialect.

"I ain't a writer," he drawls, delighted with his hill-country words. "Why, I don't even know any writers. I don't pay no attention to publishers, either. They write me a letter—if it don't have a royalty check in it, I throw it away."

His mouth, below the cropped graying mustache, signals his big joke against the literary snobs who have made his name a cult, and wish, no doubt, that he would speak with an adopted French accent and wear, perhaps, a monocle.

"I like silence," he says. "Silence and horses. And trees. You see what that big freeze last winter did to the trees in Miss'ippi? Seems like it happens ever' year. I got these cedar trees growin' along the front walk to my house. That freeze broke a heap o' branches off them cedars."

Bill Faulkner's heart is where those trees are—up in Oxford, Miss., where the big square white house is, and the stable with its four saddle horses.

He ventures sometimes to Hollywood: "When I have to, for money." He shakes his head, and deep furrows pleat his high forehead. "Sunshine all the time," he notes, with the gloom of a tragedian confronted by a monotony of stormless days.

You can see him remembering the dark swamps, the long dismal rains, the dark blue hills of his native country which he's made so familiar to the world in his books that Russians and Frenchmen can name the roads and the fishing camps of his mythical Yoknapatawpha County.

And remembering, the man of silence forgets to be quiet.

Remind him of the old days and nostalgic laughter touches his face.

"You remember the old watering places? Allison's Wells and Stafford Springs? Where folks went every summer to purge themselves of a winter of good living—eating and drinking? Why, I recollect my grandfather taking his last drink of bourbon and cussin' 'cause grandmother was makin' him go off to take the waters. A man that could have good bourbon, and havin' to follow a woman off and drink that ole muddy bitter spring water!"

Maybe, he thinks, this urge to purify the flesh belongs to the Protestant tradition he senses among his own folk: the deep-founded belief that man in this life must pay, somehow and somewhere, for whatever pleasure he allows himself.

Faulkner is an heir to this tradition, but he's more than once clashed with it. The most memorable conflict of the artist with the puritan—he's a little of both himself—happened last year when the writer felt a sudden rare urge to express himself on a public problem.

He wrote a letter to a newspaper advocating the legalization of beer in Lafayette County, where his Oxford home is.

"The puritans didn't like it," he noted wryly. "But the beer companies sure did. One of 'em wrote me and asked me could they use the letter in their advertising. I didn't care, but . . . ." He paused. "Why, you know them fellows never even sent me a case of beer. I thought I'd at least get me some beer out of it."

Yet, for all the storm his books have stirred among his neighbors, he remains bound to his own kind. In favorite book, *The Sound and the Fury,* one of his characters is asked, "Why do you hate the south?"

"I don't, I don't, I don't" the man answers.[1]

But the indignation is there, as it is in Faulkner, along with the love for neighbors and kinfolks.

He broods over names, connects them with cousins and

step-uncles and chance acquaintances of years long gone. He plays the old and endless southern game of "Are you kin to . . . ?" or "Now I knew a fellow had your name once. Lived up in Tippah County."

Tippah County is where he was born 54 years ago. "My mother was there because my father was working as agent for the railroad my grandfather built right after The War to haul the cotton out o' that country up to market in Memphis. So I was birthed in New Albany, but we moved back to Oxford when I was four and I been there ever since."

Except, of course, for New Orleans, Hollywood, New York, San Francisco, England and Sweden.

He lived in New Orleans in what he thinks were better days than these in a house in Pirate's Alley. The two years he was here were the only prolonged period in his life when he lived in company with other writers. Now a legendary lone-wolf among authors, he ate and drank and talked 30 years ago with the late Lyle Saxon, author of *Lafitte the Pirate*; Sherwood Anderson, of *Winesburg, Ohio* fame, who was Faulkner's first great booster; and the late Roark Bradford.

He misses that fabled New Orleans. It was slower, quieter in many ways, freer in other ways, and not yet a tourist center.

"And the food," he remembers. "It was better than now. Not all decorated up for tourist delight. I used to go to a little place in the Pontalba buildings. Madame something or other. Took three hours to eat dinner. Worth every minute of it."

This is his first trip to New Orleans in 10 years. He's not one to travel except when he has to, for all his nostalgic attachment to the life of a tramp.

And when he does travel, he makes tracks for home as soon as he can. He stayed only two days in Sweden last fall, when he and his daughter Jill flew over for the Nobel Prize ceremonies.

He liked the Swedes very much. He's a shy man and the Swedes are a formal people.

"They organize everything, and so I just got swept from one event to another, and didn't have to do much talking."

Except of course for the speech he delivered accepting the prize.

Faulkner's fondness for organization does not, however, extend very far. He is a staunch individualist, a lone and seemingly lonely holdout against the 20th century's passion for joining and wearing badges and uniforms.

His former fondness for football has faded as the game has become more and more a business of highly-specialized and near-professional groups.

"Why, it's like a musical comedy dance-line now," he says. "Everybody in place and kicking on the beat. The old flux and excitement of individual effort is lost in the precision team."

His brown eyes pierce behind all facades of individuals and buildings. Yet they see, as his books demonstrate, the little simple things, also.

He pauses quickly, puts a hand out to the charming southern belle he married, nods proudly at her mention of daughter, Jill, and whispers, with a glance toward the hotel bar:

"Look, Missy, it moves. Just like a circus carousel."

He's still the Mississippi yearling that "Missy" Estelle first saw astride a calico pony,[2] his eyes looking out on the world and finding it strange and wonderful and tragic.

Notes

1. The episode actually occurs in *Absalom, Absalom!.*
2. In her interview with the other *Item* reporter, Betty Jane Holder, Mrs. Faulkner had said: "The first impression I remember is seeing him with his two brothers, John and Jack, riding on their ponies. They would ride by the house on their ponies with an old groom riding behind on an old nag to take care of them."

-◄ 1952 ►-

Interview with
LOÏC BOUVARD

In 1952 Faulkner was interviewed by a French graduate student, Loïc Bouvard, then studying political science at Princeton University. The interview was originally published (in French) in the Bulletin de l'association amicale universitaire France-Amérique, *January 1954. The present translation was made by Henry Dan Piper and first published in* Modern Fiction Studies, *vol. 5 (Winter 1959-1960).*

Near the end of the interview Bouvard says, "I felt that Faulkner had talked with me freely and candidly, and that he had opened to me the deepmost recesses of his mind, and this made me very happy." M. Bouvard had good reason for satisfaction. Perhaps for no other interviewer did Faulkner reveal himself, his reading, and his ideas with quite such clarity and precision. But perhaps no other interviewer brought to a meeting with Faulkner quite the same personal and intellectual resources. M. Bouvard simply assumed that Faulkner operated on a particular intellectual level, and the interview shows that Faulkner did so.

"MR. FAULKNER is waiting for you," the secretary's voice murmured over the telephone. I thanked her, put down the receiver and walked out of the booth. I was going to meet William Faulkner. In anticipation of this visit I had carefully prepared a list of questions, but now they were all fluttering around in my head. I owed my good fortune to one of my

American friends, who was also a friend of Faulkner's. Faulkner himself was stopping at the Princeton Inn, across from the Graduate College where I lived. It was at the Inn that our encounter took place on November 30, 1952.

When I entered his hotel room, Faulkner was standing by the window, pipe in hand. I will never forget that first impression. Turning to me in a friendly way, he stretched out his other hand. "How do you do, it is nice to see you." I liked his simplicity. I noticed also that he was rather slight in build, and that he had a sport coat on over his sweater. Putting aside his pipe, he offered me a cigarette, obviously to set me at ease, and we talked about why I had come to the United States.

I kept telling myself, "William Faulkner is really there, sitting across from you!" Both his way of talking and of observing me struck me as unusual. His manner of looking at me, particularly, is difficult to describe. His eyes are small, deep-set, secretive under his eyelids—and the heavy eyebrows over them are darker than his iron-grey hair. His curved nose, small black mustache, and pointed chin all gave his face a well-bred, penetrating expression. Moreover, when he is seated, Faulkner hunches up somewhat, so that his head sinks between his shoulders; it was thus—legs crossed and elbows on his knees—that I can still picture him.

I wondered if my uneasiness would ever cease. We kept on talking, and I told him that in France we regarded him as one of the writers of our generation who has contributed most to an understanding of man. He listened attentively, and when I questioned him, he paused to reflect before he answered. I got the impression that he sought to express his ideas with the greatest precision. Then, eyeing me, he spoke very softly, in a low deep voice, with a heavy Southern accent. It wasn't at all the voice you would have expected from such a face; for instance, he never raised his voice at all. Doubtless the same contrast prevails between Faulkner's appearance and his voice as between his work and the ideas he expressed to me that day. What I am trying to say is that my reading of *The Sound and the Fury* had deceived me regarding the personality of its author. I would never have guessed that Faulkner would turn out to be this small compact man, nor that he would prove to be something of a moralist.

While we were talking of Sartre and Camus, I told him that many young people were supplanting a faith in God with a faith in Man. "Probably you are wrong in doing away with God in that fashion. God is. It is He who created man. If you don't reckon with God, you won't wind up anywhere. You question God, and then you begin to doubt, and you begin to ask 'Why? Why? Why?'—and God fades away by the very act of your doubting him." I was glad that we had arrived at this level of conversation so early, for now I felt at ease, and Faulkner himself was very much absorbed—though his manner continued to be reserved.

"Naturally," he continued, "I'm not talking about a personified or a mechanical God, but a God who is the most complete expression of mankind, a God who rests both in eternity and in the now." When I asked if he were thinking of the God of Bergson, he said, "Yes, a deity very close to Bergson's. Listen, neither God nor morality can be destroyed." I repeated this remark to myself, for he had said it with great emphasis.

Since we had brought up Bergson, I next asked Faulkner to explain his conception of time. "There isn't any time," he replied. "In fact I agree pretty much with Bergson's theory of the fluidity of time. There is only the present moment, in which I include both the past and the future, and that is eternity. In my opinion time can be shaped quite a bit by the artist; after all, man is never time's slave."

Finally we had come to the topic which I wanted most to talk about, and which I was eager to hear him discuss: Man, himself. What he had already told me about God had left me somewhat cold. After my two years in America, Faulkner's Deism was certainly not strange to me. But what he said to me that day about Man I will never forget.

And so one of the greatest artists of all time spoke to me of our human condition. "Man," he said gravely, "is free and he is responsible, terribly responsible. His tragedy is the impossibility—or at least the tremendous difficulty—of communication. But man keeps on trying endlessly to express himself

and to make contact with other human beings. Man comes
from God. I don't hold with the myth of Sisyphus. Man is
important because he possesses a moral sense. I have tremendous faith in man, in spite of all his faults and his limitations. Man will overcome all the horrors of an atomic war;
he will never destroy mankind."

Here I asked Faulkner what he thought of man's uni-
versality, and if he were acquainted with Hindu civilization.
"No," he said, "I don't know India, and know nothing about
oriental civilizations—it's one of my gaps. Man isn't universal.
In different places he conceives of God differently, and these
ways vary in time and space. Nonetheless it still holds that
man keeps creating civilizations and art, and that God exists."

Once again Faulkner was speaking to me of his faith in
God, though I personally was much more anxious to hear
him talk about art. At this point he said something that—
like the words of Paul Valéry—might be engraved on the
portals of every temple in the world—"Art is not only man's
most supreme expression; it is also the salvation of mankind."
He said this with deep conviction, and unconsciously I found
myself moved by this simple little man—a genuine artist who
with these words had just conferred such value and meaning
upon his own life. Right away I asked if he meant by all this
that the artist is the one who offers man salvation. He smiled,
guessing my thought, and said, "No. The artist is the one
who is able to communicate his message. In doing this, he
has no intention of saving mankind. On the contrary, the
artist speaks only for himself. Personally I find it impossible
to communicate with the outside world. Maybe I will end up
in some kind of self-communion—a silence—faced with the
certainty that I can no longer be understood. The artist must
create his own language. This is not only his right but his
duty. Sometimes I think of doing what Rimbaud did—yet,
I will certainly keep on writing as long as I live."

Then Faulkner talked about himself, and with that same
intensity and calm with which he had talked of God and
man. I asked him about his method of writing and he answered
with disarming candor. "Artistic creation calls for real effort.
I think Valéry was right when he spoke of its hardship. Gide

hardly needed to tell us that he admired only those books
whose authors had almost died in order to write them—for
it is always that way. A great book is always accompanied by
a painful birth. Myself, I work every day. I write entirely by
hand. I know what that 'flash' of inspiration is, but I also
try to put some discipline into my life and my work." Yes,
Faulkner is decidedly a moralist who has accepted traditional
morality at the same time that he has enlarged it by means
of his extraordinary perspective on man and art. Faulkner,
the spokesman for man's shortcomings and crises, is no less
the wise and understanding person whose remedy consists of
rigor, discipline, and order.

There still remained, of course, the topics of France and its
literature. "I love France and the French people very much.
I feel at ease in France; it is so lovely. And I greatly admire
the French spirit, even though you do tend to 'polish' people
too much. The French think too much, and in doing so,
destroy something of man's original flavor. Be careful of man
in the abstract. I think every literature pretty much expresses
whatever is possible for man to achieve in art. One finds a
great many things in French literature, but that shouldn't
prevent you from looking elsewhere, too."

So far as French influences on his own work are concerned,
here is what Faulkner told me. "I was influenced by Flaubert
and by Balzac, whose way of writing everything bluntly with
the stub of his pen I admire very much. And by Bergson,
obviously. And I feel very close to Proust. After I had read
A la Recherche du Temps Perdu I said 'This is it!'—and
I wished I had written it myself. I know Malraux because I
have read his latest books on the psychology of art. On the
other hand, I know neither Sartre nor Camus."

Then we talked about many other things, such as his
own country, the South, of which Faulkner said, "It's the
only really authentic region in the United States, because a
deep indestructible bond still exists between man and his
environment. In the South, above all, there is still a common
acceptance of the world, a common view of life, and a common morality." That word "morality" had cropped up in
Faulkner's conversation time and time again during the hour

that we had been together. But after I had left, I had the feeling of having really gotten to know the man himself who, in his novels, had created such tormented, mad, monstrous human beings. I felt that Faulkner had talked with me freely and candidly, and that he had opened to me the deepmost recesses of his mind, and this made me very happy.

I recall that it had snowed that morning in Princeton. The Graduate College reared the profile of its grey tower on the opposite side of a white expanse which I now was obliged to cross in order to return to my room, where I would write down everything I had just heard. The thing I had wanted more than anything else in the world to happen had just happened. I had met William Faulkner. And while I walked across the snow, I said over and over to myself those words which, for me at least, constitute his message: "The most important thing is that man continues to create, just as woman continues to give birth. Man will keep writing on pieces of paper, on scraps, on stones, as long as he lives. Man is noble. I believe in man in spite of everything."

--◄ 1953 ►--

Interview in

THE NEW YORKER

After completing Requiem for a Nun *in 1951, Faulkner turned his attention once again to* A Fable, *which he had conceived in the early 1940's and which had occupied him, with many interruptions, ever since. Faulkner continued to work on the manuscript during the several visits which he made to New York in 1952 and 1953. This interview in* The New Yorker *(February 28, 1953) makes an interesting companion to the piece made for the same magazine during Faulkner's 1931 visit to New York (pp. 23–24).*

FOR SEVERAL WEEKS NOW, William Faulkner has been living in town and going to work daily in the office of Saxe Commins, his editor at Random House. Mr. Commins permitted us to stop by one day last week and watch the great man in travail, and we did, and he was. We found the two men working about four feet apart in a small, warm, smoke-filled room on the third floor. The room had green walls, a maroon carpet, and a single window. Commins was sitting at a desk with his back to the window, studying galley proofs. Faulkner was sitting in a straight-backed chair at right angles to the desk, facing a wall of bookshelves; his eyes were on a level with *The Standard Medical Guide* and *The Teaching of Speech.* He was hunched over a typewriter on a stand and was a study in gray, brown, and blue: neatly parted gray hair, brown-rimmed glasses, a shirt with blue stripes, a blue tie, gray suspenders, gray tweed trousers, and brown shoes. Having shaken hands with Commins and Faulkner, we retreated to a corner of the office and watched the sole owner and proprietor of Yoknapatawpha County bring forth prose. He typed very, *very* slowly, mostly with the middle finger of his right hand, but with an occasional assist from the index finger of his left.

A tall, serious-looking girl entered the office and, without a word, crossed to the bookshelves by Faulkner's head. She pulled out a book, riffled the pages, put it back, and pulled out another. Faulkner went on typing without looking up. Commins said to the girl, "On your left, if you're looking for Aristotle." She thanked him, plucked a book from the shelves, and told Commins that she might be back later. "Any time," he said, and the girl walked out. The telephone on Commins' desk rang, and he answered it with a hearty, "Hello! Arthur! How's the play going? Still a hit?" Faulkner went on typing. Commins talked for a few minutes, put down the telephone, and returned to his proofs. Faulkner coughed, and Commins glanced anxiously at him. "Got a cold, Bill?" he asked. Faulkner shook his head, his middle finger poised above the space bar. "Think you ought to take some medicine?" Commins asked. Down went the space bar. "Isn't anythin' Ah got whiskey won't cure," Faulkner said. He lifted the sheet of paper in the typewriter and read over what he had written, then got up and stretched. "Work hurts mah back," he said. "Ah think Ah'm goin' to invent somethin' like an ironin' board, so Ah can lie flat on mah back while Ah type." He pressed both hands against his spine. "Fell off a hoss last spring," he told us. "Back's been hurtin' ever since. Ah got a very fine filly and Ah was trainin' her to trot. Ah was ridin' her mama. Had the filly on mah left side, the lead in mah left hand, when the filly crossed me. Ah didn't want to let go and Ah didn't have time to change hands, so Ah had to take the fall."

Commins fished in his wallet and brought out a snapshot, which he handed to us. "Bill jumping," he said. "Jumpin' mah daughter's mare," said Faulkner. "That mare's twenty years old. Mah daughter was in California with me in 1944, when Ah was workin' for Warner's; she was 'bout ten then. Every day on mah way to the studio to work, Ah'd drop her off at the ridin' stables. One day, she came to the studio all dusty and said, 'Pappy, Ah bought me a hoss.' Turned out it was a mare with *dis*temper. Ah had to pay a hundred and twenty-five dollars for her and seventy dollars to a vet to cure the *dis*temper and a hundred and fifty dollars for a trailer and then Ah had to pay a man three hundred and fifty dollars to pull the trailer back home to Oxford and before we got that mare into the barn she cost me twelve hundred and eighty-five dollars. Mah daughter loves that mare." He lit a cigarette and sat down at the typewriter. "Ah have a feelin' of doom hangin' over me today," he said. He typed a line, then another. The words came as if he were typing each letter of them for the first time. When he had finished a page, he added it to a pile of other pages, then went over the lot with a red pencil, marking certain paragraphs with "X"s. "Damn it!" he said softly. "Ah wish mah doom would lift or come on. Ah got work to do." Commins raised his eyebrows. "Somethin' is happenin'," Faulkner said. "Ah can feel it." Commins asked him if he got such feelings often. "Not very often, but when Ah feel it, somethin' happens," Faulkner said. "You don't *look* worried," Commins said. "Suppose it's something awful?" "Ah can bear anythin'," Faulkner said, and went back to typing. After another half hour, he got up and said he had a date for lunch. He put on a trench coat and green felt hat, and we took advantage of the opportunity to ask him why he chose to work at Random House instead of in more private quarters. "The work is gettin' itself done here," he said, heading for the stairs. "Ah don't want to disturb it." The work, he went on, is a novel that he has been writing on and off for the past ten years. He has five hundred thousand words done and he figures that if he doesn't get it finished now, he never will. At the street door, he waved goodbye to us and set off alone up Madison Avenue—a small man in a green hat, waiting for his doom to lift.

Interview with
BETTY BEALE

This interview has been extracted from a column of society gossip in the Washington Evening Star, *June 14, 1954. It merits reprinting for Faulkner's comments on the McCarthy hearings, then in progress, and on contemporary politics generally. As Miss Beale pointed out later in the column, the party was held to celebrate the engagement of Faulkner's daughter Jill to Paul D. Summers, Jr., nephew of the hosts; the wedding took place in August of the same year.*

In a letter to one of the editors, Miss Beale recalled Mrs. Faulkner's saying at the party that her husband never gave interviews. She also recalled that Mrs. Faulkner wrote to her a few weeks later, congratulating her on the interview and suggesting that Mr. Faulkner's unusual expansiveness might have been in part attributable to Miss Beale's blonde and youthful good looks. However, Faulkner was in a different mood the next time she interviewed him; see pp. 267–69.

WILLIAM FAULKNER, the literary giant of the South, spoke up at the A. Burks Summers' party yesterday on some current issues with the quiet assurance of a man who knows his own mind and has no fears in speaking it. Described as the author who writes whatever he pleases, the winner of the Nobel prize for literature said, "Nobody should be afraid to say what he thinks."

One of a handful of Democrats at a midday buffet dinner

for two or three hundred that included Senators Mundt,
Welker, Hickenlooper, Ferguson and Carlson, the distin-
guished Mississippian described the Republicans around him
as looking prosperous and worried. They are always more
reserved in their behavior than Democrats, he said, because
"to Republicans, politics is a mode of behavior instead of an
activity."

How do they feel down in Mississippi about the hearings?
"We feel shame down there just as you do here," he answered
with a level eye. People in his home town of Oxford, Miss.—
population 3,000—are watching TV just as people are everywhere else. What effect does he think the hearings will have?
"Well," he answered with a twinkle, "the Democrats at home
are watching with glee."

While her husband answered questions with an agreeable-
ness that belied his reputation for being difficult to interview,
his slim, little, dainty wife ate her dinner and chatted with
other guests. Turned out in starched gray organdy and a
fetching gray hat, she was easy to visualize against their white-
columned antebellum house in Mississippi.

"It is possible," continued her husband, whose classic
Nobel prize speech has been reprinted again and again, "in
a world situation like we have today that democracy simply
cannot work. There is too much waste motion in democracy.
The only efficient government in a state of crisis is one run
by an autocracy. The only difficulty is, man doesn't produce
a benevolent autocrat."

Then expressing more of the brooding writer, reflected
in his stories, he added: "Possibly the only thing that will save
us is defeat. . . . We in America don't take our politics
seriously enough. It's something to do when you have failed
in something else. We ought to train our people for government."

As for his great contemporary, Ernest Hemingway, he
thinks he ought to get the Nobel prize for literature. He had
other comments on this subject but asked that they not be
printed.

And to the comment that the Negro comes out best in his

writings, his reply was, "Maybe the Negro is the best. He does more with less than anybody else."

The most he has penned in one day, said the famous novelist, was when he climbed to the crib of the barn one morning with his papers, pencils and a quart of whisky and pulled the ladder up behind him. When daylight began to fail he had torn off 5,000 words.

Interview with

HARVEY BREIT

Originally published in the New York Times Book Review, *January 30, 1955, this interview was subsequently collected in Breit's* The Writer Observed *(Cleveland, 1956); the text here is taken from the latter source.*

Breit had known Faulkner long before the date of the interview (see his article, "A Sense of Faulkner," Partisan Review, January 1951), and this familiarity may have encouraged Faulkner to speak strongly—as if with a real desire to set the record straight—about his attitude to Hemingway and Hemingway's work.

WE STARTED out on a walk, and William Faulkner said, "I find Park Avenue is the best street to walk on" (though it sounded closer to "Ah fahnd Pahk Avenoo"). We headed toward it in the twilight. He was a small, slight figure, contained and unhurried, in the madding crowd that pressed anarchically ahead for Grand Central and its neighboring subway stations. He wore his Dragnet trenchcoat, an Alpine hat, and he held his pipe in a gloved hand. He looked into a variety of shop windows for long impassive moments. To me it was a foregone conclusion that he would say nothing revelatory about his recent novel, *A Fable,* which had just been honored by the National Book Award as the best fiction of 1954. Nevertheless, I asked him.

"There is nothing to say about it," Mr. Faulkner said in his unbelievably musical voice and speech. "I did the best I could, and if there's something more I could say, I'd have said it in the book. There's nothing I could add to it. I think if I would do it over, maybe I would do it better, but I always think that with everything I've done, as any artist thinks. The work never matches the dream of perfection the artist had to start with."

Suddenly Mr. Faulkner's mood changed: he grew excited. It was a small change, not greatly disparate from his earlier impassivity, but the change was apparent and dramatic, just as the modulated shift in mood in a piece of chamber music can be more dramatic than a big change in a symphony. "That's what I had in mind when I talked about Hemingway being a coward. I was quoted out of context. I had in mind this dream of perfection and how the best contemporary writers failed to match it. I was asked the question down at the University of Mississippi—"[1]

Hold on, I thought, hold on, Mr. Faulkner. Let's take it from the beginning. "Let's go over the whole thing," Mr. Faulkner said, and I knew then that this was one of those Faulkner days when I didn't need to say anything to him. "I was asked the question who were the five best contemporary writers and how did I rate them. And I said Wolfe, Hemingway, Dos Passos, Caldwell and myself. I rated Wolfe first, myself second. I put Hemingway last. I said we were all failures. All of us had failed to match the dream of perfection and I rated the authors on the basis of their splendid failure to do the impossible. I believed Wolfe tried to do the greatest of the impossible, that he tried to reduce all human experience to literature. And I thought after Wolfe I had tried the most. I rated Hemingway last because he stayed within what he knew. He did it fine, but he didn't try for the impossible."

We were walking along Park Avenue toward the Grand Central Arcade. "I hate to think that Grand Central's coming down," he said. I remembered that Faulkner long ago had written a sleepy story about Grand Central Station.[2] He nodded, recollecting the story. "I rated those authors by the

way in which they failed to match the dream of perfection,"
he said. "This had nothing to do with the value of the work,
the impact or perfection of its own kind that it had. I was
talking only about the magnificence of the failure, the
attempt to do the impossible within human experience."

It followed, then, that from other points of view the five
artists could be rated differently? Mr. Faulkner nodded in
agreement and the particular discussion was dropped. We
waited for a traffic light, and he listened with his own kind
of stillness that, more powerful than the noise around us,
subdued it. What were his plans? Was he going off again,
or staying on, or what?

"I might be going to Europe this spring—for the State
Department," he told me. "It's a possibility." He and Robert
Frost had gone to South America not so long ago[3]—that was
a good sign. "The writer in America isn't part of the culture
of this country. He's like a fine dog. People like him around,
but he's of no use."

Perhaps because of the cold war and the Soviet emphasis
on culture, our country was growing up to the realization
that its artists could make a strong contribution?

Mr. Faulkner wasn't sure. "Unless," he said, "someone
somewhere had enough sense to go to someone in a high
position and said, 'Let's see Robert Frost instead of Henry
Ford for a change.' Or someone here said to someone there,
'What can we do for you to show you a side of our country
you don't know?'

"The artist is still a little like the old court jester. He's
supposed to speak his vicious paradoxes with some sense in
them, but he isn't part of whatever the fabric is that makes
a nation. It is assumed that anyone who makes a million
dollars has a unique gift, though he might have made it off
some useless gadget."

We talked more, and I told Mr. Faulkner that I thought
of his short novel, "The Bear," as a modern *Moby Dick.* Mr.
Faulkner, rejecting the "provocation," said, "Now that's odd.
The new book we're getting together starts off with that
story." The book, we learned, will be out this year. "It's a
collection of my hunting stories, and we're calling it *Big*

Woods. I have written some remarks before each of the stories——"

Sort of commentaries? I asked. "Well," Mr. Faulkner said, shaking his head. "I think that's a bad word. I'd call them interrupted catalysts."

We came up to Grand Central and we shook hands. I told him to take care of himself. He smiled, and asked, "What're you going to do now?" I told him I thought I'd find a barber and get a shave. He said, "That's a good idea. There ought to be a good barber right here in Grand Central."

Notes

1. For the background to this paragraph and the next see above, pp. 53 and 58.
2. Breit presumably had in mind Faulkner's story "Pennsylvania Station," first published in 1934.
3. Faulkner and Frost had both attended the International Writers Conference in São Paulo, Brazil, in August 1954.

Interviews in

JAPAN

In August 1955 Faulkner, as part of a round-the-world trip undertaken under the auspices of the State Department, participated in the Summer Seminars in American Literature held at Nagano, Japan. There were several tape-recorded question-and-answer sessions with the Japanese teachers who attended the Seminars, and these interviews (plus a few with other groups) were collected and edited, with other Faulkner material, in Faulkner at Nagano *(Tokyo, 1956), by Robert A. Jelliffe, then Fulbright Lecturer at Kobe College. The texts of all the interviews in that volume are here reproduced, thanks to the generosity of Professor Jelliffe. In his Preface, reprinted here, Professor Jelliffe mentions a number of short prose pieces by Faulkner which were included in* Faulkner at Nagano; *these pieces are now readily available elsewhere, however, and they have been omitted from the present collection.*

Preface

WILLIAM FAULKNER came to Japan in August, 1955, on invitation of the Exchange of Persons Branch of the U.S. Department of State, primarily to take part in the Nagano Seminar. For a period of ten days he met with the members of that group—some fifty Japanese professors of American literature

—almost every afternoon or evening and talked to them and replied to their questions on all manner of topics. The questions ranged from the nature of Truth to the nature of Japanese mothers-in-law. The subject of his brief talks explored such matters as Impressions of Japan, Landscape, Running Water, the American Dream. In both respects, the talks and the answers to questions, Mr. Faulkner avoided the least trace of flippancy or superficiality. His every utterance was charged with utmost seriousness and simplicity. He paid his listeners the ultimate compliment of treating their inquiries and comments as springing from a concern for truth as genuine as his own.

In addition to these Seminar meetings, Mr. Faulkner was called upon to speak on various other occasions: on his arrival at Haneda Airport, at press conferences, at American Cultural Centers, and at Zenkoji Temple. It has been thought well to include these talks also in this record of his stay in Japan. And as a supplement to his own remarks and addresses, there are appended certain of the articles based on his visit here, articles originally printed in the press. In this way, so it is hoped, a fairly comprehensive chronicle of his brief sojourn in Japan will be afforded.

In presenting this account, it has been thought wise to preserve in the main the chronological order of Mr. Faulkner's talks and discussions, even though such an arrangement involves a considerable amount of repetition in the questions asked and the answers given. An alternative method, that of bringing together under similar headings all the material bearing on those topics regardless of the date of the discourse, despite its obvious advantages, would have resulted in a hodge-podge of otherwise unrelated material. As it stands, the comment from day to day can easily be resolved by the interested reader into its component topics; and the present arrangement possesses the advantage at least of recording the impromptu quality of the sessions as they occurred.

The interested reader will certainly wish to bring together from the separate transcripts of each day's doings the penetrating and illuminating comments Mr. Faulkner made on a number of his own works, many of those comments having been published, so far as is known, nowhere else. Perhaps it was the genial and informal nature of these seminar meetings that encouraged him to speak more freely and more intimately than he might have felt disposed to do in other circumstances. And as with matters of literature, his own work and that of other writers, so also with such other matters as what might be called his philosophy of life, or his impressions of Japan and of her culture, a concordance of his remarks may readily be constructed from the records of these sessions.

It has been thought wise by the editor of this material to normalize the idiomatic style of the questions asked by the Japanese participants without doing any more violence than necessary to the original phraseology. Even more so, he has been anxious to make no changes in the replies, even when they are quite obviously impromptu and colloquial in expression. He has had no desire to put words into Mr. Faulkner's mouth: he is one of the last persons in the world to need or to approve of any such effrontery. The attempt has been, instead, to present as faithful a transcript as possible of these meetings, to avoid any appearance of touching up the negative.

On occasion, because of background noise in the meeting room or because of unintelligible recording of questions—the questioners being often at considerable distance from the microphone—the responses have had to be supplemented in part and the questions have had to be inferred, in part from the replies. In such instances the editorial additions have been indicated by the use of square brackets. Only to this extent have any liberties been taken with the verbatim reproductions of these talks and colloquies.

It is hoped that this volume may serve to extend to a larger audience than those who had the privilege of listening to the living voice of Mr. Faulkner at Nagano, something of the enthusiasm and inspiration of his words.

It remains for me to acknowledge, as I do most gladly and gratefully, the help and encouragement accorded me by my colleague, Professor Junichi Nakamura. Professor Nakamura was a participant at the Seminar and a lecturer there as well. In addition, he served on several occasions as interpreter for Mr. Faulkner's interviews.

ROBERT A. JELLIFFE
Fulbright Lecturer in Literature, Kobe College
February, 1956

Interview at Haneda Airport

———

Q: Which particular aspects of Japanese culture are you most interested in?

FAULKNER: Well, their delicacy, their intellect, their intelligence. They notice things.

Q: I heard you are quite interested in the novel written by Mr. Osaragi Jiro, under the title *Homecoming*. Are you acquainted with that novel?

FAULKNER: I am not too familiar with it. I have a great admiration for Japanese culture, the culture of the intellect which we people in the West don't have.

Q: Have you read any novels written by Japanese writers?

FAULKNER: No, not since I was a young man. I remember a Japanese writer that I read when I was about twenty-two or twenty-three years old. His name I don't know.

Interview at Press Club

———

FAULKNER: I have, as every writing man has, a vast respect for the culture of the Japanese people. But this is my first visit to Japan and I am afraid that a Westerner is going to be pretty *gauche* and will look pretty stupid to the Japanese.

Q: Mr. Faulkner, will you tell us what places you visited this afternoon and what impressions you received?

FAULKNER: So far, nothing. I got here this morning after a long overnight flight and spent the day resting. I had a very nice lunch, but I've seen too little of your country. I want to see not the country, not the Japan that tourists see, but Japan [as it really is]. And I want to see how people live, what they do, and I would like to know if possible what they think. I'm afraid that a Westerner will never know what they think, how they think, but that is my hope. I would like to see the countryman, the farmer.

Q: Did you see Kabuki?

FAULKNER: No.

Q: And the fish markets, you didn't get there?

FAULKNER: No.

Q: Are you working on a novel now?

FAULKNER: Not at present, no. I have reached the age now when I work only when the weather is bad. If it's good, I stay outdoors. I like horses, boats, things like that. When the weather gets bad I go indoors and go to work. I would like to say this, I do wish I could stay longer. I think that there is something very important in Japan, the Japanese people. There's a quality that [emphasizes the importance of] man as a human being. What is the name of the Japanese whom I'm thinking of who believed that man is important? I cannot think of his name. I think there is something very valid in the Japanese people, the Japanese culture.

Q: Mr. Faulkner, you once mentioned Mr. Hemingway's world as being narrow; would you please enlighten us?

FAULKNER: I thought that he found out early what he could do and he stayed inside of that. He never did try to get outside the boundary of what he really could do and risk failure. He did what he really could do marvelously well, first rate, but to me that is not success but failure . . . failure to me is the best. To try something you can't do, because it's too much [to hope for], but still to try it and fail, then try it again. That to me is success.

Q: Would you consider that narrowness of the world [is a bad thing]?

FAULKNER: That is a difficult question, because I would have to be Hemingway to answer that. As Faulkner, I say that

it is bad, but if I were Hemingway, who stayed within what
he knew and had done a first-rate job like *The Old Man and
the Sea,* maybe. . . . But to me that is not enough, to fail is
better. To try to do more than you can do.

Q: Mr. Faulkner, do you consider human life basically a
tragedy?

FAULKNER: Actually, yes. But man's immortality is that
he is faced with a tragedy which he can't beat and he still
tries to do something with it.

Q: Have you ever [thought that man might attain per-
fection]?

FAULKNER: Yes, by changing his whole nature, [his] character. But if he did that he would stop being man, stop being
the interesting creature that he is. Now he changes his condition gradually. Nowadays, a little child doesn't have to
work; nowadays, a merchant can't sell you poisoned soup.
That's something, that's not much of an advancement, but
it's something. For I do believe in man and his capacity for
[advancement]. I still believe in man. That he still wishes,
desires, wants to do better than he knows he can and occasionally he does do a little better than anybody expects
of him. This man [is immortal].

Q: Have the living conditions of the Negro in America
improved quite a lot quite recently?

FAULKNER: Yes, they have improved quite a lot. Not as
much as they should, but they have improved a great deal,
quite a lot. I think if the Negro himself has enough sense,
tolerance, wisdom, to be still for a short time, there will be
complete equality in America. His black skin will make no
difference. But he's the one that has got to be quiet and
calm and intelligent, not the white man, because the white
man is afraid that if the Negro has any social advancement
his economic status will change. That's the whole trouble.
But now they can raise cotton and get 30 cents a pound for
it as a profit, but if the Negro's economic status changes, they
can't raise cotton and make a profit of 30 cents.

Q: Do you think [everyone in the States feels so? Or who
does]?

FAULKNER: They are the bankers who depend on the mortgages on the cotton, they are the planters who have got to make the crop, with government support, plus Negro labor. They're the citizens; they're not the people [as a whole]; they're the people who think, 'if we have this, my dollar is worth six cents less or eight cents less.'

Q: In other words, it's economic.

FAULKNER: Yes, economic, that's right.

Q: What would be your feeling about the Supreme Court's decision on segregation in schools?

FAULKNER: Well, there's really no opinion about that, it's right, it's just, but the enforcement of it [is a problem]. What to do with it, you see, and that will take a little time, and that's what I meant by the Negro himself has got to be patient and sensible. But it will come, as I see it, and maybe in three hundred years. . . .

Q: Mr. Faulkner, what do you think are the fundamental reasons why your works are more popular in France and other places than in the States?

FAULKNER: Well, probably because folks in the States don't read; everybody in the States writes, but nobody reads. I didn't mean to be facetious, I mean that people in the States really don't read much. They don't [take the time]. Our culture is production and success, that is, production has got to keep turning over to make a return on its money. The people in the States who read are the women.

Q: How many copies of *A Fable* were sold in the U.S.?

FAULKNER: Why, it sold pretty well; I think about 30,000; it was, 32,000.

Q: Have you any opportunity of reading any Japanese translations of their classic literature?

FAULKNER: Not in years, no. Yes, I must read some Japanese, but I haven't read a Japanese writer since twenty years ago.

Q: You said that if Thomas Wolfe had lived he might have come closest to making the great contribution. That would be as an American in literature?

FAULKNER: I think so, yes. His was the finest failure, mine was the next failure, Dos Passos was third, and I always rated

Hemingway last for the reason that Hemingway [succeeded in what he undertook to do].

Q: [Do you leave Steinbeck out of account]?

FAULKNER: Yes, Steinbeck is just a reporter, a newspaperman, not really a writer.

Q: [In your opinion, who should receive the] Nobel Prize for Literature?

FAULKNER: Well, my only thought was that some poet should have had it last time. I can't think of his name.

Q: Mr. Faulkner, in your Nobel Prize speech you discussed the fact that man [will prevail,] and in your recent article on privacy, you made much of the fact of the passing of individuals, at least that aspect that is involved in the outside press. Well, now, is that implied, or do you think that man will prevail only if he attaches himself to a group?

FAULKNER: No, I think he will prevail anyway. I think that the very fact that here in 1954 a fellow wrote a piece about privacy, proved that he will prevail and endure. That someone will always say, 'this is wrong. You did it, but this is bad.' Just like the people who talk about a person is ignorant, a person is greedy, there is always someone that says this is bad. Now maybe he can't do too much himself, but the fact that he gets up on his hind legs and says, "I don't like this," that proves to me that man prevails. Well, even in my own country people can get up and say, "If a Negro can get a Congressional Medal for saving your son, why can't he sit in the same class-room as your son's children?" And there are people in Mississippi who say that. Of course, it's unpleasant for them, they get into trouble and they set fire to your house and. . . .

Q: What do you think of . . . ?

FAULKNER: Fine man, who says as much as he dares say, but a fine man. A lot of people think he has got to be a little wishy-washy, but he's got to live in that country; he depended on the revenue of his paper to support his wife, his children. He's got to [be moderate].

Q: In what book [do you feel you have been most] successful?

FAULKNER: Well, the finest failure was *The Sound and the Fury,* and that's the one that to me is the [most successful] because that was the best failure.

Q: Why did you write *Sanctuary?*

FAULKNER: I needed money, and I wanted to buy a horse and I thought that people made money writing books, so I wrote a book to make enough money to buy that horse.

Q: I have always liked *Mosquitoes.* What do you think of it now?

FAULKNER: I do, too. I think it's a bad book, but I like it too, I agree with you.

Q: Did you write *A Fable* for money too?

FAULKNER: No. To try to say something which I thought was important to say.

Q: Do you think you were successful?

FAULKNER: No. But I did the best I could and I'm still around, so next year I'll try to say it again, but I did the best I could. But still it was not good enough.

Q: What phases of Japanese culture are you interested in?

FAULKNER: A culture of intelligence, which to me is the Japanese culture, just as the French is a culture of rationality; the British have a culture of [insularity], the Italians, a culture of the five senses. As I understand it, the Japanese, the Chinese, is a culture of intellect. I think that shows in your poetry, your painting.

Q: What do you mean by culture of intellect?

FAULKNER: Let me see if I can explain that. It is to see that there are certain rules which men should observe to get along best, of courtesy, of politeness, of courage at the right time. Not to be brave just for the sake of bravery but to be brave when the moment comes, which is the *samurai* position, as I understand it.

Q: [Will you make use of Japanese material for writing] while you are in Japan?

FAULKNER: No, because I'll never live long enough to write about my own country.

Q: Would you say that you have stopped writing novels?

FAULKNER: No. As long as I can find another piece of paper and somebody to lend me a pencil and to buy me a bit of tobacco, I'll keep on writing. Because as I see it one never does tell the truth as he views it. He tries and each time he fails. And so he tries it again. He knows the next time will not be good, either, but he tries it again until he does, and then he quits.

Q: Mr. Faulkner, while you are working, do you generally have regular working hours and adhere to a schedule?

FAULKNER: No, just as I feel like it. I carry a little paper and a pencil, I write . . . write a poem, sit down at a table, on the back of a bill of fare, it doesn't matter.

Interview of August 4 with
Mr. Takagi and the Editor of Bungei

MAN: Thank you very much, Mr. Faulkner, for sparing your time for this interview with Mr. Takagi and the editor of Bungei.

FAULKNER: Thank you, gentlemen; I'm honored.

Q: I am one of the Japanese novelists. Among Japanese writers, especially the younger writers, there is a great deal of enthusiasm for American literature, especially after the war. There are many questions that I would like to ask you, but since time is limited, I would like to pick out a few, and have your comments on them. There are many translations of your work, including *Sanctuary* and others, and I also have many questions on this problem of novels, so, although I don't know how many questions time will permit me to ask, I'd like to do the best I can within this short time. I'd like to have your 'message' for Japanese writers, since you are not only an American writer, but you are a writer of the world. You not only represent the United States but you represent the world as a writer. In the speech that you made at Stockholm, you mentioned that the younger generation should have more interest in the human mind than what is going on in the world itself. I would like you to explain this a little more—what you meant in that speech—you must have a message that you want to give to writers.

FAULKNER: That man is more important than his environment, than his laws and all the sorry, shabby things that he does as a race, as a nation; that the important thing is this —is man, to believe that always, never to forget it.

Q: Can you please explain a little about your works, in which things of evil or violence come in and you have used them as material in expressing your ideas? Can you give us some ideas on that?

FAULKNER: Yes—never to use the evil for the sake of the evil—you must use the evil to try to tell some truth which you think is important; there are times when man needs to be reminded of evil, to correct it, to change it; he should not be reminded always only of the good and the beautiful. I think the writer or the poet or the novelist should not be just a 'recorder' of man—he should give man some reason to believe that man can be better than he is. If the writer is to accomplish anything, it is to make the world a little better than he found it, to do what he can, in whatever way he can, to get rid of the evils like war, injustice—that's his job. And not to do this by describing merely the pleasant things—he must show man the base, the evil things that man can do and still hate himself for doing it, to still prevail and endure and last, to believe always that he can be better than he probably will.

Q: In a work by André Gide, he refers to you, and says, ". . . there is not one of Faulkner's characters who properly speaking has a soul . . . ." Now what would be your reaction to this?

FAULKNER: Well, I would say that the trouble with that is not my characters but with me, that the fault is in me, that I could not describe the soul. To me they had souls, and I was doing the best I could to show man's soul in conflict with his evil nature or his environment. Now if I didn't do that, then the fault is not the character's, but mine.

Q: What do you think of André Gide—do you like him or do you have anything to say about him?

FAULKNER: Yes—good talent, very intelligent talent.

Q: Gide has written in one of his novels about Tangier in Africa in which he dealt with this thing called evil. In that novel, Mr. Gide dealt with the problem of the soul through this medium of evil. We would like to have your comments on this.

FAULKNER: Well, I think that that is valid, yes, if one believes that he can deal with the soul by means of evil— if that's the way that seems best to him, that is valid, yes. I don't think I would do it that way, but if a first rate talent says, "This is the way that I see this—this is the way to tell this truth," yes, he has the right to do so. . . .

Q: The students of your work in Japan have mentioned in their works that you have been influenced by many people you have read when you were young, and among those are the names of Sherwood Anderson, Swinburne, Oscar Wilde. However, none of them mention Edgar Allan Poe, and I would like to know if there is any special 'inter-play' between you and Poe.

FAULKNER: I don't believe so, for this reason—Poe was one of the group of American writers who were primarily European, not American. These others—Anderson and Dreiser— they were American, so the inheritance was more direct than with Poe, because to me, Poe, Hawthorne, Longfellow—they were easterners, they were actually Europeans.

Q: I brought this up because the students of your works have mentioned Oscar Wilde, and so long as Oscar Wilde has been one of your favorites, they wondered why Poe hasn't come in.

FAULKNER: Well, I make this distinction—Wilde and Swinburne were authentic Europeans. Poe was a transplanted European, that is, there was a simple, clear tradition from the users of language in England down to my country, when the tradition wasn't too clear by the easterner who was still, in his spirit, back across the Atlantic.

Q: In your younger days, you were very interested in poetry, so since T. S. Eliot is, in a sense, American, and, in a sense, European, I would like to know how you take Eliot, that is, according to the terms you take Poe.

FAULKNER: Well, with Eliot there is this difference—Poe

dealt in prose, while the poet deals with something which is so pure and so esoteric that you cannot say he is English or Japanese—he deals in something that is universal. That's the distinction I make between the prose writer and the poet, the novelist and the poet—that the poet deals in something universal, while the novelist deals in his own traditions.

Q: I'm not very well acquainted with American literature, but a while ago, you mentioned Dreiser's name in your explanation. I think that with Dreiser, what is called 'social realism' has been the drive of his work. Then after that, T. S. Eliot came out—Eliot was more interested in the humanistic movements—'new humanism' movements. You, Mr. Faulkner, would then come after that—I mean the order would be Dreiser's social realism, next Eliot's humanism, and then your new way of handling the human mind. This is how I understand you, and I would like to know your reactions to this understanding.

FAULKNER: I agree with you. I explain that this way. In the time that Dreiser wrote, though we were in the same tradition, he wrote in a sort of isolation. Then Eliot came along, and so much more had happened in the world. There had been another war that impacted on the sensitive mentality. Then in my time—I'm still later than Eliot, so much more has happened—it's a little hard to be as free of outside troubles and anguishes as Dreiser was lucky enough to write in. That's the reason. I believe you will see the same thing in your own Japanese literature. So much has happened so that it's impossible for the tradition to hold to its own specific preciousness it had once—it's going to have to become humanitarian or conscious of sociological changes whether it wants to or not—I'd expect that in your own literature.

Q: Last of all—we Japanese are very enthusiastic about having a Japanese author win the Nobel Prize. We are doing our best to have a writer get this prize, and would like to ask you to give us a message, something that would encourage us to raise Japanese literature so that someone can get the Nobel prize. I think that what you said just now is a very good and proper message for us, but if there is any other thing that you can say to encourage us. . . .

FAULKNER: Yes—to work, to believe always in man, that man will prevail, that there's no suffering, no anguish, that man is not suitable to changing, if he wants to, then to work hard.

MAN: Thank you very much.

Interview of August 5
With the Press

MAN: Mr. Faulkner, I attended your press conference the day before yesterday; however, we would like to have a special interview with you today. We are very glad to see you here.

FAULKNER: Thank you.

MAN: We have prepared a questionnaire today—may I ask the questions one by one?

FAULKNER: Surely.

Q: First of all, you have been in Japan for about four days now—what are your impressions of Japan?

FAULKNER: Well, I have a great admiration for Japanese culture, and I am using this opportunity to prove what I was writing about, and I think I'm right.

Q: Could you elaborate a little on your admiration of Japanese culture?

FAULKNER: Yes. I think that your tradition is so much longer than our American tradition—you have had thousands of more years to train yourselves in culture and in intelligence, which we don't have, and any American will of course have an admiration for that. That's in your architecture, your poetry, your fiction, your behaviour. . . .

Q: You have studied a little bit about Japan while you were in the States?

FAULKNER: Yes, I was familiar with Japanese poetry but it was since the last war that people in my country became interested in Japanese culture. We hadn't really had a chance to be impressed with it too much, except a few intellectual people, but only since the last war, everyone has discovered that there is a Japanese culture which is probably very important.

Q: Can you name some of the Japanese poets whom you liked?

FAULKNER: Now I'm not too familiar with their names because my western ear can't quite memorize the Japanese name—I've got to see it. I was introduced to Japanese poetry through one of our American poets, Mr. Ezra Pound. That's when I was a young man; and Japanese poetry is translated in our American magazines. Your fiction is not translated too well, but almost everyone that reads poetry is familiar with Japanese poetry, but it would have to have the trained Western ear to remember the poet's name.

Q: I have heard you don't like to leave your home—you want to settle down, and you don't like to go out from your house. Therefore, we are surprised that you came on this occasion—could you tell us the reason you made up your mind to leave your native town and come to Japan?

FAULKNER: Well, that is only because I have a great deal of work which I want to get done in my lifetime and I get more work done if I stay at home and do it than by travelling around. It just happened that this was a good opportunity to visit your country to take advantage to learn at first hand what I had always believed about your people and your culture.

Q: I understand that you live at Oxford, Mississippi?
FAULKNER: Yes.

Q: And you have never seen New York or Los Angeles?
FAULKNER: Oh, yes, yes.

Q: Do you anticipate that oriental culture will create something different from Western culture?

FAULKNER: Not really different—its manifestation will be different, but the culture I think is the same. The oriental culture is much older than the Western culture, so in that way it is different.

Q: I hear that you have met some Japanese authors yesterday. What are your impressions of them?

FAULKNER: That they were much more intelligent than me,

than the western author; they are more educated, they have
a greater sense of their own traditions and their own past
than we do. You might say the Japanese are intellectual, that
they have an avocation. With the westerner, it's just a pastime.

Q: What subjects did you discuss with those Japanese
writers and critics?

FAULKNER: The difference—the surface differences between
our culture and their culture. Actually, we agreed our ideas
were the same, but there were different manifestations, but
the fundamental truth was the same. It was interesting to
see how we would do the same things but approach them
from different directions.

Q: In what way are their approaches different?

FAULKNER: Why, in the way that an inheritor of an old
tradition is different from an inheritor of a new tradition.
The westerner's tradition is not much older than his grandfather, but the oriental tradition goes back past a hundred
grandfathers.

Q: I have read your speech at Stockholm, and you say
in the speech that the author should write about the human
spirit, not only love stories or things like that, but the deep
human spirit. What do you think about this point—concerning world peace, the world situation or political aspirations or things like that?

FAULKNER: It's the duty of everyone who wants a decent
world to live in to approach it from his own particular tradition and culture, although he is interested in the same
peace, in which little children can live securely and man can
be happy, although he's got to approach it in the terms of
his own tradition and culture, which are different in the
United States, but it's the same end, the same peace that
we work for.

Q: In your Pulitzer prize-winning work *A Fable*, you wrote
about the resurrection of a soldier. The Japanese writers
consider that this is a new trend in your work. [Do you?]

FAULKNER: No, I don't think so. I simply used a formula,
a proven formula in our western culture to tell something
which I wanted to tell, but that's no new trend. I simply
used an old story which had been proved in our western

culture to be a good one that people could understand and believe, in order to tell something that I was trying to tell.

Q: May I ask a very difficult question—that question is, do you believe in Christianity at the present [time]?

FAULKNER: Well, I believe in God. Sometimes Christianity gets pretty debased, but I do believe in God, yes. I believe that man has a soul that aspires towards what we call God, what we mean by God.

Q: You don't call it God in Christianity?

FAULKNER: Sometimes, but not always. I think that the trouble with Christianity is that we've never tried it yet, but we must use it—it's a nice glib tongue but we have never really tried Christianity.

Q: Have you ever studied Japanese Buddhism?

FAULKNER: Very little. I think that's something one has got to devote a life to, that you can't just read a book on Buddhism and know much about it. You have got to study it, and that's why I say no, I never studied it. I only know what one could get from being interested in any ethics by which man wishes to make himself better.

Q: What do you think about women—in your novels always women take a very deep position—someone is felled by a woman; someone gets ruined by a woman . . .

FAULKNER: . . . and some men are improved by women. I don't think that I would make any generalization about an opinion of women—some of the best people are women, and I'm inclined to think that every young man should know one old woman, that they can talk more sense—they'd be good for any young man—well, an old aunt, or an old school teacher, just to listen to.

Q: What do you think about the Japanese girls you see on the streets when you see them?

FAULKNER: Why, I've spoken to Mr. Picon yesterday—the young ones are much prettier than I expected, somehow.

Q: Oh, is that so? What kind of beauty do you think it to be?

FAULKNER: Well, being young has a great deal to do with it—all young females have a certain charm—but there's something about their posture—their carriage—which to me is very pleasing; something about the facial structure of the young Japanese woman—it's pleasing.

Q: I understand that you were in the Royal Air Force during World War I; why didn't you join the Americans?

FAULKNER: Well, my people were Scottish. They fought on the wrong side, and they came into America, into Carolina, and my grandfather chose the wrong side again in 1861, and I thought that if I ever joined the American Army . . . (undecipherable).

Q: Just one more question—do you think that you received some effect from the works of Mr. Anderson—Mr. Sherwood Anderson?

FAULKNER: I think that he was the father of all of my works, of Hemingway, Fitzgerald, etc., all of them—we were influenced by him. He showed us the way, because up to that time the American writer had been an easterner—he looked across the Atlantic, to England, to France, but only at Anderson's time had we had an American who was primarily American. He lived in the big central part of the Mississippi valley, and wrote what he found there. Hawthorne, the others, they were Europeans, they were not Americans.

Q: Do you love the South?

FAULKNER: Well, I love it and hate it. Some of the things there I don't like at all, but I was born there, and that's my home, and I will still defend it even if I hate it.

MAN: Thank you very much.

Colloquies at Nagano Seminar

I

Q: I am interested very much in your faith that man will prevail. I am wondering if in your stay in Japan so far you found any evidence, any further reason for believing that man will prevail. Is that too big a question?

FAULKNER: No, sir. I would say to me that was put back-

ward. [You might have asked,] have I found any evidence
that I might be wrong? Because to believe that man will
prevail is a proposition that doesn't need to be constantly
proven and reproven and supported. That belief is like the
belief one has in God, Buddha, or whatever his particular
abettor[1] might be. That the only factor that might alter the
belief that man will prevail would be something that would
cause one to doubt that he may prevail. And I think now
that I am not likely in my lifetime to find anything that
would make me doubt that man will prevail. I expect to
see instances in which he has failed, yes, but they're tem-
porary failures. I think that given time he will solve most
of his problems, except the problems which he is doomed
forever to, simply because he is flesh and blood.

Q: Can you amplify on the obligations of man to make
this prevail?

FAULKNER: The obligation is inherent in the quality in
him which for lack of any better word we call his immortality.
The proof of his immortality is the fact that he has lasted
this long in spite of all the anguishes and the griefs which
he himself has invented and seems to continue to invent.
He still lasts, and still there is always some voice, some essay
saying, "This is wrong, you must do better than this." And
there is always somewhere someone that says: "Yes, that's
right, I will do better than this," even though he himself
knows that he might fail when the crisis, the moment comes
when he has got to sacrifice, that the weak shall be protected,
that man shall not be inhuman to man. He tries, I think,
to use all sorts of shabby and shoddy means and methods
to assuage himself, to say that, "Well, maybe I don't have
to work at this," but he himself doubts now and the crises
arise in which he can and does do better than he ever believed
he would and they will continue, that he will always think,
will know, that he can do better than he does and hope that
he will do better than he does.

Q: Why do you put this on an individual basis? Why do
you say there's a single voice always?

FAULKNER: It's that single voice that's the important thing.
When you get two people, you still got two human beings;

when you get three you got the beginning of a mob. And if you get a hundred all focused on one single idea, that idea is never too good. Man has got to be, if he's got to be a collection, or a gang, a party or something, he's got to be a party of individual men. To me, a proof of God is in the firmament, the stars. To me, a proof of man's immortality, that his conception that there could be a God, that the idea of a God is valuable, is in the fact that he writes the books and composes the music and paints the pictures. They are the firmament of mankind. They are the proof that if there is a God and he wants us to see something that proves to him that mankind exists, that would be proof. And if we want to stay on good terms with God, then we better keep in mind that we are, and I don't know of a better way to do it, than with the music, the books, the sculpture, the pictures, poems. That doesn't quite answer your question though, does it?

Q: Thank you very much. I have in mind that perhaps we could bring our questions to bear on both the fundamental philosophy that we have been speaking of and works of literature. This of course is an excellent foundation for that.

FAULKNER: If God can be of any good to us, he would represent certainly harmony. I don't believe anyone would dispute that. It seems to me that in no way can man attain harmony better than in the creation of something which whether he intends it or not will outlast him. That is to say, in effect, when he has passed beyond the wall of oblivion, he will leave on that wall—you know for a few years, everywhere, you saw "Kilroy was here"—well, that's what the artist has done. He can't live forever. He knows that. But when he's gone somebody will know he was here for his short time. He can build a bridge and will be remembered for a day or two, a monument, for a day or two, but somehow the picture, the poem—that lasts a long time, a very long time, longer than anything.

Q: I would like to ask a question that's more specific and not so concerned with the larger issues. It concerns the relationship of an author's fame to his material and the way the author handles his fame. Your colleague Hemingway,

it seems to me, has chosen to handle his public relationship
with the world in one way and you in another, and at the
same time it seems to me that Hemingway and another
writer we talked about, Fitzgerald, have made more use of
their relationship to the immediate world than you have.
Can you comment on that?

FAULKNER: Yes, probably they needed that relationship
with the world more than I did. That is, I don't think that
[the fact that] they needed the relationship with the world
that Fitzgerald and Hemingway established and obviously
wanted had anything to do with the value of their work.
It may be that the same composition of hormones and genes
and what have you in them, which produced the sort of
work they did, produced the need to establish that sort of
relationship with the world that was typical of them.

II

Q: Speaking of [poetry], mention was made, Mr. Faulkner,
the other day, of the difference of American literature and
French literature. There are a number of similarities between French and Japanese hardships. Edgar Allan Poe is
popular in France, so he is in Japan, or at least used to be,
because Poe's artistry is exquisite. His finesse appeals to our
sensitivity as well as the Frenchman's. At one time in Japanese literature, poets used to sing long poems resembling
somewhat Walt Whitman in the volume of the voice and
in the representation of nature. But our population increased
and it became accordingly smaller, our poets came to sing
only [shorter] poems. However, the names of poems are of
secondary importance. The poet may sing of the Rocky Mountains or sing make-believe, provided the poem is good. Your
literature, allegorically speaking, is of a larger piece, feeling
at home in the vast ocean, but ours is of a small fish living
in a big stream. That is what I think.

FAULKNER: I agree with that. How much do you think
that environment, geography, tradition and everything that
makes up one ethnic racial group might have to do with the
individual produce? That is, my idea is that the sums of
years that have produced the Japan of my time was the

power which took the idea and refined and refined and
crystallized it until it became just this faint shadow of the
tree on the rock, when my own country, which is new,
which is still in a certain amount of turmoil, it doesn't know
yet where it's going, it's not even an integrity, racially or
ethnically, even. And so its literature will, as I see it, inevitably
reflect that condition. That's what I meant the other day
when I spoke of my belief that environment shaped culture
rather than culture created environment. But as you so
rightly point out, the value of the article is not at all in its
size. And so it's really not too important, the size or the
shape of it, not even who made it. It's the truth and the
result. That's my belief.

Q: The [integrity] of the Japanese character. Did you
think it before you came to Japan?

FAULKNER: Yes.

Q: Are you still thinking of us as a rational people?

FAULKNER: Rationality?

Q: Yes.

FAULKNER: Well, I think of the Frenchman as the man who
makes a fetish of rationality. To me the Japanese is a man
who has made a fetish of intellectuality, that he prefers that
all the frayed ends of the idea be trimmed off, that it be
complete and intact, and exquisite and refined. But I still
think, if you will pardon me, that sometimes that leads one
into an impasse, where all he's got left is intellectuality,
there's nothing in it any more. It doesn't always happen,
but it's possible.

Q: There's an obvious typographical error here. I think
the typist left out a phrase. You haven't seen this, Mr. Faulkner, in its final form?

FAULKNER: No, I haven't.

Q: As I remember your original manuscript, it says you
believe that the Japanese culture is a culture of the intellect,
and the culture of the French is one of rationality. The typist
in copying said the Japanese culture is a culture of rationality.
There has been a mistake in typing; I think that's what caused
the problem.

FAULKNER: No, your version, which you just spoke, is what

I had in mind. That the Japanese culture is one of the intellect; the French culture is [one of] rationality. They prefer to be rational than right. Or just, or anything else, but they would be rational first. They like it.

Q: That would be, then, that the Japanese culture, for instance, is a culture of the intellect as the French is a culture of rationality, and the British culture, etc. This is a typographical error.

Q: Some of us have been asking Mr. Faulkner to amplify or interpret further some of his own earlier comments. If I may add to that kind of topic, I for one (I think others, too), would like to know exactly what you have in back of your mind, Mr. Faulkner, when you use as the measure of successful accomplishment in literature the standard of attempting the impossible.

FAULKNER: That's what the phrase "Kilroy was here" means. Man cannot live wherever he knows that. He will do the best he can to be physically immortal as well as immortal in spirit; and to try to do more than he knows he can do, is the right aim. To do better than he knows he can do makes something better than it is. All artists, all writers, deal in the same truth because there's not very many different phases of it, and it has been said before, said marvelously so many times before, and it is not enough just to want to say that as good as it has been said, to say this time just a little better, because you know you can't do it, but you can try.

Q: Speaking of the environment, I think that your South is very complicated. Do you think we can understand that your [style] is rather complicated, at least for us, because your environment is complicated?

FAULKNER: No, sir, I don't quite hold that. I think that the theme, the story, invents its own style. I think that if one spends too much time bothering too much about his style, he'll finish with having nothing left but style. That the theme he is trying to tell, if it's worth telling is something that has moved and stirred him so much that he's got to tell it and he's got to say, "Kilroy was here," he's got to tell all the truth in that one time because he may not have another chance. And he tried before and it wasn't quite good enough. This time he will try it again to make it better, and he's not deliberately trying to be obscure but he's trying to get everything into it this time that wasn't in there before. Maybe this time it will be right. Now that's the difference between the Japanese and the American. The Japanese is older and has been an artist longer and he has decided that refinement and refinement and refinement until only the essence is left, is right. The westerner, who has not been an artist very long, maybe he will find that someday, but so far he hasn't. Especially the American, whose culture is of mass production and in that way his environment may affect his style without actually creating that style, it's his temperament. And lack of practice, I wouldn't say initiates, but lack of practice [influences]. Occasionally there would be one like Hemingway, who through instinct or through good preceptors learned that he could do better by holding to a supple, undeviable style, and he trained himself not to be a stylist but to tell what moved him in that method which his preceptors said, "This is a good method." He has stuck to that. He was right to do it, probably, because what he's done is very fine. But the others, Wolfe, for instance, and myself, for instance, we didn't have the instinct, or the preceptors, or whatever it was, anyway. We tried to crowd and cram everything, all experience, into each paragraph, to get the whole complete nuance of the moment's experience, of all the recaptured light rays, into each paragraph. That's why it's clumsy and hard to read. It's not that we deliberately tried to make it clumsy, we just couldn't help it.

Q: Mr. Faulkner, may I add that we have new movements in Japan, too. You talk about refinement, but in poetry, for instance, we have new movements, too. The new generation will not be contented with what they have inherited from the past. They have things they want to express and things of their own, and for that, it is said, the theme brings out the suitable expression, and so I think the new generation, too, will not be contented with the old refined style, style of expression.

FAULKNER: I think so, too. And I think what is primarily responsible for that sort of alteration in the sound, the style, the shape of work, is disaster. I think I said before that it's hard believing, but disaster seems to be good for people. But if they are too successful too long, something dies, it dries up, and then they have to collapse with their own weight, which has happened with so many empires and dynasties; but disaster is good for man. But if it does nothing else it reminds him who he is, what he is. And so I'm sure you're right that there will be a new pattern in Japanese writing, poetry, painting.

Q: Would simplicity of style [result from absence from disaster]?

FAULKNER: I don't quite understand, tell me again.

Q: The simplicity of style that's characteristic of Hemingway's writing. . . .

FAULKNER: I wouldn't think so. Of course, I don't keep abreast of literature enough to answer really, but I wouldn't think so. But I'm not, as I said, a literary man in the proper sense. And I have read not for style, to see what style meant really, or method meant; I read because what I read was about people who behave as I believe people should behave.

Q: I mean not in ideas, but in the use of words.

FAULKNER: Then that I don't know too much about, either, because in your sense, I'm not even an educated man. I didn't like school and I quit about sixth grade. So I don't know anything about rational and logical processes of thought at all. I didn't have enough mathematics to have a disciplined mind.

Q: Mr. Faulkner, [just what do you mean] when you say our culture is that of intellect? For our Japanese critics, Japanese literary critics, are always telling us that the one thing we Japanese lack is intellect. Maybe your definition of intellect is different.

FAULKNER: I tried to explain a moment ago that by intellect I mean the processes of the mind which must follow a reasonable, I mean, a mathematically reasonable, pattern. That is, if one thing is thought, then another thought must follow that, and another thought must follow that. It's not too important what the thought is about. But one thought must follow another just like one chess move must follow another.

Q: Mr. Faulkner, do you mean logic by intellect?

FAULKNER: No, sir. Logic needs intellect to function but I don't think that logic and intellect are the same thing. If I understand what logic means, it's to take a series of thoughts or ideas that continue to a logical conclusion. Or to a conclusion that is inevitable, assuming that one has stuck to the premise. Intellect is the business of taking that premise and following or fitting the next idea that fits it, the next idea that fits it, the next idea that fits it. There could be an error somewhere in that but the process of the intellect goes on.

Q: In your definition, does logic presuppose conclusion?

FAULKNER: No, it's not interested in conclusion, it's interested in its own process.

Q: [Do you think the arts are] going to decay?

FAULKNER: No, if they do, then man is finished.

Q: [Do you think they are likely to flourish?]

FAULKNER: No, I don't; I do not, I think that they are, well, they never flourish. That is, if I have the right comprehension of what you mean by flourish. But they exist and they endure. Otherwise, man himself wouldn't have lasted this long. That comes back to the single voice always somewhere saying, "You must be braver than you may be and are; you must be more compassionate than you are; you must be more truthful than you are," and there's always enough to say, "Yes, I will." And so, we get rid of the tyrants that way, we get rid of a great deal of the misery which we create for ourselves, a condition of keeping cool, of little children who don't have to work in sweat factories any more. There's a certain amount of protection against a merchant selling one poison food, the condition of women is better, the condition of the people who were slave people is better. That's some advancement. The artist has more freedom, at times he had to please some lord or baron for his daily bread, he had to speak ideas which pleased some powerful person; he doesn't any longer. The philosopher can say what

he wants and he knows nobody will take him out and build
a fire under him. That's some improvement. And even when
he knew the fire would be built under him, he still said
what was truth. And when it's easier to say truth, it seems
to me reasonable that more people will say truth. And when
disaster comes and we learn, as we do, that man does learn,
that's another proof of his immortality, that there's certain
ways of living that we cannot continue or we must perish,
then he changes them.

Q: Mr. Faulkner, [how do you feel] about Robert Penn
Warren's idea of death?

Faulkner: The only book of Mr. Warren's that I ever
read was *All the King's Men,* and the best thing, I thought,
in that book was a story he threw in, and I don't know why.
That's all of Mr. Warren I have ever read.

Q: Would you repeat that, please, Mr. Faulkner? We
didn't get that.

Faulkner: I never read but one book of Mr. Warren's.
It was called *All the King's Men,* and the only thing good in
that book, and that was very good, was a story which he put
into the middle of it. I don't know why except he thought
it was an awful good story himself, that's probably the
reason. But for me, I would have kept that story and thrown
the rest of the book away.

Q: We are getting close to the end of the present session.
The question that was just asked and answered leads me to
ask what we might take as one final question, Mr. Faulkner,
this afternoon. Several members of our group I have heard
wondering about your earlier confession that you haven't
particularly kept up on present-day literature, but that you
were content to re-read many of the books that were of
interest and value to you some time ago. The participants
are wondering if you would mind telling us just what some
of those books would be.

Faulkner: No, sir. I read *Don Quixote* usually once every
year. I read *Moby Dick* every four or five years. I read *Madame
Bovary, The Brothers Karamazov.* I read the Old Testament,
oh, once every ten or fifteen years. I have a complete Shakespeare in one volume that I carry with me and I read a little

of that almost any time. I read in and out of Dickens some every year, and in and out of Conrad, the same way, some every year.

Q: This policy, I am sure, will lead at our next meeting to further questions, and as you can see, Mr. Faulkner has dodged no questions, so we need not, I take it, hesitate to ask him anything, however profound, that may come into our minds.

FAULKNER: Please don't, for to tell the truth, I'm learning, too. I'm learning a great deal more about Japanese than I knew, which is what I hoped and intended when I came to your country.

III

FAULKNER: Let me ask your apologies for this interruption, too, and to promise you that it is in what I think we all agree is a good cause so that people will know what goes on at these seminars at Nagano. Too few people know what this means, what it could mean. I spoke to Dr. Yoshitake, Dr. Honda, this morning, and asked their advice, and they were kind enough to allow me a chance to talk to the junior professors, which so far I hadn't done, and that is what I hope we might do tonight, that we could start a discussion under the auspices of the senior professors so that the junior professors could talk to me. I think it's very important that people communicate as individual to individual, not as the representatives of groups. Dr. Yoshitake, Dr. Honda were kind enough to give me the chance, this chance, to talk to the junior professors. Dr. Yoshitake, would you like to explain any more than I have; is it necessary?

PROFESSOR YOSHITAKE: Yes, I think so. It is not necessary for you to explain the program. We have plans made, we have various people who [wish to ask question]. Yesterday evening, when you mentioned those books which you read, you said nothing about more recently made works. I should like to know how you think of such items, chiefly your opinions as [Proust], Joyce, and [Auden]. Are you quite indifferent to them, and generally speaking, quite indifferent to European culture, traditions?

FAULKNER: To me, Joyce was touched by the divine [af-
flatus]. Proust I have read. The names I mentioned yesterday were the names of the men who I think influenced me.
When I read Joyce and Proust it is possible that my career
as a writer was already fixed, so that there was no chance
for it to be influenced other than in the tricks of the trade,
you might say, but I think the bad [habits] had been established. When I named the writers that I'd read, I did not
mean by that that I had not read anything else and did not
read anything else, but they were the ones that, to me, had
been masters, and I felt towards them the same loyalty and
affection and respect the young student feels towards his
professor, his master, which doesn't mean that the young
student doesn't exchange ideas with his contemporaries. Joyce
was, well, in a way, a contemporary of mine; Proust, almost
a contemporary of mine, that is, he was writing towards the
top of his talent at the time when I was writing towards
mine. No, I did not mean that I did not read these people
and, of course, I have a great respect for their talent. I meant
only that I had named the ones which I felt were my own
masters, that had influenced me.

Q: Mr. Faulkner, sir, yesterday, you told us the books
which you are now reading or which you have read and
you mentioned the Old Testament, but you didn't mention
the New Testament. I want to know the reason why.

FAULKNER: The reason is, to me the Old Testament is
some of the finest, most robust and most amusing folklore
I know. The New Testament is philosophy and ideas, and
something of the quality of poetry. I read that too, but I
read the Old Testament for the pleasure of watching what
these amazing people did, and they behaved so exactly like
people in the 19th century behaved. I read that for the fun
of watching what people do. The New Testament I would
read for the reason that one listens to music, or one would
go to a distance to see a piece of sculpture, a piece of architecture. That to me is the difference. One is about people, the
other is about the aspiration of man within a more or less
rigid pattern, such as the pattern of the art formed by
philosophy.

Q: Mr. Faulkner, to tell the truth, I have not yet read your recent novel, *A Fable*. According to some critics, written on *A Fable*, it's slightly different from your previous novels. Then, if you don't mind, will you tell us the relation between [your earlier works] and *A Fable*?

FAULKNER: I'm inclined to think that [all of a man's] work has such a definite relationship that he doesn't in mid-career change his stride, or his purpose. It may have for the moment, for the sake of one particular work, have what you might say is a different attitude, a different point of view, but it is basically directed towards the same point, and this was—I think I've spoken of this once before—it is the desire of the artist before he dies to say all he possibly can of what he knows of truth in the most moving way; that I used that form, I used a story, which had been proven to be one that did move man, which was that part at which the father must choose between the son's sacrifice or saving the son, as one of the most moving tragedies which can happen to the human breast. I used terms which were familiar to most people which saved me a little trouble there. But it was principally to try to tell what I had found in my lifetime of truth in some important way before I had to put the pen down and die.

Q: How would your American younger generation think of European culture against your culture? Do they still think of European culture as a superior one or do they feel that American culture is independent and can stand by itself?

FAULKNER: No, I think the American younger generation is badly confused, maybe more confused than any other national younger generation. I think that they are not too afraid that when the moment, the crisis, comes that they will live up to the demands to be made on them, but they like to think that by taking a nihilistic attitude towards it, it looks well. Of course they don't want to face it, but basic-ally, they are as sound, I think that all young men, young people everywhere, are sound, that they listen to their elders, and in America, the elders talk one moment about a fear of war, the next moment they talk about weekends²—remove the fear of war by continuing production. They don't want to face the fact that man has got to accept freedom or accept servitude—one of the two completely, that there cannot be degrees of human freedom, and so much of the economy—a certain amount of it—is based on an inner quality[3] of man for various reasons—one very serious one is the color of skin, which you in your country are free of. It's no longer a question of caste, it's no longer a question of money, but now it's a question of skin, and they wish to continue an economy in which they can make a certain profit, because a certain amount of the population, because of the color of skin, is compelled to live in a little [humbler] fashion, to have a little less, to accept a little less.

Q: Do you think that [if America had] economical equality it will help very much to get rid of the racial prejudice?

FAULKNER: Actually, in my country, I think there's a desire everywhere that it be got rid of, that such a condition is in itself a sickness, and no country can exist with an internal sickness, that there are—a minority—other people whose economy depends on that sickness, and they will drown themselves to the fact that no nation can live very long sick, it has got to suffer the operation which will remove this sickness, this cancer. In time, that cancer will be removed. It's —I prefer to think that this is the only practical way to do it—that people must be calm, that people, the victims of the injustice, must be the ones that will have the most patience, that people really must be patient, they must be capable of waiting rather than to be frightened into taking irrecoverable steps.

Q: In this country, Somerset Maugham, the British writer, is very popular, and his works are widely read, and his value as a storyteller is highly appreciated. If you care for him at all, what do you think about him?

FAULKNER: That's true in my country, too, yes. I read Maugham when I was a young man, and occasionally I still read Maugham. Some of his early books I think had more strength than some of his later ones; to me there's a kinship between Maugham and Thomas Mann, that in Maugham's earlier works there was something of the quality that Mann's books had, and to me, except for maybe *Death in Venice* or a short story called ["Rain" (?)], Maugham never quite touched Mann's books again, and I think that Maugham never quite touched some of his earlier works again, though the talent is there; it's quite a good talent, but it reached its peak before he died, which is unfortunate, that a man should reach that peak and then die, because it's very difficult to stop writing, that writing or any form of art is probably the worst place that one can receive from the Gods—once he's touched that, he's never satisfied.

Q: Mr. Faulkner, I understand in the story "The Bear" treating the American scene, and I presume in your latest book, *A Fable,* you developed the same feeling on a larger and a more generous scale, and my question is, does your conception of wilderness cover the whole modern civilization?

FAULKNER: No, not actually. I see your point, I see what you mean, but no, it doesn't, because to say that wilderness is the whole modern scene is a little more of an intellectual idea than I had. The wilderness to me was the past, which could be the old evils, the old forces, which were by their own standards right and correct, ruthless, but they lived and died by their own code—they asked nothing. But if I understand that you mean wilderness in the sense that people speak of the present day jungle of cities where crime can exist, no, it doesn't mean that sense at all. To me, the wilderness was man's past, that man had emerged. The bear was a symbol of the old forces, not evil forces, but the old forces which in man's youth were not evil, but that they were in man's blood, his inheritance, his [instinctive] impulses came from that old or ruthless malevolence, which was nature. His dreams, his nightmares; and this story was to me a universal story of the man who, still progressing, being better than his father, hoping that his son shall be a little better than he, had to learn to cope with and still cope with it in the terms of justice and pity and compassion and strength.

Q: Mr. Faulkner, do you mean a living force by nature?

FAULKNER: Yes, yes, mind that spawns and produces, it doesn't care whether it makes a poetess or bricklayer, or lion or serpent, but it still will produce something—a force, a blind force, that by its own standards is neither good nor bad.

Q: I would like to know what the puny, tiny mongrel dog symbolizes.

FAULKNER: That little dog in that story to me symbolizes the thought of loyalty, the thought of courage, that because it was loyal and believed that it was loyal to something which in turn was loyal to it; that there's nothing, no bad influence in it, mongrel though it was, raceless, casteless, with no ancestors to boast about and no hope of future, but it was still loyal and brave, and because it loved what it was loyal to, it believed that loved one was capable of that loyalty, and so no bad influence was in it at all.

Q: Mr. Faulkner, in "The Bear" and other short stories of yours, your English is pretty understandable to me; however, in most of your novels, your English and style is too difficult for me, and it has puzzled us a great deal, and I think our literature is something reciprocal—the writer writes and the reader reads it, and I mean that when the writer writes, it is not yet literature, and when the reader reads it, it is passive literature, but the literature itself exists in the process of giving and taking, and so this might be very possible; but I myself would appreciate it very much if you would be kind enough to teach us, to make your English a little bit more easy. I know some Japanese writer who, when he became a writer, wrote in very difficult style; gradually he, well, he changed, or maybe his style became easier, I don't know which, but anyhow, his style changed a great deal, and he began to write in an easier style. And also I think of the recent changes in paintings and sculpture maybe, the very abstract and the surrealistic pictures, and those things are, well, not understandable to me and well, I myself don't like them. You see, I heard you in Nagano at a press conference, and your style, your best one, and your only style—I apologize—what do you think about it?

FAULKNER: Well, I agree with your first statement that it takes two to make the book, the poem. What I said in the first conference about my style being the best one, I meant by that, as I said before, that anyone in writing is writing about truth and there's only one truth, and any one writer

worth his soul is never satisfied with the job he's done because it wasn't as moving as he wanted it to be, so he tries
it again. It's the same truth, but it has taken a different
story, there's different people in it, different characters in it,
different situations, and they compel the style. That is, he's
still trying to tell that truth in such a truthful way that if
he dies tomorrow, he will have said that and would be sad,[4]
and unless he is trained so that he can control his method—
and there're not too many artists, western artists, that are
trained that way—there were few, there were sculptors, there
were few painters, there were few musicians, like Mozart, that
knew exactly always what they were doing, that used their
music like the mathematician uses his formula. Anyway, he
knows exactly what he's doing, but all artists, they can have
the urge, the desire, the need, but they don't have the—whatever the quality that Mozart, Hemingway, had, and when
I said the best, that meant that at the time I was doing the
best I could to tell this truth. Now, I agree with you, when
it's difficult for the reader to understand and the mistake
is not his but mine—it failed again, and so I try again.

Q: Mr. Faulkner, what tobacco do you smoke?

FAULKNER: Tobacco that was blended for me by Dunhill
in London when I was about nineteen, twenty years old;
I've been smoking it ever since. They have the number
down in a big book; they've had that book for two hundred
years I suppose—and they look in the book and read off the
formula and mix it up.

Q: Mr. Faulkner, I know that you lived once [in New
Orleans, near] Mr. Sherwood Anderson in the same apartment. I would be very delighted if you will tell me some of
the first impressions you received.

FAULKNER: Why, he was one of the finest, sweetest people
I ever knew. He was much better than anything he ever
wrote. I mean by that he was one of those tragic figures
that had just one book, which was *Winesburg, Ohio.* He
wrote that and then he found later that that was all, and
there was someone else who died too late, and he kept on
trying to write *Winesburg* again and that was all. To me,
Winesburg should have been worth a lifetime, he should

have been contented with it. When I met him, it was by
chance. I hadn't seriously thought of writing, then. I was
working for what we called a bootlegger—this was in the
days when there was prohibition in America, and a raw type
of rum would be brought up from the West Indies and be
changed into Scotch Whisky and gin and whatever you
wanted to have. I was—I ran a boat that would go down
into the Gulf of Mexico and bring back the rum to make
into the bottled whisky. I didn't need very much money
in those days and I would be paid a hundred dollars for
each trip, which was a lot of money in 1921, so I would loaf
until I ran out of money again, and I would write. And I
met Mr. Anderson—we would meet in the afternoon, we
would go around the city, talk to people—he'd talk and
I'd listen; then in the evening, we would meet again, we
would go somewhere, we would sit over drinks and talk
until we went to bed. The next morning, he would get
home writing. We would meet again in the afternoon, again
in the evening, the next morning he was at home writing,
and so I decided that that was about as pleasant a life as I
knew, and if that's the way you live being a novelist, I would
try being a novelist, too. So I wrote a book called *Soldiers'
Pay,* and when I started I found out that writing was fun,
and I was at mine all day and at night, too, and I hadn't
seen Mr. Anderson for three or four weeks, and he came
to see me—the first time he ever came to see me—and said
that he hadn't seen me in some time, and I said, yes, I'm
writing a book. And he said, I'll make a trade with you.
When you finish it, if I don't have to read it, I'll tell my
publisher to take it. So I said [all right]. I finished the book
and he told his publisher to publish it, and the publisher
took it—that's how I got to be a writer. But he was a very
nice man—he—except for that tragedy—he was successful in
our American terms and his fault is, he was an insurance
man, and he decided suddenly that he wanted to be a writer
and an artist. He gave up that success, gave up his home—
had a family—left it all to be a writer. He wrote that one
book and then there was no more, and that was his tragedy,

he'd got success, he gave it up. I mean success in American terms, he gave that up, and then had just the one book. Very sad. But I think that *Winesburg* is a very fine work, I think [*The Triumph of the Egg*] is a very fine work—some of the stories, the short stories—but after that it got worse and worse and he tried and he tried and he tried—that was the tragedy. And I think that's what he died of.

Q: Mr. Faulkner, who are your favorite poets, if any?

FAULKNER: Oh, the English poets of the [Elizabethan period]—most of the Elizabethans. I like some of the later ones—I read Pope with a great deal of pleasure, Milton, but my favorites are Shakespeare, Beaumont and Fletcher, Marlowe, Marlowe probably more than Shakespeare. One of my favorites is Campion, Thomas Campion. I know just a little of the French poets, but I know very little of any poetry outside of English. The German—there are great Germans, of course—Goethe was a [great one.]

Q: Don't you like John Donne?

FAULKNER: Yes, all the Englishmen.

Q: Are you composing poetry now?

FAULKNER: No, I wanted to be a poet—found out very soon that I could not be a good one, and so I tried something that I might be a little better at. I look at myself as a failed poet.

Q: In "The Bear" you quoted from Keats. Did you like him?

FAULKNER: Yes, yes.

Q: Mr. Faulkner, I want to know your opinion about Caldwell, especially in connection with his plain, simple style, because it's so popular here.

FAULKNER: For plain, simple style, it's first rate. There was a thought or a certain moving power and quality in his first book, *Tobacco Road,* but after that, it gradually grew towards trash, I thought. But in the first book there was a very moving power, that those people even at times when I —well that was my country, too—close to it—I didn't quite believe in them, there was still something human and moving, even though I never did quite accept them as actual people.

Q: You said there is a short story, "The Man from the South,"[5] and according to some critics, the hero of that story is you. . . . Do you identify yourself?

Faulkner: Yes . . . That was in the beginning, when he first began to realize his tragedy. I think when a writer reaches the point when he's got to write about people he knows, his friends, then he has reached the tragic point. There seems to me there's too much to be written about, that needs to be written about, that needs to be said, for one to have to resort to actual living figures.

Q: May I take it that there is a symbolized feature of truth—there is a symbol of nature or truth for women?

Faulkner: The story itself, I hope and intended, told the truth. "The Bear," as a story, was a truth of the bears and animals, was a natural force which represented not a deliberate evil, not a satanic evil, but the quality of evil in sample[6] size and force which exists, which man has got to face and not be afraid of, that force itself has certain rights which must be respected. That force must not be reduced by trickery, it must be reduced by a bravery comparably as strong as its power.

Q: I think that Stephen Crane is still alive in American literature.

Faulkner: Stephen Crane, yes. That was another case of man who had one book, a very fine book. It's sad that the writer can't accept the one very fine book, but apparently he can't—you've got to believe that if you keep on you will write that well again or that better again—luckily Crane didn't live long enough to drive him to the anguish and the unhappiness that it drove Anderson to.

Q: Excuse me, will you repeat the name of this book?

Faulkner: *The Red Badge of Courage.* Is that in Japanese, Dr. Yoshitake? *The Red Badge of Courage*—is that in Japanese? The Stephen Crane book?

Professor Yoshitake: Yes, we have it.

Faulkner: Who's the translator?

Professor Yoshitake: Mr. Yamaya is going to translate it.

Faulkner: Well, you had two good books to translate, anyway.

MR. YAMAYA: We are very fortunate to have two good writers for translation.

MODERATOR: Thank you, Mr. Faulkner. I think we'll close the session now until tomorrow. Thank you for a very interesting discussion.

FAULKNER: Let me thank Dr. Yoshitake and Dr. Honda for giving me the chance to talk to the juniors here tonight. Thank you very much.

———————

Q: Mr. Faulkner, we hear that you mentioned in Tokyo something like primogeniture. Do you regard it as a duty or as a burden?

FAULKNER: Well, a responsibility, not a burden. If we understand burden in the same sense. You mean by burden, something that one abhors and does not like—I think that anything worthwhile is a burden. To be always truthful is something of a burden. To be always courteous is something of a burden; and maybe a certain amount of burden, or a responsibility of burden, the knowledge that one will accept burden, not shirk burden, is good, once you have that. Does that answer you, or do you understand what I was [referring to]?

Q: I heard once at the commencement of [some] college you gave a short speech, and you [placed Thomas Wolfe] first of American—contemporary American—novelists. Could you explain this?

FAULKNER: Yes; that wasn't at the speech, it was at a meeting of students something like this—I mean at a school. They were not faculty people like you, they were graduate students, and I was asked for my opinion of my contemporaries in American literature. They named the ones of my time about my age; they were Hemingway, Dos Passos, Thomas Wolfe, Erskine Caldwell, and I said that in my opinion we had all failed for the reason that I've just spoken of, that I think that no poet, no writer, is ever satisfied with what he has done, that it wasn't quite good enough, that the next time he will do it, that up to that moment we had all failed, and I rated us not by our accomplishments but by the splendor of the failure, and I rated Wolfe first, not by what he'd accomplished but because he made the—he dared most—in my opinion. I rated myself second because I dared most, second. I rated Hemingway last because Hemingway through good fortune or through good preceptor, had developed a style where he was quite at home, where he did not make mistakes, and that he did not risk as we've risked, but that's—remember, the rating I gave had nothing to do with the work—it was only in my own idea of the splendor of the failure that we'd made, because I believed at that time that none of us had done his best work, you see, that if we lived long enough we would do the good work, some of us, maybe one out of the five would do the good work, the best work of our age, our time, I hoped. That's what that meant.

IV

Q: I have been given the honor of speaking first. This morning when you gave your suggestion that we should choose one of your works which is most popular in Japan, we discussed [the matter] and *Sanctuary* was chosen. First, I would like to ask you to give your frank opinion of our choice, that we have chosen *Sanctuary*. Would you expect it, or be disappointed? We would like to hear.

FAULKNER: I think that that's a very good subject to start with. I think we should find plenty of discussion in that book. I suppose you know how it came to be written. I believe I wrote an introduction that explained that. If anybody's not familiar, I'd be glad to tell you about it.

Q: We read it, but if you will explain it more fully, we would be very happy.

FAULKNER: Well, I had been writing books and getting a lot of pleasure out of it and one day it occurred to me that maybe some money might be made out of writing. And so I thought of the story which I was most confident someone would pay money for, and I wrote it. I sent it to the publisher and he wrote back saying, "Good Lord, we can't

print this, we'd both be in jail!" And so, I forgot it and I
wrote two more books. They were published and then one
day in the post I got the galley of *Sanctuary*. That was two
years after. And I read it and it was so badly written, it was
cheaply approached. The very impulse that caused me to
write the book was so apparent, every word; and then I said
I cannot let this go. But they had made what they call the
plates, which is the metal imprint which the book is taken
from. And the only way to rewrite that book was to break
up those plates and make new prints. The publisher at that
time was a young man, too, just starting out in the business,
and he said, "I haven't got the money to do this." And I said,
"You can't print it like this; it's just a bad book." And so
our agreement was that he would pay half the cost of the new
plates and I would pay half. And my half was $270 and I
didn't have $270 at that time. And so that was the first lesson
I got, not to write cheaply; always do the best that I could.
The book was published, was very popular. The first time
I was to make a lot of money. And just before I got the money,
the publisher went bankrupt. And so I got my full deserts
for that and that taught me a lesson—from then on, if I
were going to write, to write as honestly as I could—a lesson
that I am very grateful for now. So the book, as it stands,
is the best I could do with it.

Q: Mr. Faulkner, could you please give me the privilege
of disbelieving your statement just now. I can't believe your
statement that it was badly written. According to my understanding, maybe I'm too simple-hearted, but I find something deeper beyond the surface. According to me, it seems
to be unjust. As you wrote it, I can't help having the feeling
of the universal injustice of [the world]. Take this case:
the hero of the story, Popeye, got killed because not his killing
the policeman, because of another reason, and I couldn't help
feeling the injustice in law and I couldn't refrain from
feeling terribly impressed with the injustice in the world.
And I just shook myself in that sense. Would you comment
on that?

FAULKNER: Yes, your point is well made. Remember, the
one you read was the second version. At that time I had

done the best I could with it. The one that you didn't see was the base and cheap one, which I went to what sacrifice I could in more money than I could afford, rather than to let it pass. The one you saw was one that I did everything possible to make it as honest and as moving and to have as much significance as I could put into it. And I'm glad that your comment has told me that you saw that I was right.

Q: So would you give me the privilege to believe that your statement concerning the money business was part of it true?

FAULKNER: Yes, to this extent, that the artist had better not bother about the money. That is, he takes his art one moment away from the value of the work and begins to think of it in terms of the money, then he has debased his art, his craft, and he deserves the worst that can happen to him.

Q: One of the participants asked you, how are the ideas [about life to be presented]. You answer that the way in which you have written is the best way to express them, and I ask you to explain more in detail about it.

FAULKNER: The answer to that, it seems to me, was expressed in this gentleman's discussion a moment ago when he said that he had found in *Sanctuary* an exposition of the terror and the injustice which man must face and which he must combat if he is to live with himself, with his soul, if he is to sleep in peace at night. The Stockholm address was, I hoped, exactly what it said. I wished to use that moment to speak to the young writers, the ones who some day would stand in that fortunate position, to remind them that the things to work toward, to write about, were the verities which later he would never be ashamed of. That a man, not only the writer, but man in his life, whatever that life is, must remember those verities, he must try to live up to those verities, whether he always can or not, and that the poet's duty is not just to record his triumphs and his defeats but to remind him always that his triumphs are truly his triumphs, the triumphs not of that individual, but of all men.

Q: I want to know your view of women. You write of lots of women who are various types of women in your novels and your stories. Of course, they are the women in the South and

not in the North. Is there any difference between the women
in the North and in the South?

FAULKNER: No. I think there's no difference between
women anywhere. Just as I think there's no difference between men anywhere. The women that have been unpleasant
characters in my books were not created to be unpleasant
characters, let alone unpleasant women. They were used as
implements, instruments, to tell a story, which I was trying
to tell, which I hoped showed that injustice must exist and
you can't just accept it, you got to do something about it.
That when you are brave you may not get the reward for it,
but the bravery is its own reward.

Q: Mr. Faulkner, I would like to ask you a problem. What
kind of readers or audience did you expect while you are
writing a novel? There is your answer that you have written
your works for your own view or for yourself, but so far as
a writer wants to publish them, it seems to me writers must
expect some kind of readers in mind. Do you expect Southern
readers or much larger readers?

FAULKNER: Now that I can't answer because of one time
in my life I was so busy writing, I wrote so seriously, that I
didn't have time to stop and think, "Who will read this?
Will he like it, or won't he like it?" Because I was so busy
trying to write something that would please me, that would
suit me, that would be in my estimation the best. Each time
it was not, and I had no time to stop and think who will
read this, what will they think, because at that time I was
furiously engaged in writing the next one, hoping that that
would be the one that would suit me completely, knowing
it wouldn't and I would probably have to write another one
as soon as that was done. I don't mean to say that wasn't
fun all the time I was doing it; it was fun. But it was [after
I] got old and began to slow down that I became conscious
there were people that read the books. And when I found
that people read the books and got pleasure from them and
found in them something of what I tried to put in, I was
very pleased, I was very flattered. Though they found things
in those books that I was too busy to realize I was putting
in the books. They found symbolism that I had no back-

ground in symbolism to put in the books. But what symbolism
is in the books is evidently instinct in man, not in man's
knowledge but in his inheritance of his old dreams, in his
blood, perhaps his bones, rather than in the storehouse of
his memory, his intellect.

Q: Whenever I read your novels I feel that you have been
obsessed by the idea that women are causes of all evil and
troubles. For instance, taking the example from this story,
Clarence Snopes said to Horace Benbow like this, "Half the
trouble in this world is caused by women." For instance,
Miss [Myrtle] was saying, "If us poor girls causes all the
trouble and get all the suffering. . . ." Would you say something about that?

FAULKNER: Yes. You'll remember that those two opinions
came from the sort of people whose opinions one would not
put too much faith in. One was a base opportunist whom no
one would dare trust very far, the other was a woman who
belonged to a class, a profession, which had been debased;
well, the profession depended upon a certain abasement, but
before a masculine world. In comparison or opposition to
them, I like to think of some of the characters I invented or
wrote which to me are some of the best. One was the Negro
woman, Dilsey, in *The Sound and the Fury,* who had taken
care of a family who were decaying, going to pieces before
her eyes. She held the whole thing together with no hope of
reward, except she was doing the best she could because she
loved that poor, otherwise helpless, idiot child. There was
the old woman in stories of our Civil War in the middle
of the last century who held a family together, did the best
she could to keep the Negroes fed and clothed, to look after
the mothers a little more while the menfolks were off galloping around the country waving their swords after glory.
And the opinion that women cause the trouble is not my
own. I think that as fine an [influence] as any young man
can have is one reasonable old woman to listen to, an aunt,
or neighbor, because they are much more sensible than men,
they have to be. They have held families together and it's
because of families that a race is continued, and I would
be sorry to think that my work had given anyone the im-

pression that I held women in morally a lower position than men, which I do not.

Q: Mr. Faulkner [the young lady who asked the question], likes to know if Emily is your ideal woman, or do you like Emily or not?

FAULKNER: I feel sorry for Emily's tragedy; her tragedy was, she was an only child, an only daughter. At the time when she could have found a husband, could have had a life of her own, there was probably some one, her father, who said, "No, you must stay here and take care of me." And then when she found a man, she had had no experience in people. She picked out probably a bad one, who was about to desert her. And when she lost him she could see that for her that was the end of life, there was nothing left, except to grow older, alone, solitary; she had had something and she wanted to keep it, which is bad—to go to any length to keep something; but I pity Emily. I don't know whether I would have liked her or not, I might have been afraid of her. Not of her but of anyone who had suffered, had been warped, as her life had probably been warped by a selfish father.

Q: Mr. Faulkner, what does the loss symbolize in the story?

FAULKNER: Why, it's the loss which, the grief which might come to anyone, and one must have the training to face loss and griefs.

Q: Mr. Faulkner, I think she means "rose."

FAULKNER: Oh, that was an allegorical title; the meaning was, here was a woman who had had a tragedy, an irrevocable tragedy and nothing could be done about it, and I pitied her and this was a salute, just as if you were to make a gesture, a salute, to anyone; to a woman you would hand a rose, as you would lift a cup of *sake* to a man.

Q: I think you have an ideal woman in your mind. And what type of woman is your ideal woman and in which novel or story can I find your ideal woman?

FAULKNER: Well, I couldn't describe her by color of hair, color of eyes, because once she is described, then somehow she vanishes. That the ideal woman which is in every man's mind is evoked by a word or phrase or the shape of her wrist, her hand. Just like the most beautiful description of anyone, a woman, since we are speaking of women, is by understatement. Remember, all Tolstoy said about Anna Karenina was that she was beautiful and could see in the dark like a cat. That's all he ever said to describe her. And every man has a different idea of what's beautiful. And it's best to take the gesture, the shadow of the branch, and let the mind create the tree. So, that's why I couldn't begin to describe my ideal woman, which of course I have.

Q: In your works, with your variety of characters, are you concerned with psychological type story of Jung, one of Freud's disciples, or do you create such characters entirely due to your observation and imagination?

FAULKNER: A writer is completely rapacious, he has no morals whatever, he will steal from any source. He's so busy stealing and using it that he himself probably never knows where he gets what he uses. Probably no writer can say, "I was influenced by so and so." He can say, of course, "So and so encouraged me, I admired his work," and he might say, "I was influenced by him and no one else." But that writer is wrong, he is influenced by every word he ever read, I think, every sound he ever heard, every sense he ever experienced; and he is so busy writing that he hasn't time to stop and say, "Now, where did I steal this from?" But he did steal it somewhere.

Q: Mr. Faulkner, my question is rather irrelevant, but let me ask you, what part of the dialect did you use in your work?

FAULKNER: I doubt if I ever used any dialect, except possibly the one that I speak myself. That is, the dialect is a good deal like something I said about style. The moment, the character, the rhythm of the speech, compels its own dialect. One moment the character can speak as a countryman, then when the need comes he will speak as a poet, but still in the phraseology of his background. I think to set out to write in dialect is as wasteful as to set out to write in style. That is, if one is busy trying to create on paper living people, he hasn't got time to bother too much about style or about dialect.

Q: I think your way of speaking is a little bit, I'm not sure, but is it hillbilly talk, or colloquial hillbilly talk?

FAULKNER: My characters, you mean?

Q: No, I mean your way of speaking.

FAULKNER: No, I can't say. No, it's not what I would call hillbilly talk. It's not university talk. I don't know what it would be.

Q: Well, your intonation or your stream of speech is somewhat different from the so-called [standard speech].

FAULKNER: I would say that it is probably a rhythm that pleases my own ear. That is, I am not trying to make sounds with my mouth which sound good to me. But all the time that I speak there's possibly an auditor here that controls and checks just like the stock on the [?], so that it pleases something in my own ear.

Q: And when I read your novels, sometimes I hear in my ear your voice. After I met you your voice recalled it, page after page. And I wish if you record some of your works like Thomas [Mann] very recently, it helps us readers very much.

FAULKNER: There has been some of it recorded. When I get back home I will send a record here. Who shall I send it to, Professor? To the Embassy, I think. Yes, I will do that when I return home.

Q: I find in your novels some Scotch expressions; do Americans who come from Scotland live in your town?

FAULKNER: Yes, the people in my country were mostly of Scottish origin. We have lived remote from railroads, communications, until a few years ago, and so our talk, our expressions, are identical to ones you hear today in Scotland. We say, for instance, not to 'clean' a room but to 'redd' a room, as the Scot does. Moreover, one who steals cattle is a 'reaver', just as in Scotland. In all the dialect of that section, you find any number of words, terms just like those used in Scotland, for the reason we are of Scottish descent.

Q: Mr. Faulkner, you met a lot of Japanese women since you came to Japan. What is your impression of them?

FAULKNER: Well, of course, if I had visited Japan before, I might be able to answer that question better. As I have seen the Japanese women in the short time I have been here, there is not too great a difference that I can see between American women except the fact that most Japanese women can speak English and few American women can speak any language except their own, and not always that very well. I don't see too much difference. And my impression is that they are of a quality of courtesy which is not feminine. It's in all Japanese I have met. They are a little gentler perhaps than American women. I mean by that, they're not so abrupt. Their manners are better, put it that way, than American women.

Q: Do you have any idea of writing a story taking a theme on this country now?

FAULKNER: Probably not. I doubt if I'll live long enough to ever get done all the writing I want to do about my own country. But if I do live to be 100-odd years old and use up my [materials] I may turn to Japan.

Q: Mr. Faulkner, in *Sanctuary,* they couldn't prevent the beating. In *Intruder in the Dust,* they could prevent the beating. Does that mean you found some reason you could save the Negro from beating in your latter work?

FAULKNER: People can always be saved from injustice by some man. The story I was trying to tell in *Sanctuary,* it was necessary that this man, tragic though it may be, should not be saved. The story I was trying to tell in *Intruder in the Dust* was this Negro, who because of his black blood was already doomed, could be saved by a little child and an old lady. Anyone can save anyone from injustice if he just will, if he just tries, just raises his voice.

Q: And in some of your stories, the Negro and young boys are always congenial to each other. Does this mean that the young boys, only young boys, could find good quality in colored people and then after they grow up they have some kind of crisis and couldn't see the color of the people as they are?

FAULKNER: Yes. It means that if the problem of black and white existed only among children, there'd be no problem. That that child as he grows up becomes a victim of economic pressure. The whole trouble between the black and the white is not in anything racial or [ethnic]. It's an economic fear that if the white man allows the Negro any sort of advancement whatever, the Negro will take his economy away from him. That is, if man for a moment could be set in abeyance and a generation of black children and white children allowed to grow up together, the problem would vanish, I think.

Q: We find in your works not a few characters mentally deformed and crippled, congenitally or by environment. As you know, some noted writers and thinkers of modern times, for instance, Rousseau, declare we should return to nature to recover our whole and proper humanity because I dare say they thought civilization gave our humanity [a wrong slant]. Do you hold such an idea, and if you do, to what extent and in what relation to civilization do you support such an idea?

FAULKNER: No, I don't hold to the idea. I don't hold to the idea of a return. That once the advancement stops then it dies. It's got to go forward and we have got to take along with us all the rubbish of our mistakes and our errors. We must cure them; we mustn't go back to a condition, an idyllic condition, in which the dream [made us think] we were happy, we were free of trouble and sin. We must take the trouble and sin along with us, and we must cure that trouble and sin as we go. We can't go back to a condition in which there were no wars, in which there was no bomb. We got to accept that bomb and do something about it, eliminate that bomb, eliminate the war, not retrograde to a condition before it exists, because then if time is a [forward] and continuous thing which is a part of motion, then we have to run into that bomb again sooner or later and go through it again.

Q: Every lady and gentleman has a time to speak in connection with the words that have been told to Mr. Faulkner. Do the names of your characters have a specific meaning?

FAULKNER: No, my characters, luckily for me, name themselves. I never have to hunt for their names. Suddenly they tell me who they are. In the conception, quite often, but never very long after I have conceived that character, does he name himself. When he doesn't name himself, I never do.

I have written about characters whose names I never did know. Because they didn't tell me. There was one in *Pylon*, for instance, he was the central character in the book, he never did tell me who he was. I don't know until now what his name was. That was the reporter, he was a protagonist.

Q: Mr. Faulkner, how much weight do you put on the form of novels? We find various kinds of forms you have taken in your novels; some are [simple in plot, some are involved].

FAULKNER: The answer to that is like the names of the characters, that a novel compels its own form. Sometimes the novel knows from the first exactly how it wants me to write it, and I have written books in six weeks; I have worked nine years on another because I didn't know how it wanted it written. I would try it, that would be wrong, I would try it again, that would be wrong, until I would realize I had done it the best I could, I'd better put that one away and write another one.

Q: In *Wild Palms* there are two kinds of stories and they are entangled. What kind of effect did you intend in that story?

FAULKNER: To tell the story I wanted to tell, which was the one of the intern and the woman who gave up her family and husband to run off with him. To tell it like that, somehow or another I had to discover counterpoint for it, so I invented the other story, its complete antithesis, to use as counterpoint. And I did not write those two stories and then cut one into the other. I wrote them, as you read it, as the chapters. The chapter of the "Wild Palms," chapter of the river story, another chapter of the "Wild Palms," and then I used the counterpoint of another chapter of the river story, I imagine as a musician would do to compose a piece of music in which he needed a balance, a counterpoint.

Q: Mr. Faulkner, in the introduction to the [Portable Edition] of your work, Mr. Malcolm Cowley says in *The Sound and the Fury* that you have not overcome presenting the frustrations and suffering after death. Am I wrong?

FAULKNER: You're right. I wrote *Sartoris*, then I wrote *Sanctuary*. *Sanctuary* couldn't be printed as I told it, then

I wrote *The Sound and the Fury* and *As I Lay Dying*, then *Sanctuary* was published.

Q: And, Mr. Faulkner, why did you begin to consider the Yoknapatawpha County as an [epitome of your] work?

FAULKNER: I think it was because about that time I realized there was a great deal of writing I wanted to do, had to do, and I could simplify, economize, by picking out one country and putting enough people in it to keep me busy. And save myself trouble, time—that was probably the reason. Or it may have been the same reason that is responsible for the long clumsy sentences and paragraphs. I was still trying to reduce my one individual experience of the world into one compact thing which could be picked up and held in the hands at one time.

Q: Were you any changed in your view of life before you went to the war and after you came back from the war? I ask you this question because the war must have given you a deep impression upon the mind.

FAULKNER: Well, yes, it did. Of course, everything that one experiences impresses the mind. When I went to that war I was more or less a child, and anything that happens to the mind of a child impresses it. And war is very likely to make an impression on any mind. But I don't know that it made any uncommon impression. I don't know that it altered very much what I might have gone into otherwise. It's possible it did, but that's a question that no one can answer. I prefer to think that it would not have, that I would have been more or less what I am now, with war or without war, though I don't know.

Q: Mr. Faulkner, so far almost all questions came from juniors; may I go ahead and [speak for] our seniors?

FAULKNER: After all, youth should give place to age in some points.

Q: Speaking of your county, Yoknapatawpha, could you just explain, what shall I say, the origin of Yoknapatawpha? I'm not saying, you may say Yoknapatawpha calls itself. But Japanese wonder about the origin of Yoknapatawpha.

FAULKNER: Of the word? Yes, it's a Chickasaw Indian word. They were the Indians that we dispossessed in my country.

That word means 'water flowing slow through the flatland', which to me was a pleasant image, though the word in Chickasaw might be pleasanter to a Chickasaw ear than to our ear, but that's the meaning of it.

Q: Mr. Faulkner, it seems to me that you are one of the most, or one of the very rare writers of the world who have most strong belief in immortality of mankind, immortality of man's soul. May I ask what has made you so, is there any [experience] or special event, or your culture, your education?

FAULKNER: I have noticed in young people in America— I don't know how true it is with young people in your country —but there's a certain feeling of shame about admitting the idea of immortality, that it's a little archaic, the idea. That one should be up with the times, with the modern age, and to think of immortality is not only old fashioned but it implies a certain amount of ignorance. But maybe in my own case it's ignorance in the sense that I am not a trained thinker, not a school man, but I don't feel the shame about believing in immortality that I might feel expressing a belief in it if I were an educated man and could refer to philosophy. That's a bad answer, but that's the nearest I could explain it myself.

Q: How about the older generation?

FAULKNER: [Short answer, unintelligible].

Q: In your novels, there are some ideas of [human values], for example: *pieta, gloria, virtus*, etc. Have you studied Latin literature in your young years?

FAULKNER: I didn't, because I doubt very much if the Latins invented glory and pity and integrity. I think that the Latins, like all the people, inherited a knowledge of glory and pity and integrity. I don't think they invented it, and I don't think that one has to have studied any literature to believe that glory and pity and integrity are important and valuable. I've seen ignorant people that didn't know the words, that acted on the belief that they were valuable and important.

Q: But you have quoted Horace in your *Soldiers' Pay*.

FAULKNER: Well, I like to read Horace, yes.

Q: Have you read some other Latin writers?

FAULKNER: Yes, when I was a young man I read a great

deal of poetry and I have probably quoted lots of it in my work and I still read it. For the Latin, I taught myself a little of Latin, reading poetry, just like I [did with] French, reading Flaubert, Balzac, Laforgue, Verlaine.

MODERATOR: It is my ungracious function to call attention to the fact that this particular session should now terminate. Just a short time ago Mr. Faulkner expressed to us his great belief and trust that the artist always feels, that he may hand down to posterity something immortal, and as he himself phrased it, in the language of the late war, "Kilroy was Here." I am a little bit afraid that if I am at all remembered in connection with the Nagano Seminar, it will be in terms of "Kill-joy was here." But perhaps I may be partly excused if I tell you at this time what Mr. Faulkner's next subject is going to be. He has consented to read to us one chapter of the work on which he is at present engaged, a chapter that has so far been read or heard by nobody else. And that new book is to carry the title, *The American Dream*. For the following session, which must be the final one, Mr. Faulkner is going to talk to us on his impressions of Japan.

v

Q: Mr. Faulkner, we never expected you to come to Japan. Whatever got you here?

FAULKNER: When I received this invitation, I declined because your culture was foreign to my culture. I didn't think that we would understand each other. Then someone from the Department in Washington said, "If you knew how anxious the people in Japan are to see you, and if you realize how much good you might do by going, you wouldn't hesitate," and I thought that people should come to know one another, should make efforts, if there is anything that people of one nation can give to people of another nation, they should make that effort to do so. Even when they themselves doubted the result of it.

Q: And what strikes you most in Japan, may I ask?

FAULKNER: First is your beautiful scenery of your country. Next is the politeness, the courtesy, of the Japanese people to make a stranger welcome to the country.

Q: Now, Mr. Faulkner, the South of your country and Japan have something in common, that is, an old tradition. You seem to have much interest in the old tradition of Japan. Now what aspect of our tradition do you find homogeneous with yours?

FAULKNER: We had at one time a tradition of an aristocracy something like the Japanese *samurai,* and also a peasantry which was somewhat like the Japanese peasantry, that was the connection I saw between our two peoples to make us understand one another possibly.

Q: We think the troubles of the South stem partly from the old world; are we right?

FAULKNER: Yes.

Q: And what modification do you think that European tradition has undergone?

FAULKNER: The tradition which we inherited was intelligent, an intellectual tradition when it was transposed to our country which was a new, virgin, seething country. It was transposed just a little in order to exist in a rough, awkward land, and out of that, I think, came benefits to us from our European heritage.

Q: And Indians and Negroes play an important part in your work. What kind of meaning do they have in the [Southern] tradition?

FAULKNER: They represent the dispossessed, the people who racially or ethnically have received injustice from the hands of people who were more fortunate than they, and my use of them in my work is from pity, that I believe that people should not be treated unjustly or with injustice just because they happen to be red in color or black in color.

Q: Now, is there any author, American or European, from whom you may have received the greatest influence?

FAULKNER: I can't say. I think like all artists, all writers, I have received influence from every artist and writer before me, Japanese, French, English, Russian, that I ever read.

Q: Very interesting. What do you mean by Japanese authors; whom do you mean? Could you mention?

FAULKNER: No; to me the author is not important, it's the work. I never had a favorite author, I don't know what it means to have one, it's the work. To me, the story, the poem, is much more important than who wrote it. The Japanese literature that I read when I was young and read a lot, I remember the stories, I remember the people in those stories, but I don't remember who wrote them.

Q: Among contemporary American writers, whom do you like best?

FAULKNER: That question gets the answer that I just gave. To me the writer is not as important as the work, and some obscure [authors] have written things that I admire, some of the best have written things which I don't like. So I can't say that I have a favorite author. But the work to me is the important thing.

Q: How do you think about Mark Twain, Mr. Faulkner?

FAULKNER: In my opinion, Mark Twain was the first truly American writer, and all of us since are his heirs, we descended from him. Before him the writers who were considered American were not, really; their tradition, their culture was European culture. It was only with Twain, Walt Whitman, there became a true indigenous American culture.

Q: Do you mean, Mark Twain was the first founder of your national literature?

FAULKNER: Yes, in a sense. Of course, Whitman was in chronology the first, but Whitman was an experimenter with the notion there might be an American literature. Twain was the first that grew up in the belief that there is an American literature and he found himself producing it. So I call him the father of American literature, though he is not the first one.

Q: Now, Mr. Faulkner, we Japanese students of American literature regard both you and Mr. Hemingway as the two masters of American fiction of today. We should like very much to hear your frank opinion about Ernest Hemingway.

FAULKNER: A very fine talent, a man who knows exactly how to do what he wants to do.

Q: And how do you think about his style?

FAULKNER: His style is a perfect style in the sense that it suits exactly what he wants to do with it. He can control it, it never falters. So, if a style can be perfect it seems to me it must be the style that the man can use exactly and never fail nor falter with, which I think Hemingway does.

Q: As you know, a lot of people consider that both you and Mr. Hemingway show the extremes, I mean.

FAULKNER: Yes, I think so, too.

Q: Now, Mr. Faulkner, in your second speech you suggested that young writers shouldn't forget the problem of the human heart in conflict with itself. But as you know, the present situation, I mean, cold war, industrial confusion, etc., the present situation seems not entirely favorable for young writers to devote themselves to those problems. Now, Mr. Faulkner, in what way do you suggest they can follow your advice?

FAULKNER: I think they must follow that advice. The man or the woman, the writer, has no choice in when he will be born. I agree with you that this is a bad time to write, but that should not deter the man who has been given talent by God, heaven, wherever talent comes from. That should not deter him, and the difficulty of the work, if anything, should improve the quality of the work. But he must remember always that the important thing is the work. It's too bad he must live in a time when work is difficult, but let that not stop him.

Q: What kind of work can we expect from you in the near future?

FAULKNER: I hope better work than I have done. I think that one is never satisfied with the book, the poem, he has just finished, which is the reason he writes another one. And I believe as long as he or I live I will still try to write the good book which up to now I have never quite done.

Q: Are you right now working on some fiction?

FAULKNER: Not at present, but I am still writing. But it's not another work of fiction in the sense that I wrote ten years ago.

Q: What's your hobby, may I ask? You know a lot of people, and Japanese people are quite interested in what your hobbies are. Do you still enjoy aviation or hunting?

FAULKNER: Yes, I still enjoy aviation, but it has become

so mechanical that the pleasure I had once is gone. One has to be a mechanical or technical expert to fly any more. The days when anyone with an airplane and a tank of fuel could fly where he wanted to is past. And, yes, I like hunting. I suppose that if I have a hobby, it's horses. I like to raise and train horses.

Q: Do you own some horses?

FAULKNER: Yes.

Q: How many?

FAULKNER: I have five.

Q: And what kind of horses?

FAULKNER: One I'm training for a jumper. I have one that I had trained as a hunter, that is, that I could ride through the country after hounds, after game; the other one that I am working on now would be just a, what we call, a school jumper, to jump just for exhibition. The others are work horses. They will draw carts, carriages, things of that nature.

Q: Why do you like horses, may I ask?

FAULKNER: I think I inherited it. My father was a horseman. Well, my first memories are of horses, of being on ponies in front of greens. And my children are the same. They were on horses in front of greens before they could talk, almost. I think it's just, it's a family heritage that we all get as we grow up.

Q: Mr. Faulkner, is there any connection between your literary works and horses?

FAULKNER: In a sense, yes. I believe I learned from horses to have sympathy for creatures not as wise, as smart, as man, to have pity for things that are physically weak.

Q: I am very interested in that fact that you love horses because Sherwood Anderson was also interested in horses, and I think there is some connection between two of your interests. Of course, now you don't have spotted horses. You know we studied the little piece, very interesting piece, "Spotted Horses," in the seminar and we enjoyed it very much. And speaking of animals, I think you know we read and discussed "The Bear." Could you make any comment or explanation about "The Bear"? It's very famous and, what shall I say, it's very popular among Japanese scholars. I wonder if you could make any comment or explanation about that wonderful piece. I mean, "The Bear."

FAULKNER: Yes, that was symbolism. That was the story of not just a boy but any human being to grow, as he grows up, to compete with the earth, the world, the bear representing not evil, but an old obsolescence that was strong, that held to the old ways, but because it had been strong and lived within its own code of morality, it deserved to be treated with respect. And that's what that little boy did. He learned not about bears, from that bear, but he learned about the world, he learned about man. About courage, about pity, about responsibility, from that bear.

Q: I keep thinking that piece is the boy's initiation to life and nature.

FAULKNER: That's right, his discovery of the world, of life.

Q: What did you mean by the bear? Taking it this way, the bear is symbolic of nature itself?

FAULKNER: Yes, symbolic of nature in an age when nature in a way is being destroyed. That is, the forests are going, being replaced by the machine, and that bear represented the old tradition of nature.

Q: Does that nature include both evil and good?

FAULKNER: Yes, sure. Its own morality. It did things that were evil, by a more intelligent code, but by its own code they were not evil and it was strong and brave to live up to its own code of morality.

Q: In conclusion, let me ask you about your style from translator's standpoint. So far, I myself have translated many authors, British and Americans, but you are the most difficult writer to render into Japanese, except perhaps James Joyce, whose *Ulysses* I translated with some of my friends about ten years ago. I think the difficulty with you maybe lies in your style, objective and subjective combined, with so many implications and symbolic meanings. Now, Mr. Faulkner, I'll only ask you two questions in this connection. Is your style the result of very conscious efforts, studying various kinds of new experiments and prose techniques, or is it quite natural for you, and you can't help writing as you do?

Faulkner: I would say that that style is a result of a need, of a necessity. This is what I mean, man knows that he cannot live forever, he has only a short time to live, there could be in a man's mind, in his heart, a desire to express some universal truth and he knows he has only a certain number of years to express that truth in, and so in my own case anyway, it's the compulsion to say everything in one sentence because you may not live long enough to have two sentences.

Q: And secondly, do you think your works can be translated into foreign languages without losing their artistic merits?

Faulkner: I think they can be translated into any language provided the story I told was valid and true. Now in another language it may, the construction, the style, may have to be changed, of necessity. I think that's not too important, that when it won't translate into any language the fault is not the translator's nor the language, it's in my original, that I did not tell that truth that I was trying to tell. To me to translate the style, the method is not too important. It's to get the sense of it.

Q: What you mean is, any bad translation can't spoil and destroy the truth expressed in the literature?

Faulkner: It may be the worst time he had had to live through yet, but that must not deter him. He must still not take the easy way, he must accept the difficulty of telling what is important and valid no matter how bad the time is, that's all that means.

Q: So you mean this is self-explanatory?

Faulkner: [Yes].

Q: They say you are not so interested in what is called "literary classification." You have been called a lot of things, such as naturalist, traditionalist, symbolist, etc. I wonder what school you feel you belong to.

Faulkner: I would say, and I hope, the only school I belong to, that I want to belong to, is the humanist school.

VI

Faulkner: As Professor Jelliffe said the other day, this is a chapter from what would be a book. It's in the nature of essays. One has been delivered at University of Oregon last spring and was printed in *Harper's Magazine*. This is another more or less complete section, which would be another chapter.[7] This has no very close application in your country, because this problem doesn't exist in your country. But I hope you will see that the problem is more than just a local one in the United States, that it is a problem that affects all people because it is a choice that has actually, basically, not so much to do with racial discrimination as with a choice that people must make between freedom and not being free. So with your permission I will just read it without any more explanation.

[Mr. Faulkner read his "essay" from *The American Dream*.]

MODERATOR: Mr. Faulkner, we have all been made quiet and even solemn by this affirmation of the American spirit. We are greatly moved by the correspondence between this statement and the statement of the same truths in so many of your stories. Our silence is a tribute, you may be sure; but if you are willing at this time, I think there may be some members of our group who would like to make comment or even raise questions.

Q: The chapter you have read just now sounds like, in some parts reminds me, of what you wrote in *Intruder in the Dust*.

FAULKNER: I'm glad you see that, because *Intruder in the Dust* was an effort to show in action what this speaks of in theory. Yes, you're quite right. That to theorize about an evil is not enough. Someone, somewhere, must do something about it. Even if it took a little boy and an old frightened woman. But somebody did do something about an injustice. And somebody somewhere must do something to rectify, cure injustice, rather than just philosophize about it.

Q: I think in *Intruder in the Dust* you talked about hate of the South. I think you suggested a way of solving the complicated problems of the South in *Intruder in the Dust*.

FAULKNER: Yes, people have got to do it, not theories. People have got to say: "No matter how weak I am, I myself, Smith, will not put up with this."

Q: Mr. Faulkner, you said that we don't have that kind

of trouble, racial trouble, in the Far East; we have a little of that same kind of trouble among Japanese and Korean people living in Japan. So we are very much conscious of racial problems.

FAULKNER: Yes, probably racial problems to some extent do show up everywhere and probably anyone's own personal problems do seem the most serious. So that is very likely an incorrect statement to say that only we are troubled with such problems. It just happens that ours at the moment is one that is a blot not only on the American face but it's on the face of all humanity. Probably, I'm sure, that there are economic problems that exist everywhere, in all countries, and if that is an economic problem, as I attempted to say, based on an obsolescence like an inequality of man, then it would have to go anyway. What I don't like is the fact that these people who insist on that economic balance not being disturbed, use such base means. If they would come out and be honest and say, "we don't want to change this because it will cost us money," at least you respect them for telling the truth. You wouldn't think very highly of the type of truth he believed in, but you'd respect him because he told the truth. But he won't say that, he says the Bible says that the Negro must not be our equal, that if the Lord wanted him to be our equal, the Lord would have made him white —foolish, silly things like that. They would tell you that a different kind of blood runs in the Negro's veins from the white man's veins. Everybody knows that blood's blood. Any student in biology could tell them that. No, I object to the baseness of their reason, not the baseness of the motive, because man will always fight for economic reasons, but let him be truthful about it.

Q: I was in New Orleans, April of last year, that's when the decision of the Supreme Court [appeared] against the segregation issue. I ask your opinion of some townspeople of New Orleans. They're for gradual integration in the school system. They thought that the immediate change in the system would throw the community into confusion, so they told me. Now, in what you have just read you emphasized the economic condition is basic, if I am not mistaken, but

I think there is some other problems besides the economic factor, for example, [customs] and morals of the colored people. I should like to know how you think about those problems.

FAULKNER: It is a situation that simply cannot be changed overnight for the reason that it is not basically a moral problem. It is an economic problem, and if it were changed overnight it would mean turmoil, confusion, because it would be an upset of a working economy. It will have to be gradual, but the gradual process which will change it is, in my opinion, people that will say things like this, will believe things like this, and keep on to gain a little, a little and a little, to keep it always in people's minds that no matter what they say about the threat of the Negro, because he is a black man, to the white man, it simply will not stand up if you measure that against "shall we be slaves or shall we be free," and we can't be half-slave and half-free, we got to be either one or the other, and if we are going to talk to—I mean by we, Americans—talk to other people around the world about freedom, let us practice it, let us keep our own skirts clean, so nobody can say, "Well, you talked to us about freedom, look at your own country." That the time is coming, before rapid communications, airplanes, so that people could cross half the world in twenty-four hours, a country could conduct its affairs without much regard for other countries, but that's not true any more. That one nation's trouble now is everybody's trouble. One nation's freedom is every man's freedom.

Q: I am sorry to repeat the same kind of question. You said you object to the baseness of their reasons, not their motives. Does this mean that the nature of man is, what we secured first we don't like to share with others? Do you admit that kind of human nature first?

FAULKNER: Yes, man, his instinct, wants to hold what he has at any price. It takes his conscience to tell him, "You must relinquish some of this," but his instinct, his nature says, "Hold it, you got it, it's yours, it's mine, I want it, I've got it, so I keep it." That's not anything to be at all proud of, but since it is his nature, I would not apply the

word base to that, but when he pretends that his reason for
that is some high moral one, then that is the baseness.

Q: You always talk about truth. Could you give us your
definition of what you call truth?

FAULKNER: Yes, truth to me means what you know to be
right and just, truth is that thing, the violation of which
makes you writhe at night when you try to go to sleep, in
shame for something you've done that you know you shouldn't
have done. That to me is truth, not fact. Fact is not too
important and can be altered by law, by circumstance, by
too many qualities, economics, temperature, but truth is
the constant thing, it's what man knows is right and that
when he violates it, it troubles him. Well, I doubt if he
ever does toughen himself, toughen his soul, to where it
doesn't trouble him just a little and he'll try to escape from
the knowledge of that truth in all sorts of ways, in drink,
drugs, various forms of anesthesia, because he simply cannot
face himself.

Q: Will you distinguish between truth and ideal?

FAULKNER: Well, an ideal is a hope, an aspiration, it
could be an impossible dream. Truth is not an impossible
dream, it's not an ideal or aspiration. Truth is a quality
which one must accept or cope with. That is, he must accept
or spend all his life running from it.

Q: I think most of the readers and students of literature
have deep interest in making approach to the secrets of the
writer. And, naturally, the diary [kept by] Somerset Maugham
and memos are very interesting and useful and helpful for
them. Do you keep a diary? Do you make notes and have
you any intention to publish them?

FAULKNER: No, I never have kept notes. There have been
times when I have made notes, simply as a carpenter would
pick up a few sticks and put them temporarily aside because
he would need them. Then when I used those notes, I threw
the notes away. I never look on them as of any value. They
are the scraps a woman might trim off after she has made
the dress. She doesn't keep those scraps because they have no
value, the valuable thing is that complete dress. And some

of those notes have no place in that dress, in that book, and so I throw them away. I never kept them.

Q: Could you tell me your best story in your own estimation?

FAULKNER: In my own estimation, none of them are good enough, that's why I have spent thirty years writing another one, hoping that one would be good enough. And so my personal feeling would be a tenderness for the one which caused me the most anguish, just as the mother might feel for the child, and the one that caused me the most anguish and is to me the finest failure is *The Sound and the Fury.* That's the one that I feel most tender toward.

Q: Going back to the notes, did you make any when you wrote the first section of *The Sound and the Fury?*

FAULKNER: No.

Q: Would you tell us something about the time you wrote the first section, it seems to be so complicated, and I wonder if you wrote it just as you did *The Wild Palms.*

FAULKNER: That began as a short story, it was a story without plot, of some children being sent away from the house during the grandmother's funeral. They were too young to be told what was going on and they saw things only incidentally to the childish games they were playing, which was the lugubrious matter of removing the corpse from the house, etc., and then the idea struck me to see how much more I could have got out of the idea of the blind, self-centeredness of innocence, typified by children, if one of those children had been truly innocent, that is, an idiot. So the idiot was born and then I became interested in the relationship of the idiot to the world that he was in but would never be able to cope with and just where could he get the tenderness, the help, to shield him in his innocence. I mean 'innocence' in the sense that God had stricken him blind at birth, that is, mindless at birth, there was nothing he could ever do about it. And so the character of his sister began to emerge, then the brother, who, that Jason (who to me represented complete evil. He's the most vicious character in my opinion I ever thought of), then he appeared. Then it needs the protagonist, someone to tell the story, so Quentin appeared. By that time I found out I couldn't possibly tell that in a short story. And so I told the idiot's experience of that day, and that was incomprehensible, even I could not have told what was going on then, so I had to write another chapter. Then I decided to let Quentin tell his version of that same day, or that same occasion, so he told it. Then there had to be the counterpoint, which was the other brother, Jason. By that time it was completely confusing. I knew that it was not anywhere near finished and then I had to write another section from the outside with an outsider, which was the writer, to tell what had happened on that particular day. And that's how that book grew. That is, I wrote that same story four times. None of them were right, but I had anguished so much that I could not throw any of it away and start over, so I printed it in the four sections. That was not a deliberate *tour de force* at all, the book just grew that way. That I was still trying to tell one story which moved me very much and each time I failed, but I had put so much anguish into it that I couldn't throw it away, like the mother that had four bad children, that she would have been better off if they all had been eliminated, but she couldn't relinquish any of them. And that's the reason I have the most tenderness for that book, because it failed four times.

Q: I made a thorough study of the first section and I felt that it was humanly impossible to write it down from the very beginning without any notes, but you did that?

FAULKNER: One time I thought of printing that first section in different colors, but that would have been too expensive. That was about 1930, I think, and at that time they had not advanced the printing of different, separate colors as they have now, and that would have been almost prohibitive in color. But if it could have been printed in different colors so that anyone reading it could keep up with who was talking and who was thinking this and what time, what moment in time, it was. To that idiot, time was not a continuation, it was an instant, there was no yesterday and no tomorrow, it all is this moment, it all is [now] to him. He cannot distinguish between what was last year and what will be tomorrow, he doesn't know whether he dreamed it, or saw it.

Q: You mean to say you wanted to print one whole first chapter in different colors?

FAULKNER: Yes.

Q: In modern editions we have some italic letters.

FAULKNER: Yes, that was the next recourse because italics were easy to be cut into the plates but color would have been prohibitive.

Q: Which work do you like best, all your life?

FAULKNER: I just answered that; none of them are good enough. So, I like the one which caused me the most trouble. That is *The Sound and the Fury*. But none of them are good enough, as good as I am convinced I could do if I had my life to live over and could write them again. But that is impossible, so all I can do is use the rest of my time to write one that will be good enough, which I'm sure I won't do, but I'll probably try.

Q: This is maybe a bad question, but what [part of your reading] would you think gave you most influence on your novels?

FAULKNER: Every bit. That is, I don't know one that influenced me more than another. I know that all my life I have been very fortunate in being very interested, completely interested, in living, in seeing, listening, experiencing, imagining; I've never been bored in my life.

Q: We all know your ability to describe things, persons, etc. So I wonder [why] you drew the picture of the coffin in *As I Lay Dying*? Was it just for fun or were you experimenting?

FAULKNER: I would have to see the book again, I don't remember that. The trouble is I didn't draw it, as I remember, though I may have. But that was thirty years ago and it's been thirty years since I read that book, so I'd have to see this book again.

Q: Or perhaps, the symbol of the eye. I think that was in *The Sound and the Fury*. The picture of the eye with the eyelash.

FAULKNER: I would have to see that, too.

Q: I was just wondering whether you were having fun at that particular moment.

FAULKNER: I may have been, I can't remember either one of them. The only drawing I ever did in any of my books, I did make a map of Yoknapatawpha County which was printed in the back of one, I forget which now.

Q: Mr. Faulkner, what is your favorite hobby?

FAULKNER: Horses. I breed and train horses.

Q: Your next, second choice?

FAULKNER: Hunting, probably, is the second one, then sailing.

Q: How about drinking?

FAULKNER: Well, drinking, I consider drinking a normal instinct, not a hobby. A normal and a healthy instinct.

Q: Well, Mr. Faulkner, I have stayed away from my home for two weeks and I am to some extent homesick. How about you?

FAULKNER: I don't think that I know what homesickness is either, in the sense you mean it. There are some times when I would like to hear rain on the roof of the back porch at my house, but I don't especially want to go back there to hear it because I can imagine how pleasant it sounds from here just as well as to be there and hear it.

Q: Mr. Faulkner, in one of our sessions you named in rapid order four books which you wrote fairly quickly and published fairly quickly, *Sartoris,* etc., then you pointed out that you had taken as much as nine years on one book, and I'd like to know if you still write as much as you did in that brief spurt, or do you write less, more carefully?

FAULKNER: I think, yes. I think there's a period in a writer's life when he is, well, simply for lack of any other word, fertile and he just produces. Later on, his blood slows, his bones get a little more brittle, his muscles get a little stiff, he gets perhaps other interests, but I think there's one time in his life when he writes at the top of his talent plus his speed, too. Later the speed slows; the talent doesn't necessarily have to fade at the same time. But there's a time in his life, one matchless time, when they are matched completely. The speed, and the power and the talent, they're all there and then he is—the American says, he's "hot"—which of course can't last forever, and so at my age probably any writer writes less, not that he writes more carefully, maybe he is a little more difficult to please than the monitor in everybody's mind that judges, passes on what he does, that may be a little more severe than it was once.

Q: Is it possible that the theme of the book that took nine years has something to do with the length of time it took to create it?

FAULKNER: That's a very comfortable belief to hold, that it wasn't because my powers had failed that it took nine years, but I like to believe that I simply wasn't quite ready to write that book when I got the idea. That it took nine years for that book to gestate, and that I had to learn a little more than I knew when I first had the idea.

MODERATOR: The nearer the time comes for Mr. Faulkner to leave us, the harder we all find it to let him go, in any one of these sessions. If there are no other questions at the moment, we'll look forward to our next meeting.

VII

FAULKNER: I was very happy to have a chance to give you my impressions of your country[8] in the short time I have had to form impressions. If I could stay longer these would run into a book, probably.

MODERATOR: Well, ladies and gentlemen, this is the last chance for you to speak to Mr. Faulkner. Please speak something, all participants speak something, to Mr. Faulkner.

Q: I think there is much difference between scenery and the landscape of your country and ours. What kind of impression did you get from the scenery around here, or in Japan?

FAULKNER: Why, your scenery, it's beautiful, but I think the faces are better. I have never been much of a sightseer or traveler, I've never owned a camera and never been too interested in the pictorial, I much prefer to look at faces. And speculate on what's behind those wrinkles, what's behind that expression, what that life could have been that that face shows. What that living, that anguish, or hope or suffering, or whatever it was made that face look like it does. But your scenery is beautiful. This section of Japan, of course, is the one I know best, but your mountains are magnificent. We drove yesterday, and you could see all possible gradations of light from yellow through green into the blues, azure, lilac, on to purple, all with one look of the eye, and the good, rich fertile land where your rice grows—it's nice country.

Q: I think we are in the best season, too. To you are our faces more interesting than other faces?

FAULKNER: Oh, all faces, it's only incidental that the face is Japanese or Scandinavian. It's the face, the life, the same life, the anguish, the same anguish, the triumph, the same triumph. Doesn't matter what it is.

Q: Mr. Faulkner, I would like to ask a question in connection with Japanese faces, Japanese expressions. When Lafcadio Hearn came to this land more than sixty years ago, at first he was puzzled by Japanese smiles. He found Japanese smiles enigmatic, but after some stay in Japan he found much significance in that smile. What do you think of our Japanese smiles?

FAULKNER: Mr. Hearn, of course, had been in your country longer than I have. I haven't seen any particular significance in the smile as a smile. To me—this is, you understand, a quick impression that I've got from a very short stay and probably an unwarranted impression—it seems to me it's more modesty than anything else, it really has nothing to do with what might be going on behind the face, that it's almost a gesture, not really a smile. Because there's a difference [between a laugh and] a smile. When something amusing has been said, interesting, then it's different. But the smile which I see most often is, so far, I think it's a nervous grimace more than anything else. That's probably wrong but that's my thinking.

Q: That's a more realistic interpretation of the Japanese smile than Mr. Hearn's.

Q: Mr. Faulkner, you have always told us your interest is with the people, the common people, and didn't you notice too many people in Japan?

FAULKNER: Well, in a sense there are too many people everywhere. I mean by that that we have not yet taught ourselves to use people as valuable commodities, that if we had given the time to using people to the best of their capabilities and possibilities that we have to making machinery and making things that simply are big and that travel fast, then I think the earth would be a better place to live. Yes, there are too many people everywhere, too many people wasted, unused.

Q: Too many people in Japan?

FAULKNER: No more than anywhere else, but there are too many people everywhere. Too many people wasted, unused, that provision has never been made by us to see that all people have enough to eat, that all people have a chance to go to school. There's no reason why this age shouldn't take care of the population of it, if we just used some sense, had some sense about it, were interested in people.

Q: Mr. Faulkner, I hope you will write about Japan.

FAULKNER: Well, since I have found so much that is pleasant to remember, to write about, in Japan, if I stayed longer I'm afraid that's all I would do. I would write about Japan till all the Japanese people would be sick and tired of it. They'd wish I would go back home and stay there.

Q: I suppose this is a first-time experience for you to attend a seminar like this. How do you find Japanese students?

FAULKNER: Well, I would have to speak in general. I approve of the idea of seminars. I wish that it could be more universal, that more people would have a chance to gather as intellectuals, that is, people interested in ideas, and in that gathering, that meeting, come to know one another as people. When people meet as politicians, it's under a preconception to begin with, and they never get to know each other as individuals, there's little chance to express opinions that don't depend on mass, but on what I believe and what I think would be best that all of us do. As we can do when we gather like this under the aegis of culture or education or whatever it is.

Q: My question has nothing to do with this speech, but

you have done a few screen scripts. Do you think a screen script a promising form of literature? What do you think about the future of the movies?

FAULKNER: Well, it's promising, but in my opinion, that's all, just promising. The reason is, there's no chance for the individual to make something as he himself thinks it should be made. That it's made by too many people, too many forces comment, not only difference of individual opinions about what's good, but there's the tremendous cost in money which must be considered. And that's why I don't think it is as yet a very good medium; it's promising, it could be the best, so that when the story is made, you can see it, hear it at once. For that, it's marvelous, but until they can be made by individuals, then it just promises. The good ones apparently emerge by accident, are not the work of anyone, but nobody of the people concerned know, themselves, as to what happened that this turned out to be first rate. They can't be repeated every time, where one does learn something from a book, a poem, in which he himself has worked alone, so at least he can avoid mistakes, but in motion pictures, you can't. Nobody can promise to produce another of your *Rashomon*. You might hope to, but there's no assurance that you can repeat that or better it or even equal it. But the book, you can, you do hope that maybe you can better it, or if you are careful, at least equal it. Unless the talent is faded.

Q: I am very glad you have got better acquainted with us, the cultural persons of Japan, but I hope you will have the opportunity of getting acquainted with various villages and farmers in this country if possible while you are in Japan.

FAULKNER: Yes, Doctor, I would like very much to stay longer. I think that nobody really comes to know a country in a month or even two months. It takes longer than that. You got to know something of the language, you got to be accepted by all the people. It's easy enough to be accepted in a group like this because we meet on a culture of ideas, but it would take a long time for the Japanese farmer, say, to accept a stranger, or a Japanese fisherman.

Q: In your first talk, you said ours is a culture of the intellect, and we have seen and heard quite a lot of things since then. Do you still believe that ours is a culture of intellectuality, or rather is there going to be some modification or something like that?

FAULKNER: Well, they were just generalizations. Of course, that's not a complete summation of any one culture. It's reducing it to what might be called a workable typification, just for discussion, for talk. No, that's not a real complete summation of any character, and anyone would be foolish to think he could make that assumption. That was simply a workable typification of a culture to distinguish it from American, from English, from French culture.

Q: When we enter a temple, we feel at peace and appreciate the quiet beauty of a temple. But the Shinto temple is rather crowded. What is your impression of the Zenkoji Temple?

FAULKNER: Of great age, of tradition, a little puzzling to the westerner. It was impressive, I got the feeling that the people there believed in it, got some comfort from it, something very important from it. But what, of course, I don't know because I'm a westerner and I could never understand. I can see that what your people get from that temple comes in a different form from what the westerner gets from his, though I would like to think that basically they are related. It takes a different form, a different observance, possibly a different attitude of approach. So that's a question that's a little difficult for the westerner because it's like the Japanese language, there's nothing really to measure it against. They're both temples, both have walls and roofs and they are fixed on the earth and there's something of ceremony in them, and all ceremony is in a way alike because it's ceremonial. But for no other reason. So that's something I can't say, that would be another impression that would not be an impression of an idea at all but a sense.

Q: In your speeches you tell of the old woman who sells peanuts, but in this country peanuts are rather expensive and the Japanese are more frugal and eat only beans.

FAULKNER: Well, you would have to excuse that, too.

Remember that this is another matter of the alien, that in the short time that I've been here, my impressions—I think the impressions are true, but the mechanics, the machinery —may not be true because I don't know enough of Japan for that. So that sort of thing is not a deliberate mistake and the ignorance will have to be excused because at that time I was too busy with what I thought were much more important impressions than to say, are these peanuts or are these beans?

Q: When you visited the Zenkoji Temple, some days ago with the Japanese doctors, I heard you have seen the Bon dance, the Japanese folk dance. Will you kindly tell me the impression of the dance?

FAULKNER: That was an interest in seeing the people, not Japanese people, but all people express themselves by their own poetry, and that's what I thought that I saw. That the Japanese himself was expressing there in his own simple terms, which little children, old people, everybody understood, the poetry of his race, of his tradition, his religion, his work.

Q: We couldn't quite catch you that time. This dance is the way to express what?

FAULKNER: To express the poetry of his culture. And I could see, or I thought [I could], the gestures with which he expressed his pleasure, his joy in breathing, in being alive, his love of his own people, to be with them, doing something together with fifty or sixty or a hundred of them, all of them enjoying what they were doing because they were doing it together, moving in supple, expressive terms of their tradition, their past which is the poetry of a race, of a people.

Q: This is again a question of translation. Through translation we can know truth and contents and the thought of the original, but we can't translate the style and the expression of the original. What do you think?

FAULKNER: That's true. Sometimes style and expression simply will not translate. As I believe I said before, translation owes something not only to the writer, but to the translator. That the translator gives something of his own to that work, that the translator gives something of Japan to the work which was conceived in English, in America. If it's a good translation, and a good translation can even be made of work which itself is not good, and make it gain something from the translator who then becomes more important than the writer. That was the case of FitzGerald and the Persian poem of Omar Khayyam. To the English ear, FitzGerald is probably better poetry than Omar wrote. Though to the Persian, Omar of course would be better than FitzGerald.

Q: Then the translation is sometimes better than the original?

FAULKNER: Yes. Though the germ of the poetry, the truth, must be there to begin with unless the translator himself has written a new poem, a new work.

Q: Mr. Faulkner, would you kindly excuse me when I call you a countryman, not a city man? I, myself, am a countryman, actually come from the South of Japan, and one of the troubles in the South of Japan is the people, especially the intellectual people, aren't contented staying in the country and they are so anxious to make a quick pilgrimage to the culture, for instance. I don't object to that, it's a good thing to go to the horizon, the intellectual horizon, but they go up there and never return. I am very much concerned with that. In addition, I may say that I myself, believer in the community, still have a kind of uneasiness. I am telling one experience of mine which is when I was told that my speech is a Southern dialect, I should have agreed, but I wasn't [happy]. Could you kindly argue some advice to this emotional [reaction]?

FAULKNER: I think that may come back to my quick opinion of what to me constituted your Japanese culture, that's the culture of the intellect, of ideas; and people in this country, in Japan, are more interested in ideas as ideas, not so much wisdom or even information, but ideas, simple ideas. I would say it's maybe a national, perhaps a racial characteristic. And for that reason the countryman has not the chance to exchange ideas or to indulge in intellectual talk. That's why he comes to the cities for the reason that he knows he can find there other people that he can discuss ideas with. That's just an assumption. I would say that may be the reason, I don't know. I rather believe it would be true of all people who are interested in ideas of course, not only your people but mine, too, but I think that more Japanese, or every Japanese, has more interest in ideas, perhaps than, or in the process of ideas, let's put it, than the westerner.

Q: [You spoke of the mountains. Is that your chief impression of Japan?]

FAULKNER: No, everywhere I have been in Japan, I have been conscious always of the sound of water or that water was flowing, and I have seen children along the road, they like to play in water, they sprinkle the streets, and always there is water in motion, there's the sound of it, everywhere. This country is to me, a stranger who's never been here before, almost as full of the constant sound of water as [living by the] sea. I'm conscious always of water, the flowing, the sound of it, of people moving in water, living very close to water, that water is a very important part of their lives, not just to drink it, but the fact that there's water, the fountains, the wells, the wetting down of the streets every morning when I walk.

Q: This is very interesting for me because I have never experienced that impression in Japan.

FAULKNER: That is because, of course, you live here and you wouldn't be consciously suddenly aware of it as a stranger would, coming here.

Q: Have you written these [impressions of Japan] in this room of Gomeikan?

FAULKNER: Yes, I wrote it yesterday.

Q: Did you typewrite it yourself?

FAULKNER: Yes, I typed it up because nobody can read my script.

Q: I've heard you can't read your manuscript yourself after one day.

FAULKNER: Yes, I have to write it again then.

Q: Is it because you write too fast?

FAULKNER: Yes, I can't write as fast as I need to, and I begin to make symbols because at the time it's plain to me, and I say, "Oh, I'll remember what that is," but then to-morrow of course I don't.

Q: May I ask what foreign countries you have travelled in?

FAULKNER: Only in Europe, never before in this part of the world. That's the continent of England, Scandinavia, but never before east of Greece.

Q: I think your visit to Japan added something to you, but I want to know was it positively or negatively?

FAULKNER: Why, I had hoped that this paper you have in your hand would prove that it has done something to me in a very positive way. It was at least positive and urgent enough that I had to sit down and put on paper impressions which seemed to me so important that I didn't want to risk forgetting them. So I would say that's a very positive way, and I imagine after I have been away from your country for a while, I will have still more impressions which right now I don't even know I have. I will remember things that now I don't know that I do remember, but I am sure they're stored away and I will dig them up in time, put them down, too.

Q: Have you found us Japanese to be too serious a people who don't like a joke?

FAULKNER: Now, that, Doctor, I can't answer because I don't know your language, you see, so I can't say. I know that you are very polite and courteous people, and so I don't know what you would be among your friends, when people do laugh and talk, when you [forego your customary] courtesy. The humor, the wit I've seen I have appreciated, some of it I probably have missed. So I'd have to come to Japan and live a long time and know Japanese people better before I can answer your question.

Q: We may seem to you very courteous people, but we do like to joke very much among ourselves.

FAULKNER: Yes, I'm sure you do.

Q: Mr. Faulkner, what is your impression of us Japanese scholars?

FAULKNER: Now that's a question like you would ask my impression of Japanese songs. I think that [people are

scholars] by vocation or avocation, but they are primarily
people. I think that cultured people are cultured by vocation and avocation, but behind that they are still people,
and I doubt if there is any one name that a tenth of you
would fit completely, let alone all of them. So my impression of you would be first of individuals. There are certain
of you, I don't know how, but I have been able to communicate with better than others. I don't know how, don't
know why, except that all people are primarily themselves
and a little different from all other people, that no matter
how much they might want to, people simply won't fit into
a mold or type.

Q: When you wrote these impressions you got the idea
from taking notes or just from your memory?

FAULKNER: Well, I saw the face and when I had the pencil
and paper I found out what I thought when I saw that face.
I just remembered the face. Though, very likely when I saw
the face, the whole thing was instantaneous, but I didn't
bother to remember it, but when I got the pencil and paper
and thought to myself, "What did this face evoke in me?"
that's what the face evoked in me.

Q: I understand, of course, naturally your sympathy with
the South, but frankly speaking, your way of treating the
South is quite, does look quite strange sometimes, and it
seems to me you are both [Southern and American], and
frankly speaking, this is my own experience, whenever I
make a lecture in American literature, most of my students
wonder why your characters—I am now thinking of *Sanctuary,*
and *Intruder in the Dust*—I am wondering why your characters must reach an absolute pitch of degeneration or dam-
nation. Could you explain that?

FAULKNER: Yes, I think the reason is simply that I love
my country enough to want to cure its faults and the only
way that I can cure its faults within my capacity, within my
own vocation, is to shame it, to criticize, to try to show the
difference between its evils, its good, its moments of baseness, and its moments of honesty, integrity and pride, to
remind the people who condone the baseness that there were
moments when it was glorious, when they as a people, their

fathers, grandfathers, did fine, splendid, glorious things. Just
to write about the good qualities in my country wouldn't
do anything to change the bad ones. I've got to tell people
about the bad ones, so that they'd be angry enough, or shamed
enough to change it.

Q: That's why you've got to take up the extreme cases?

FAULKNER: Yes, probably. I'm not really a sociologist,
though I assume that that is perhaps the reason behind it.

Q: This is again a question about your South. Do you
think your attitude towards this South has ever changed
from the very beginning? Is there any development in your
way of, in your philosophy of life?

FAULKNER: Well, my attitude towards it would have to
change because in the country I come from, as in yours,
it's either moribund and doomed or itself changes. So, the
attitude, the point of view, the feeling toward that country
must keep pace with it. There are things in my country
that I don't like, that have become more apparent so that
one has got to hate it a little more than one did twenty
years ago or thirty years ago because it's worse now than it
was then. There are other things which are better than they
were then, and so I love my country more but the balance
is probably the same. I think that one never loves a land,
a people, or even a person not because of what that person
or land or place is but despite what that person or place
is. That perfection, you'd have great admiration for it, but
no warmth for it, not enough warmth to want to change it
or to amend it.

Q: Remember that one of the characters in your *Intruder
in the Dust* says the North and the South of the United
States are two different nations and, well, according to my
interpretation, the North is part of the United States and
the South is the other part of the United States, but if I
remember correctly one of the characters in *Intruder in the
Dust* said that the North and South are two different nations.
Am I right?

FAULKNER: Well, now you must remember that that was
that character's opinion and it need not necessarily be mine.
I'm writing about people, not trying to express my own

opinion, so that could have been his and I would have dis-
agreed with him possibly. I don't remember the context from
which that came but that's possible that that was his own
opinion.

Q: If I remember, I heard that gentleman mention two
people, but to my understanding I think, watching them, the
Southern people [resent the criticism of the Northerners].

FAULKNER: But that's my belief anyway, yes, that one
state, one precinct has no business compelling another state
or precinct to correct its ills; that never works, but the
precinct, the state itself must correct those ills.

Q: Is that kind of antipathy about the Southerners against
the Northerners still prevalent in the Southern States?

FAULKNER: True, only among the old people who can
remember something of the Civil War between 1860 and
1865. They're usually women who were children during the
ten years after that war when we were an invaded land,
invaded by people speaking our own language, which is
about the most savage war that you can have. When people
speak different languages, they seem to be much more decent
in war than when they are divided and speak the same
language, then they seem to have no mercy on each other.
And some of the old ones can still remember that, the fact
that our houses were looted by people who spoke our language.

Q: The racial troubles between the white and the Negroes
are rather fatalistic so far as it concerns the superiority complex of the white people, don't you think so?

FAULKNER: Not really, no. It's economic. The Southern
farmer can make more money when he can have peonage
to do the work. If he can keep the Negro in a position where
he will be content with less food than the white, man to man,
will live in worse quarters than the white, man to man, will
be satisfied with inferior schooling, then he will continue to
work for less pay than the white man gets. The white man
in my country is afraid that if he gives the Negro any advancement, any social advancement at all, the Negro man
will stop working for the low wage and then he will get less
when he sells his cotton, that's all it is. But they will use
religion, they will use all sorts of nonsense about the white

man having been created by God better than the black man
to justify this position. It's not that at all. It's purely and
simply they want the black man to keep on working for less
money than they'd have to pay a white man to do that work.
That's all.

Q: Your work, *A Fable,* is dedicated to your daughter Jill
and I am sure you are most fond of your daughter, but why
did you dedicate your book to her?

FAULKNER: Why, that was the year she was twenty-one
years old, she had been the youngest of the children and
she had inherited lots of my traits. That is, she liked horses,
too, and she spent a lot of time with me for that reason.
With horses and with farmwork. And when she was little,
she was more or less under my feet all the time 'cause she
just liked the land, she liked dirt, she liked animals, and
she listened to me for advice more than the others did, and
for that reason I was more interested in watching her development because I had a chance to see, "Am I any good
at this business of leading a child's development of character?" and this was just a gesture toward her when she became of age and was no longer under my thumb. It was just
a way of saying, "Good-bye to your childhood, you are grown
now and you are on your own." That's all.

Q: I have heard you don't like to speak about politics,
but if you don't mind, I would like you to speak in brief
about your writing on communism or communism government.

FAULKNER: I don't like any form of totalitarian government. In theory, I thought that communism would be very
good for people, only I don't think that communism as I
understood it twenty-five years ago exists any more. This
is not the communism that I thought I understood, this is
something different. I can't see the difference between this
and Germany, ten years ago, fifteen years ago, of any monolithic state in which men use the mass of peoples just like
the rich men in my country established their power and their
aggrandizement on beaver pelts. It seems to me that the
totalitarian people use people just like they use beaver pelts,

just for their own power. And I agree that democracy as we talk about it in my country is a very clumsy, inefficient way for people to govern themselves, but so far I don't know a better one.

MODERATOR: Just as soon as Mr. Faulkner leaves us, we shall all be reminding ourselves of innumerable other questions. But even as it is, if some time there should be a P.S. to this document we all hold in our hands, and if Mr. Faulkner should permit himself to give us his impression of the Nagano Seminar, I suspect that part of that impression would be the questions drawn from all parts of the universe, touching on earth and heaven. We shall all be happy to have as a memento these impressions in mimeographed form. Long after they have been carefully filed away, we shall all remember the tone of his voice and his presence here among us and the fact that we wish, all of us, that he might stay longer.

FAULKNER: May I take this opportunity, Dr. Yoshitake? I'm going to leave Nagano tonight and some of you I won't see again, many of you I won't see again, and I want to thank you for the warmth which you have given me since I have been in your country. They say to part is to die a little —not to die, but to leave something, perhaps. So when I go I will have left something in Japan and in its place I'll take something back with me to my country, something of the courtesy and the warmth of the Japanese people.

Interview at Zenkoji Temple

FAULKNER: I am most honored to be received here this afternoon.

ABBESS: We are very glad that you came despite the heat.

FAULKNER: Thank you. I hear there are many national treasures in the temple here.

ABBESS: The Buddha statue over there is a national treas-

ure—it is called the Maedachi Buddha. The building also
is a national treasure, as is the Buddha that is deified inside
it.

FAULKNER: May I ask how old the temple is?

ABBESS: This temple is one thousand four hundred years
old and the present abbess is the one hundred and nineteenth
abbess. The temple was established to serve the Buddha
statue in the main temple.

FAULKNER: That was in the time of what emperor? What
dynasty?

ABBESS: In the period of the Emperor Kogyoku, in the
year 1212 according to the Japanese calendar, which is different from the Christian calendar, when the Buddha came
to Japan.

FAULKNER: The books in the library—could you tell me
what they are?

GUIDE: They haven't such a big library because this temple
was burnt about one hundred years ago. Also, again in the
Meiji era, it was burnt again, so the library isn't so big. As
a matter of fact, it was burnt eleven times since it was established long ago.

ABBESS: The Buddha came to Japan in the era of the
Emperor Kinmei—not as mentioned earlier. What was your
purpose in coming to Japan and how long are you going
to stay in Nagano?

FAULKNER: I came to Japan to come to know more about
the Japanese people and Japanese culture, of which we know
something in my country, and admire, and I will be here
three weeks more.

ABBESS: Are you going to visit Kyoto and Nara?

FAULKNER: Kyoto, yes. Three weeks is not long enough to
come to know Japan—I would like to stay a long time.

ABBESS: In regard to religion, are you studying Christianity
or Buddhism primarily?

FAULKNER: I'm interested in all religions as a form of man's
behaviour. The scriptures that he lives under—I think all
morality that makes people behave is based on religion.

ABBESS: Is this your first visit to Japan?

FAULKNER: Yes. My first visit for myself, but I have known Japanese history, Japanese art, Japanese literature a long time.

ABBESS: I feel very much assured that you have so much understanding towards these things.

FAULKNER: Thank you very much—it is very kind of you. I wish that more people from my country could know your country better than they do. I wish that more people from my country could know your people and your country—we should know each other better, it's important that we should.

ABBESS: Can you eat this kind of Japanese cake?

FAULKNER: I've never had it before. I'm sure I can because I like all Japanese food.

PICON: Mr. Faulkner was quite skilful the first time he used chopsticks.

FAULKNER: Could we ask if the big straw sandals are used for anything—you remember the big straw sandals on the path that leads here?

ABBESS: Farmers living near the temple donate those sandals, wishing that their feet become very strong like those of the huge sandal—it is the symbol of power, so they wish to be very strong like that.

FAULKNER: Japan is so old that people from my country expect everything to have a legend or a story even when it doesn't.

ABBESS: Well, about those slippers, there isn't such an old story connected with them—the farmers merely hope to get strong. You are giving a lecture or something in Nagano?

FAULKNER: I attend the seminar in American literature.

ABBESS: It must be very trying for you in this hot season.

FAULKNER: No, this season is like the season at my home —very pleasant here.

INTERPRETER: I asked if that screen over there is one of the national treasures, but it isn't—still, it is very old.

ABBESS: This one over here is a manuscript of a very old Japanese story.

INTERPRETER: Thank you for all your trouble.

ABBESS: Thank you very much for coming.

Meeting with Nagano Citizens

FAULKNER: All of you here have known American soldiers. I am not a soldier, and I would like to talk to you not as a soldier and only incidentally as an American.

I would like to speak as one man, a stranger who has been made welcome in your country, who would like to give to the Japanese people what he hopes is a better picture of America than maybe soldiers do.

I would like to take back to my country something of my visit in Japan with the Japanese people that would do what might be possible, that relations not between Japanese and Americans but between simple human beings might be the better for my visit.

I think we have had too much of people making speeches, making lectures to one another. I think that what we need if we are to make this world any better for all of us is for people not to make speeches, lecture to one another, but to talk to one another. I would like this evening for any of you who would like to ask me questions about my country, to ask them, or who would like to tell me something about your country so when I go back to mine, I can say this is what Japanese men and women told me about Japan, about what the Japanese people think about Americans, and what the Japanese people think we should do, that conditions that we have known in the last ten years will never happen again.

Q: Which one of your works do you advise us to read first, and which next, and so on?

FAULKNER: Thank you, that was very good English. I'm ashamed when I hear the Japanese people speak my language, and I can't speak theirs. I would suggest—the title is *Intruder in the Dust*. I suggest that because that deals with the problem which is important not only in my country, but, I think important to all people.

Q: Which next?

FAULKNER: I would say next, any that is available in translations in Japanese. The works deal with my country because
when I was writing, that's the only country I knew enough
about to be familiar enough with to write about, and they
all, I would like to think, give a true picture of my part of
America. I could suggest other books that may give a better
picture of America than mine do if I knew what part of
my country you would like to know about—then I could
suggest titles. Let me say this—I would suggest that the translator of the works might be a good one to ask that question,
that any work when it is translated, the translator must give
something, that no work can be translated literally, that the
translator himself, between that work in English, in my language, and the finished translation in Japanese, that man
has given something to it, and I think that he would be
better to ask which one to read to know about America than
to ask the writer.

Q: [The original question as worded by the questioner is
somewhat difficult to understand, hence, the question has been
re-translated from the Japanese interpretation given after Mr.
Faulkner's reply.]

Although your home is in Mississippi, many of your works
illustrate Alabama, or the cities of New Orleans and Memphis.
Have you any particular feelings about these places?

FAULKNER: No, that is only because most of my country lies
between New Orleans and Memphis. New Orleans is the big,
important city that in my country is like Tokyo here. That
is, Nagano would be Memphis, Tokyo would be New Orleans,
because Tokyo is the larger city. My country would be between Nagano and Tokyo. They were important in my work
only because they were the big cities—the life in my land,
the land I know, is country, it is farmland. These cities
happened to be the big cities in that part that I knew.

Q: Who do you think were the five greatest American
novelists up to the end of the 19th century?

FAULKNER: Mark Twain, Herman Melville, Theodore
Dreiser—the next two would be difficult to choose—there
are some works of several people which are first rate. I

can name the ones that I was impressed with and that probably influenced me to an extent that I still like to read—one a woman, Willa Cather—I think she is known in Japan—Sherwood Anderson, Sinclair Lewis.

Q: May I ask you why you did not mention Hawthorne and Henry James?

FAULKNER: For this reason—to me, Hawthorne or Henry James are not truly American writers. Their tradition was from Europe. They wrote in the tradition of European writers. They were not true Americans in the sense that I mean—indigenous American writers who were produced and nurtured by a culture which was completely American, such as Whitman and Mark Twain, the poet Sandburg. They were products of a nation which did not develop, did not begin to develop, until after the eastern seaboard was a cultured region, where the tradition (which after all, to me) was a European tradition.

Q: The scene of soldiers drinking liquor which appears in the beginning of the book *Soldiers' Pay* made me recall an occurrence which arose just after the end of the Pacific war. When I was standing on one of the platforms at Nagoya, some American soldiers came along and forcibly held my neck, making me drink whisky. They then passed the bottle among themselves, drinking from the same bottle that I had drunk from. Since considerable time has elapsed since the time that *Soldiers' Pay* was written of, and since things are quite peaceful now, I don't imagine that such things happen nowadays. Could you tell me whether such scenes can be seen?

FAULKNER: I wouldn't say that that is typical of American soldiers. If I said that was typical, I'd say that it is probably typical of all soldiers, that in this gentleman's case, these were young men who had never been this far from home before—they were in a strange country, they had been fighting in combat—suddenly combat was over, they were free of being afraid, and so they lost control temporarily. They wouldn't act like that always every time—it was the relief that anyone who has been a soldier and knows what it is

to be fighting—when he gets over being in fighting, he's really
not accountable for what he might do. He won't mean to
misbehave, but he himself isn't accountable for what he will
do after he has been under fire and has been fighting, and
then suddenly sees, "Why, I'm still alive, I wasn't killed!"

Q: My question is a childishly simple question, but as
I'm greatly interested in you as a writer, I would like to ask
you about your life as a writer—how do you write your novels?

FAULKNER: I am not really a writer in the sense you mean
—my life was established before I began to write. I'm a
countryman. My life is farmland and horses and the raising
of grain and feed. I took up writing simply because I liked
it—it was something very fine, and so I have no plans—I look
after my farm and my horses and then when there is time
I write, or if I have something that I want to write, I will
find the time to write it, but just to be a writer is not my
life; my life is a farmer, so in that sense, I'm not a writer
because that doesn't come first. I always find time to do the
writing, but I do other things also.

Q: What connection is there between the titles *Absalom,
Sanctuary, The Sound and the Fury,* and the characters in
these novels? Is there any connection between these titles and
the characters that appear in these novels?

FAULKNER: No, the names are symbolical rather than litera-
tive. The names have a little connection with the story or
the characters—the names represented an idea. In *Sanctuary,*
that meant that everyone must have some safe secure place
to which he can hurry, run, from trouble. *Absalom, Absalom!*
came out of the Christian Old Testament. The story in that
book was of a man who wanted a son and lost that son.
That title came from the cry of King David, who said, "Absalom, oh, my son Absalom!" when his son died. *The Sound
and the Fury* came from a passage in Shakespeare's *Macbeth,*
that has produced titles for a dozen books. It's a speech of
Macbeth's when he was told that Lady Macbeth was dead.
He said "Dead? There should have been a time for such
as this; tomorrow and tomorrow and tomorrow creep in this
petty pace from day to day, and oh, how[9] yesterdays lead

but to dusty death. Out, out, brief candle; life is a poor player, who struts and frets as upon a stage, and then is gone. It is a tale told by an idiot, full of sound and fury, signifying nothing."

Q: In Macbeth's "sound and fury," there is no article before "fury." Why did you place a "the" before "fury"?

FAULKNER: For emphasis. Sound and Fury wasn't quite enough for the ear. The ear said it needs rhythm, emphasis —*The* Sound and *the* Fury.

Q: Mr. Faulkner, I would like to hear about the mother-in-law and bride relationship in your country, because here in Japan we have a lot of trouble between the mother-in-law and the father-in-law and the young bride who comes in the family.

FAULKNER: Well, that seems to be a universal trouble— that's not Japanese and it's not American. That is, it happens everywhere, unless you will find some mother-in-law who's very wise, very sensible, so wise and so sensible that she can admit that when her daughter's old enough to marry, or her son, that son or that daughter's old enough to run their own business, and you don't find many women, or men either, for that matter, like that. From what little I have been able to learn of Japan in the short time I've been here, I think that the mother-in-law in Japan has more power than the mother-in-law in America, because of a tradition which says that the older parent commands respect because that parent is older—there's a tradition of respect towards the elders which is not so strong in my country.

Q: That's quite true, Mr. Faulkner, too strong.

FAULKNER: Yes, I agree with you, and I can say that because I am old enough to have children, married children, and grandchildren, and I know that my principal duty to them now is to stay out of their lives, to let them alone; when they want help from me, they come, and I try to give them just what they ask for, but never to give them advice, that if I haven't taught them by this time to run their lives, it's too late, now. I try always with my children to remind myself that respect is like love—it's not something given, it's something that must be earned, and I do not expect my children, my grandchildren, to give me respect and love. I must earn it from them.

Q: Many American soldiers marry Japanese girls when they leave after they have been in Japan—in the same way, many marry Koreans; but do you favor international marriages? It doesn't matter in places like Europe where the customs are more or less similar with those of America, but with the orient. . . .

FAULKNER: There, I think that the parent of the average American soldier has had very little experience of people. He knows only vaguely where Japan is, he has certain ideas about Japanese people that simply are not true because he had no basis to get his information from, and when he hears that his son has married a Japanese girl, he's shocked, because he believes that he is—well, this boy has married someone who is alien, who is, in his sense, not really a human being; but it doesn't take long before they find out that this Japanese girl is just another girl, that she's just like the American girls that they knew, that there's no difference, and if the son is happy, from what few cases I know, that's all that's necessary. It takes a little adjustment—the girl has got to be patient to give these old people time to find out that a Japanese is not different from anybody else, that people are fundamentally people, that young people are fundamentally young people, that young men and young women fall in love; it doesn't matter what their nationality is.

Q: You say you are a farmer rather than a writer, so, as a farmer of America, what were your on-the-spot impressions of Japanese farmers, especially farmers in the mountain areas that you went to the other day? Do they look happy or unhappy—do they look well-fed or bad-fed? I'm a farmer myself.

FAULKNER: I only passed through the country of the mountain farmer. I was taken on a short trip with one of the officers in your Department of Agriculture, but that was in the valley, so what little I have learned of farming in your country is from the valley farmer, who has what looks to

me very good land, very good rich land. I noticed that his
methods are very much like ours—we raise rice in my country
—our paddies are a little bigger than yours because our land
is a little bigger. We don't make quite as much—we measure
by the acre, you measure by . . . what is your. . . .

INTERPRETER: We have entirely different measurement. . . .

FAULKNER: Well, we don't make quite as many kilograms
as you do, but we can have more land; we can use machinery
—the machine will transplant four rows to each section, so
one man on each three sections will transplant twelve rows
of rice, while you have to do it by hand. The only difference
is—it's the same nature, our column is different, because
with us the machine is cheaper than the labor—you have
more labor, and so it's cheaper for you to do it by hand
than to buy that machine, but the process seems to be the
same. Your beans look like our beans, your corn is like our
corn, though we have more of it. I have been in the home
and met only one farmer—he was an apple raiser and he
struck me as being very prosperous. Now the gentleman from
the Agricultural Department said that he was a little above
the average farmer. I don't know about the average farmer,
because I would have to be in your country a whole summer—I couldn't just see one farmer or two farmers, no.

Q: I am a designer and feel that in designing—a desk or
furniture—it has become simpler these days—is that so—do
you feel that way?

FAULKNER: Yes, I would say more functional, whether the
function is the result of the simplicity, or the simplicity the
result of the function—I don't know. Of course, in my country,
so much of the shape of the design depends on the machine
that makes it, so that's like the question of the chicken
and the egg—I wouldn't know which comes first though.
Yes, it is simpler because it is functional. It takes up less
room, maybe less weight.

Q: I have heard that you will be speaking of your impressions of Japan to the people attending the seminar—
however, would you tell us of your impressions about Nagano
—the scenery, the people, and such things?

FAULKNER: My impression is that of a busy prosperous

city not too large, which is based on agriculture, on your farms, your silk, your rice, your apples, not too much manu-facturing—that I haven't seen. I would say that it is a very pleasant place to live in. It's within a reasonable distance of a big city, if you need a big city. I've seen too little of your country, but it strikes me that this is a very nice part of Japan to live in, though I've seen too little to say—that's just the impression I've got from the two weeks.

INTERPRETER: We shall close here.

Meeting at Tokyo American Cultural Center

MISS DEAN: We are indeed pleased that Mr. Faulkner found time during his visit to Japan to meet with us at the Tokyo Center. It appeared for a while that only the partici-pants of the Nagano Seminar would be fortunate enough to talk with him, but he decided to come here this evening. Mr. Faulkner has declared to some of us that he is not a literary man. We should not dispute his words, but for a nonliterary person he has had tremendous influence upon the literature of his own country and on others, and has written what has been judged to be outstanding literature. His words are greeted with great interest and at times there have been cries from those who were disturbed, but this has always been the case when individuals show the nonthinking world a facet of itself that some prefer to ignore. A man who can think and after thinking present with words to others the truth has always been a catalyst for action. He has by writing literature shown a segment of life, encouraged talk and constructive thinking and action. We all have read some of Mr. Faulkner's works and we know of him at least through the imagery he has woven and given to us. In recent weeks we have been reading his statements in the paper and because we are always interested in ourselves, in the familiar, it has been exciting to read his statements about things Japanese. In this I number myself with you because of my interest in Japan. His visit to Nagano and its reflection in the paper this past week was fascinating to me, for that is one of my favorite places. If you know the temple, the city, the people, you can see all the background and appreciate even more the thoughts and feelings there behind his skillful work. It is fortunate, I think, that Mr. Faulkner came to Japan with a definite purpose and destination for his first visit rather than as a casual visitor. For he met with people from all parts of the country and visited a Japan that is as distinctly Japanese as his imaginary county is distinctly a section of Southern America. In all of his writing you recognize reality stated with beauty and clarity. When I mentioned before I could see Nagano in his impressions, it was because he stated impressions I recall, that is as a writer, one who can say eternal verities and bring to his reader's eye and heart, the place, the person, the emotion felt. Usually, as a librarian, I introduce to patrons the words and thoughts of writers. It is with great honor I bring to you tonight the first author that it has ever been my privilege to introduce to patrons. Nobel and Pulitzer and National Book Award prize winner, Mr. Faulkner.

Would some of you now like to ask some questions? Mr. Faulkner has said that he will be happy to answer the questions that you ask on literature, his writing, or on America.

Q: I would like to start the questions by asking Mr. Faulkner to give us the reason for his change in literary style from his earlier. Like the use of very short sentences and very succinct style to the later long sentence type of literature.

FAULKNER: I think that the work the writer is trying to do commands, compels, its own style; it may be when style changes, it must change as anyone grows, because the only alternative to growth is death. That maybe, as the writer gets old, he realizes that he has shorter and shorter time in which to write before the day comes when he will be tired or will realize that he can't say what he wants to say and so maybe he tries to say all he has not said yet in each sentence, in each paragraph, because maybe he won't live long enough to do another. It may be that's the reason, that he gets along and he hasn't said it yet, so he'll try it this way. He changes his style. It's something like the man who will write a book on the back of a postage stamp or a prayer on the head of a pin, to get it all said in one compact bundle before he quits.

Q: Do you plan to continue to write?

FAULKNER: The worst habit anyone can form is writing. You can form other bad habits and you can cure yourself but you never cure yourself of writing. And so you keep on writing lots of times long after you've got nothing more to say. So I imagine that I will continue to deface paper as long as I can get the paper and the pencil.

Q: Do you hear what is being said about you and your works?

FAULKNER: Yes, I think when a man is young, he is busy writing, doing the work and he hasn't got time to pay too much attention to what is said about him, because he is so busy finishing one job which is not quite good enough. He knows that, he will take up another. Later on, when the blood gets slower, just like the athlete that can't move as fast as he could once, he has more time to become aware of what people think, and then it becomes more important to him what people thought because that is the only measure of whether he has wasted his time or not, is what people think. And if what he has said causes people to want to talk to him, to ask him questions, if young people are interested enough to come where he is and want to know what his experiences were, then that is a reward for what he did; at least whether the work is good enough to please him, it has interested someone, someone to come and ask him questions and talk to him. For the result of his experience, as a writer or experience in breathing, yes, that's important.

Q: We would appreciate it very much if we could hear from your own mouth, what authors, whether American, British or French, influenced you most. If any.

FAULKNER: I'm convinced that every writer is influenced

by every word he ever read anywhere, from the telephone directory up, or down. The advertisements, the newspapers, the books; and he probably can't say with any truth, "This influenced me more than another." He doesn't know, but everything he ever read has influenced him. I could not say who nor what influenced me. I could only say the ones that I like, admired, that I hoped in my time I could compete with, maybe better, but at least do something they would not be ashamed to read; but I think that everything you read influences you as a writer.

Q: What do you think about the idea called a writer is a [member of the lost generation]?

FAULKNER: Now, that was a phrase that was coined by Gertrude Stein speaking of the younger writers in Paris in her time. They were Scott Fitzgerald—Hemingway wasn't too well known then, and I think she meant by that, well, at her age there'd been a dreadful war which had destroyed lots of young men, it had changed the pattern of the time of the world just as the last war did, and from her point of view, she believed that the young people who had survived that war had been permanently hurt by it, that they were a lost generation. I had never agreed to that; I think that a certain amount of disaster and trouble is good for people. And I don't believe that Hemingway, or Fitzgerald, either, ever really considered themselves as belonging to a lost generation. They accepted her terminology which sounded good, it was something nice, a type or tag, you might say, but I don't believe any writer ever considers himself a member of a lost generation. He considers himself a member of the human race, that he may have picked out a better time to have lived if he had the choice, but that's not too important, either. That there's no reason to say, "Well, this is a bad time, we have gone through a bad war and there's nothing for the young man to look forward to, to hold to." I don't hold to that, because people are very tough and they can go through disaster, they can suffer the dreadful aftermath of war, but people are tough, they survive that, people are the toughest things in creation. Man even survives his own disasters; and if you want to write, then it doesn't really matter whether it's a bad time or good time, you still write.

Q: I think every literature has its own social background. Every literature is much influenced by society and some environment, and I don't mean to deny the importance of environment, but I'm beginning to think what is more important is the writer. [Do you agree?]

FAULKNER: As I see it, the writer has imagined a story of human beings that was so moving, so important to him, that he wants to make a record of it for his own satisfaction or, perhaps, for others to read, that story is a very old story, it's the story of human beings in conflict with their nature, their character, their souls, with others, or with their environment. He's got to tell that story in the only terms he knows, the familiar terms, which would be colored, shaped, by his environment. He's not really writing about his environment, he's simply telling a story about human beings in the terms of environment, and I agree that any work of art, any book, reflects its social background, but I doubt if that were the primary consideration of that writer. That reflection or that background was simply the story told in the terms of its own environment. If he is merely telling a story to show a symptom of a sociological background then he is first a propagandist rather than a novelist. The novelist is talking about people, about man in conflict with himself, his fellows, or his environment.

Q: [Do you not think the present age is darker than earlier times were?]

FAULKNER: Well, the darkness of the world, I agree with you it is darker at times than at other times, and this is a very dark time. But I am still convinced that man is tougher than any darkness. That man's hope is the capacity to believe in man, his hope, his aspiration toward a better human condition. The fact that man always hopes toward a better human condition, I think that the purpose of writing, of art, is a record. The reason that the books last longer than the bridges and the skyscrapers is that that is the best thing man has discovered yet to record the fact that he does endure, that he is capable of hope, even in darkness, that he does move, he doesn't give up, and that is not only a record

of his past, where he has shown that he endures and hopes
in spite of darkness, but it is a promise of the validity of that
hope. That that is one thing in which he can show tomorrow
that yesterday he endured. He knows that since his own
yesterday showed him today that he endured, was capable
of hope, was capable of believing that man's condition can
be bettered, is his assurance that after he is gone someone
will read what he has done and can see what man yesterday
was capable of believing and of hope that man's condition
can be changed; and man's condition does change. There
are evils of yesterday that don't exist any more, the evils
of today will be gone tomorrow by the advancement, women
will have more freedom in this country than they had once.
There will be a time when the older people that get the
world into wars won't be able to get the world into wars any
more for the young people to get killed in. That will come,
it will take time, it will take patience, and it will take a
capacity of people to believe that man's condition can be
improved, not as a gift to him, but by his own efforts. That
he can do it.

Q: [I should like to ask how you came to write] *A Fable*.

FAULKNER: That was again the writer who had imagined,
who had heard of a story that was so moving, so true to him
that he had to put it down. I was primarily telling one of
the oldest and the most moving tragic stories of all as it had
been written thousands of times, that is, the father who is
compelled to choose between the sacrifice or saving of his
son. It came, incidentally, out of a speculation which a lot
of people besides me have probably wondered at: Who might
have been in the tomb of the Unknown Soldier? And if that
had been, if Christ had appeared again in 1914-15, he would
have been crucified again. To tell that story, the thought
was if I could just tell this in such a powerful way that people
will read it and say this must not happen again, that is, if
Providence, Deity, call Him what you will, had tried to save
this world once, save men once by the sacrifice of His Son,
that failed, He tried it again and that failed, maybe He
wouldn't try it the third time, and so we must take warning
because He may not try to save us again that way. Though

that was incidental, I was primarily telling what to me was a tragic story, of the father who had to choose between the sacrifice or the saving of his son.

Q: Do you really think it necessary to explain a particular story or novel [or to] correct [the style]?

FAULKNER: I feel a need to. As I said before, when a young man begins to write he is so busy writing that he himself doesn't really have time to read it again because he is busy on another. He reaches a point where he works slower and when he finds that what he has written is misunderstood not because of any fault in the story, but simply in the way he told it, then he does feel the need to correct that, if he can correct something baffling about the style so that it leaves what he was trying to say plain and clear, yes. Then he wants to correct it. Otherwise, he wouldn't be sitting here answering questions like this.

Q: I want to ask you from what center do you estimate [the relative importance of the contemporary authors you mentioned].

FAULKNER: The way I made that judgment was this. My own feeling is that the work that I have done was never as good as I wanted it to be, hoped it would be, which is the reason the writer writes another one. If he wrote one book and that was all he had hoped of it, he would probably quit. But it's not, so he tries again and so he begins to think of his own work as a long series of failures, that is, it was the best he could do, but none of it is perfection, which is what he wants, and anything less than perfection is failure. I was asked to rate my own contemporaries, that was Hemingway, Dos Passos, Caldwell, Thomas Wolfe, and I said I could not because I believed they would feel as I did that what they did were failures, that the only way I would rate them was by the magnificence of that failure, that I rated Wolfe first because he tried the hardest to do what he knew he couldn't do. I rated myself next because I tried next to Wolfe to do what I couldn't do. I rated Hemingway last because he had found out early in life what he could do and he stayed within that pattern; that this judgment had nothing to do with the value of the work, it was only in what I would call

the magnificence, the splendor, of the failure. That was what
that was. I think that the writer must want primarily perfection, that that is his one chance while he has breath, to attain
perfection. He can't do it in his life because he can't be as
brave as he wishes he might, he can't always be as honest
as he wishes he might, but here's the chance to hope that
when he has pencil and paper he can make something as
perfect as he dreamed it to be.

Q: Of your own works, what is dearest to your heart?

FAULKNER: The one that was the most gallant failure was
The Sound and the Fury. And that one I wrote five times
and it's still not finished.

Q: I ask the opposite question, which one do you like the
least?

FAULKNER: The one that gave me no trouble, that I wrote
in six weeks without changing a word, that was *As I Lay
Dying*. That's pure *tour de force,* that was no trouble.

Q: [What of the] future of Japanese literature?

FAULKNER: Yes, I'm glad that question came up. A hundred years ago there were two cultures, two economies in
my country, the United States, and ninety-five years ago we
fought a war over it and my side were whipped. We were
invaded, we went through something of your own experience,
only our invaders made no effort to help us. And I think
that there were young men in my country then who said
as the young men in Japan are probably saying to themselves today, "What have we to hope for, to hold to, where
shall we go?" In my own country shortly after that there
was a resurgence of writing so that now when anyone speaks
of American literature, they think right off, "What Southerner
has published a book now?" Because everybody in my country
writes books and some of them are good books. For instance,
me, a Mississippi countryman, was of value enough for young
men and young women ten thousand miles away to listen to
me talk. And I think that that is what is going to happen
in your country. I think that a certain amount of anguish
and trouble is good for people and that I look for that to
come out of your country, a group of very alive or important

writing. It may take fifty years, but that's what I look for.

Q: [What is the best way to learn to write?]

FAULKNER: My belief is that nobody can be taught any-thing, that one must learn. I would say if I had a class of young people that wanted to write, I would make available to them everything that was ever written, with no distinction of time, period, style, but everything. Anyone who wants to write must read everything, trash, the best, the worst, everything, because he will never know when he will find something he can need and he will use because any writer is a thief and a robber. He will steal from any source, and he must read, should read, everything. And I think all there is to do is not to bother to try to teach him, just make it available to him, so he can get it. So if he is puzzled by it, explain it to him if he wants an explanation, but let him read everything.

Q: Well, of course, it's very good to read everything you can get hold of and get what we like out of them; but then [our students] say, "Be a little bit more specific and give us just a few examples of [the best models"].

FAULKNER: Well, I think if the books were available, the student himself would take care of any time element. I don't believe that to set specific chores of that nature would do any more than to teach him a specific style. And I don't think that style is very important. My belief is that the work itself demands its own style and if anyone is interested in style, then he can learn that, but then he is not really in-terested in writing, he's just interested in making a book. You will have to use a certain judgment in the individual. If he showed certain tendencies, then a teacher could guide the tendencies. But I would say to make the books available, let the student come and show some particular bent, some particular interest. But mainly to have the books so that a pupil can read and answer his own questions. If he be-comes interested in method and can't answer his own ques-tions from the books he reads, then let him come to the teacher and say, "Why did this writer write this scene in this particular way?" which becomes a matter of craftsmanship then. But it takes complete freedom of spirit to be the writer. He's got to make his own mistakes, he's got to learn, himself. I don't think you can teach him. He's got to have the desire to learn, the patience to learn and an infinite capacity to experiment, to make mistakes, to throw the mistakes away and try again.

Q: I understand that your books were read in France and more appreciated in France before you were recognized as a great writer in the United States. Is that because of the subject matter? For instance, you wrote about [a little known part of the] population in the South. Or is it because generally a prophet is not recognized in his own country?

FAULKNER: It's a little of course according to the adage about the prophet in his own country. I think it is to a great extent due to the fact that we Americans think that we are too busy with too many other important things to waste time reading to find out what we want to read. We let some-one else tell us what we should read, and that saves our time. And so when your reputation comes back from people whom we consider had plenty of time to do all of his preliminary reading, that saves us the trouble. It's not that we don't have the taste and don't appreciate it, it's simply that our culture tells us that we are too busy to waste the time look-ing through books to find which one we should read. We let somebody else tell us which one would be best.

Q: I think the answer is cited in your own books, but [the racial] problem [still bothers us. We should be happy to have you tell about the] history of the South.

FAULKNER: The racial problem in my country is an eco-nomic one. Our economy of raising cotton depends on a system of peonage, that is on a system of labor that would be content to accept a little less for the work it does than it might and should, and so our problem is not based on any hatred of another race, it's simply a fear that if we give the inferior, what we call the inferior, race any more social advantage, he might be dissatisfied with his economic status and he might want to change that. I think that in a few hundred years the Negro in my country will vanish any-way. He will be assimilated into the white race simply be-

cause there are more white people. He has a force, a power
of his own that will enable him to survive. He won't vanish
as the Indian did, because he is stronger and tougher than
the Indian. It will take a great deal of patience on his part
for a few years more. He'll simply have to wait until a few
old people in the South die, that's really what will have
to happen. When the problem becomes one of the younger
people, the problem vanishes, the younger people that have
served as soldiers with Negro soldiers, there's no problem,
there's no problem among the children, they play together
and sleep together and eat together. It's only when they get
old and inherit that Southern economy which depends on a
system of peonage do they accept a distinction between the
black man and the white man, and it's simply because they
are afraid that the black man, if he has any social advancement he will quit his present economic status and since he
has learned through many years of having to do with less, to
work what land he owns with inferior tools, and still send
his children to school, still keep a home. That if he has a
chance he may take the white man's economy away from
him, that the white man will have to work for less money
because the Negro will own the cotton land and the cotton.

Q: [Do you believe it is an economic problem, then?]

FAULKNER: In my opinion, yes. That because of the fear
of the economic upset, they will vest it with all sorts of
extraneous moral reasons, but they are not worried about
those moral reasons, they are afraid of the economic upset.
There are certain ignorant people that can be led to believe
that one man is better than another because the Christian
Bible says so, they believe all sorts of delusions about him,
that he has different sort of blood in his veins, which is
not so; any student in chemistry could answer that question.
But it's primarily, I think, economic. There's a class of white
man that hates the Negro simply because he's afraid that
the Negro will beat him at his own job, his own economic
level, and he would feel the same toward anything that
he believed would beat him at his economic level. It could
be a piece of machinery. He would hate that too.

Q: I think [there may be other reasons for the white man's

hatred of the negro]. They are equals legally and politically, but still I think they—there is something hidden or latent in the thoughts of the people that they can't mingle or they can't mix with the colored people. I mean social. And I think this is also one of the important elements of the problem besides economic factors, and I felt that was especially clear in the Southern states.

FAULKNER: If you remember that our latent refusal to mix never appeared in youth, in childhood, only in middle age, that in youth and childhood there's no problem, they seem to mix; I grew up with Negro children, my foster mother was a Negro woman, I slept in her bed and the Negro children and I slept in the same bed together. To me they were no different than anyone else. I noticed that with my own children. It's only when the child becomes a middle-aged man and becomes a part of the economy that that latent quality appears.

Q: I was not quite satisfied by your answer, so may I trouble you again? The word caste sounds to me [a degrading term] and because I felt when I travelled around the States the difference of the acting toward the Negro in the North and the South, and in the North I felt strongly that the difference, the social status, on the surface, is much less than it was in the South. For instance, in the Tennessee Valley Authority, I saw a [unintelligible] on the air. I saw two [?], one is for the Negro and one for the white.

FAULKNER: Well, I would say the reason there is more prejudice in the South is that the economy is less complex. It is an economy of producing cotton, primarily. In the North, it would be a separate competition for jobs and the white man would hunt for any designation which would knock the greatest number of his competitors for his job in it. And if there were more of them had black skin, he would use black skin, particularly if that has already been offered him. If there were more of them had three hands, he would be against people who had three hands. But in my opinion, it's still economic.

Q: I would just like to make a statement rather than to ask a question. As an American myself and as the first mis-

sionary, Negro missionary, from my board to come to Japan,
I would like to say that it is not a caste system, as much as
it is economic condition. If a man is able to improve himself
in America, whether he has a black skin or white skin, he
can do it. Much different, I would say, than what I witnessed
this summer in Osaka visiting the poor and aged people
in Japan. I feel that the American Negro is much better off
than the people in Japan who are set aside in segregated
villages, or segregated areas. I would say that the American
Negro is not in a caste, but in a class which can be improved
if he himself applies himself. Mr. Faulkner says you can
make for yourself your position in life.

FAULKNER: I agree with that and I am grateful to you for
expressing it a little better than I was able to. I think that's
quite true and I think, as I said, a great deal of the prejudice
in my country is the knowledge the white man has that the
Negro can improve himself and will even faster than the
white man through idleness wants to. But I still believe that
it is basically an economic fear.

Q: What is your opinion of Negro writers?

FAULKNER: There was one that had a great deal of talent,
named Richard Wright. He wrote one good book and then
he went astray, he got too concerned in the difference between the Negro man and the white man and he stopped
being a writer and became a Negro. Another one named
Ellison has talent and so far he has managed to stay away
from being first a Negro, he is still first a writer. And I think
that he will go far. There are others that don't have the
talent of those two, that's the reason that I mention those
two, that they have the talent in the sense that, well, Hemingway, when he was a young man, had the talent, or Fitzgerald;
but Wright, as I say, became more interested in being a Negro
than in being a writer and that destroyed him. And the
writer has got primarily to be a writer first, everything else
must go by the board. Let him be a writer first, then let him
be honest, brave, or whatever, but let him be a writer first.
It's a terrible burden that the Negro has to carry in my
country. It's astonishing that any of them can disassociate
themselves enough from that problem and that burden to

make anything of a talent. And when one does, I think it implies a very fine talent, that it is strong enough so that he can accept the fact that he is a Negro and then stop worrying about it and be a writer. Much more difficult than the white man. The white man hasn't got that pressure on him all the time to remind him what he is by the color of his skin, by social condition, by status.

Q: In your novels, and maybe in your poems, truth often has been spoken of. I wondered if there is a difference between truth in poetry, and truth in a novel? Is the integrity of opinion in a novel different than, say emotionalism or . . . ?

FAULKNER: Not in the fundamental truth. The poet has more license, at the same time more strictures because of the medium he is compelled to use, which is a refinement. Where the novelist has a certain space in which to make errors and mistakes, the poet doesn't. But I think that that truth is the same truth though the poet is allowed a little more freedom in images, but the truth is the same and the poet cannot violate that basic truth any more than the novelist can.

Q: [Don't some novelists use the technique of poetry?]

FAULKNER: Very well; Conrad has done it at times. Almost every American writer of the Mississippi Valley has used it, Sherwood Anderson; the Americans east of the mountains more tend to the European and they don't need to resort to lyricism. They have a more expressive, a more precise, rational concept of the material they use, so their kinship is more to the French writers. But the so-called primitive, which would be the uncouth or middle westerner, is more prone to resort to lyricism.

Q: I think that there's no doubt about the fact that any author cannot escape from the environment in which he lives and I think in your works you often write about the South, and I am wondering if you are intentionally trying to reflect or project the South in your works or do you unconsciously do it?

FAULKNER: It would be unconsciously done. Any writer is primarily telling the story. Of course he reflects his own background, his own heritage, his own tradition, and if he writes in terms of what he knows and what he knows is restricted, in my own case, then naturally his work will give a picture of that background, that social background. Now that may be a little warped for emphasis though that won't be deliberately done to warp the picture of that background, because the background is incidental. He is trying primarily to talk about people in conflict with their own consciousness, their own hearts, with one another or with that environment.

Message Given at Nagano

WHEN I FIRST RECEIVED this invitation to visit your country and participate in this seminar, I declined it with thanks and regrets for this reason—that the Japanese people were the heirs of a national history centuries old—a history which had produced a tradition of centuries of education and discipline of the intellect until discipline of the intellect had become a national character of the Japanese. A national character and trait which I believed they held more important and higher than any other.

While I was descended of a national history not yet two hundred years old. A national history still being created by a country which had not yet been completely opened and explored. A country still partly virgin. A country still in the seethe and turmoil of being opened and developed and in a sense civilized.

And therefore there could never be any real contact between the Japanese people, particularly the scholars and literary people, and myself. Because we would have no common ground to meet on. We would respect each other—I never doubted that. I would respect their old, proven civilization of intellectual discipline which I knew they had. And I believe they would respect whatever was valid and true and honest in my work, but that we had better let it go at that. We had both better let my works speak for me while I stayed in my own western tradition and culture.

Then I discovered that I was wrong. It was shown to me that the Japanese people really and actually wanted to see and to know me—the man, the human being. I realized for the first time that apparently a human personality had been transported ten thousand miles by means of my written works and that the alien and older and in their cultural sense wiser people than I wanted to see and know that individual human personality.

Once I had realized that, naturally but one course remained. That was to beg the privilege of retracting that refusal. I did so. But even then when I reached your country, I was frightened. I believed that you would be expecting something of me which I knew I did not possess. You would expect that literary man which I knew I was not, but which you, inheritors of your long tradition of a culture of discipline and what I will call orthodoxy, a conventionality of intellectuality, could never believe that a man who wrote in an occidental tongue books which oriental people could want to read and understand, could not be.

And once more I found that I was wrong. My welcome here, my continued welcome here, has proved that the Japanese intellectuals did not even want another intellectual. What they wanted was just a human being who spoke not their same intellectual language, but who could write books which met their standards of what writing must be, yet who in trying to communicate, human being to human being, spoke in a mutual tongue much older than any intellectual tongue because it is the simple language of humanity—of mankind, of man's hope and aspiration which has enabled him to prevail above his condition and fate and his own self-created disasters.

Plot Complications
Result of His "Ignorance": Faulkner*

WHAT POSITION SHOULD novelists hold in society? What should be the theme of their works? What, above all, should be the relation of man to society?

These and other subjects were discussed across a table Thursday [4th August] among an eminent American novelist, a Japanese authority on American literature and a foremost woman social critic of Japan.

They were: the Nobel Prize winner WILLIAM FAULKNER, now in Japan, MASAMI NISHIKAWA, professor of Tokyo University and Miss SHIHO SAKANISHI. The conversations follow:

SAKANISHI: The Mainichi newspapers have two big editions —a Japanese edition and also a fairly large English edition. The readers of both editions are very anxious to hear about you and American literature.

First of all, could you tell us what prompted you to come to visit us? We are extremely pleased and we know that you are going to lecture at the Nagano Conference but considering how busy you are, we would like to know what interest you have in Japan.

FAULKNER: I answered that at some length this morning. I wish we had a transcription of that. To see something of your culture I have heard about all my life and this was a chance to see how it met my preconception of it.

NISHIKAWA: Mr. Faulkner, if I remember right, you were first introduced to Japan before the war, and after the end of the war, your works have been translated—for example, *Sanctuary*, etc., and even *Fable* is being translated by an eminent writer and novelist, Mr. Tomoji Abe, but I am afraid you are not so widely read as Hemingway or Steinbeck because we find it very hard to translate your works into

* From the *English Mainichi*, August 5, 1955. Reprinted by permission of the publisher, the Mainichi Newspapers. [This note was in original text.]

Japanese. So the translation is not always good, and it is very difficult for readers.

SAKANISHI: Those who have read it appreciated it very deeply and they felt here is an American writer who has something in common with their spirit. You see, in this country, the public has taken up a keen interest in French literature, but American literature has always been rather difficult for them to understand: probably there are certain basic differences in points of view—Puritan spirit is rather alien to us, the optimistic democratic idealism is another difficulty we have had to face in this crowded society. Your vastness and your enormous possibilities and opportunities given to everybody is rather incomprehensive, but your having brought a conflict of the spirit so well presented in your novel made us realize that your writings touch us deeply and touch our problems, too.

So far in the very short visit you have, I wonder if in talking to the writers and critics you have come to feel any similarity or akinness to your ideas and ideals.

FAULKNER: Well, they seem to be interested in what I thought of Japan more than what I thought of idealism. That seems to have been the general tone of the question you asked me of Japan and Japanese culture more than what I thought about ideas, about man in general.

SAKANISHI: Well, that is probably very true, simply because just at present after the surrender, we were extremely self-conscious.

FAULKNER: Yes, I assumed that. That was obvious from the question. Yes, that was quite obvious from the question.

SAKANISHI: But as you come to know more of the Japanese, probably you will find that we are always discussing more or less intangible things, not exactly the matter of spirit as you use it but the matter of mental attitude, ideological differences rather than concrete physical matters and, of course, our tendency has always been putting too much emphasis on these intangible things, forgetting how to reach a certain conclusion or harmony between the spiritual things and physical things. I think in this morning's *Asahi*, you mentioned the fact that in Mississippi you have a family, a big family—it was translated as "kazoku"—for whom you are responsible, and that interested the Japanese very much. Could you tell us something about it?

FAULKNER: Yes, we are country people and we have never had too much in material possessions because 60 or 70 years ago we were invaded and we were conquered. So we have been thrown back on our selves not only for entertainment but certain amount of defense. We have to be clannish just like the people in the Scottish highlands, each springing to defend his own blood whether it be right or wrong. Just a matter of custom and habit, we have to do it; interrelated that way, and usually there is hereditary head of the whole lot, as usually, the oldest son of the oldest son and each looked upon as chief of his own particular clan. That is the tone they live by. But I am sure it is because only a comparatively short time ago we were invaded by our own people —speaking in our own language which is always a pretty savage sort of warfare.

SAKANISHI: So you hold together a community as a unit. It is very interesting. It was a type of living we always maintained till rather recent times in this country and I suppose still we go on maintaining these clannish ideas which give solidity to a certain extent to the social life. But is this mostly among the farmers or can that be maintained among the industrial field?

FAULKNER: No, it is regional. It is through what we call the "South." It doesn't matter what the people do. They can be land people, farmers, and industrialists, but there still exists the feeling of blood, of clan, blood for blood. It is pretty general through all the classes.

SAKANISHI: In the United States, do the writers more or less concentrate the theme or the main topic of their work in certain locality? Is that the general tendency?

FAULKNER: Well, I don't know because I am not really a literary man. I don't know any writing people and I am not really too interested in writing people. I am a farmer, a country man and I like to write. Though there is a colony of writers who gravitate toward the big cities, like New York, and their social life is a life of books but in my county that does not exist. The individual is primarily a farmer and after that he is a writer, unless of course he is a school man or scholar in the university.

SAKANISHI: Mr. Faulkner, when you are not writing, what do you do?

FAULKNER: I am a farmer. I like horses—I breed and train horses. That is what I like to do more than writing.

SAKANISHI: Breed horses? Oh, really! Just at present there are a few Japanese writers who own race horses but they don't breed horses.

FAULKNER: The writer that owns horses must be a pretty successful writer.

SAKANISHI: In your Nobel Prize speech which was a great interest to us and which was translated extensively in this country, you mentioned the physical fear we are faced with today. It is very true in this country. We not only have physical fear but also spiritually we are completely upset. We lost sort of bearing in this world.

Now, if I remember right, you said we have to overcome this because fear is not going to get us anywhere, but the problems that our writers and publishers are discovering are: "Could we do it by individual effort?" For, at this present age, we are so bound together by fast means of communication and all kinds of scientific improvements and no individual can cope with his own problem.

FAULKNER: Well, there is tremendous pressure on all of us to belong to groups. We are told we must belong to a group of artists. We don't believe that. I think the individual can be tough enough to protect himself. He does not have to belong to a gang today. It may be a little easier to belong to a group, but I don't think he has any business belonging to any group. If he belongs to a group of artists, he should do that just for the pleasure he gets out of exchanging ideas but not to defend themselves as artists, a lot of artists themselves, as against industrialists. I think the salvation of man is in his individuality, that he has got to believe that he as integrity is important and not as a group is important.

NISHIKAWA: You said in your Nobel Prize speech that you believe in the immortality of man not only because man will endure but also because man will prevail. Do you mean by "man will prevail" that justice will prevail in this world?

FAULKNER: I believe that justice won't prevail, but I believe man, through his immortality, intends and wants to do better than he probably will, but at the crisis, he himself will sacrifice his life that justice will prevail. He is constantly doing that. That he has got to work as a man is what he can never slacken if he believes in justice, in truth, in freedom, in liberty. He has got to work at it. That is the price of peace. He must always work at it vigilantly, never fail in vigilance, to be ready to sacrifice. It seems to me there is something I have noticed in the younger Japanese writers I have talked to, a doubt that they can stand alone, individually yet, that they have got to confederate. If I have done any good talking to them, I have tried to tell them that they don't have to confederate. They can confederate as artists, but they must stand on their own feet.

SAKANISHI: That is one thing we have to think really seriously. Now the post-war tendency is to congregate no matter what the purpose is, just get together like animals and I think it is very dangerous.

FAULKNER: That's right.

SAKANISHI: I am so glad to hear you expressed your opinion to the young writers. Now there is another tendency in this country which to us is constantly puzzling, but that is an easy way for the newspapers and journalists to solve the problem. If anything sensational or vital happens, they always get hold of a novelist to ask his opinion. Now there is a mass drowning of school kids and a novelist is called upon by telephone or by interviews to see what he thought about it as the highest authority in the matter of events. He gives out his opinion.

FAULKNER: To me that is a symptom of your culture and I think a very good and an important one. In my country, an artist is nothing. Nobody pays attention to him. He has no part in our ideology and our politics, but in an old culture, an artist is a wise man, is important and looked up to with respect which I think is fine. I wish it were true in my country.

SAKANISHI: Really.

FAULKNER: In my country, instead of asking the artist what makes children commit suicide, they go to the Chairman of General Motors and ask him. That is true. If you make a million dollars, you know all the answers.

SAKANISHI: There is another recent tendency. For a very long time the writers very seldom took any interest in politics or social events. They more or less secluded themselves and considered themselves high above. But now such established writers as Hirotsu and a few others take up the matter and write all the social problems in novels. There was a group of workers who organized themselves and derailed a train —Matsukawa and Mitaka incidents. The left-wing writers took the matter up and wrote extensively criticizing the court decision and prejudice against a certain political party. I think the Japanese were more or less in sympathy with the attitude of the writers trying to help the underdogs, but on the other hand, some of them feel that writers are involving themselves too much in politics and events are a little too dangerous because if they are good writers and they take an unfair attitude or criticize the established government too much, it will create distrust.

We are wondering if in rather recent times, there was such a tendency in America. We remember that at one time some of the critics and writers took up such social problems.

FAULKNER: True but they were not first rate writers. They were more people who thought it was a nice idea to be a writer and they would do anything that would foster their position as being writers. The ones that were first rate writers were too busy writing to bother with them.

NISHIKAWA: How about Upton Sinclair?

FAULKNER: Mr. Sinclair was a second rate writer with a first rate message. He was so busy trying to tell the world his message, that he didn't take the time to make himself a first rate artist. Though he was first rate man, he was not a first rate writer.

NISHIKAWA: Most of his important works were translated in Japanese almost 20 years ago, and widely read.

SAKANISHI: Now in the 20's and 30's, the first rate writers in this country wrote for the upper class intellectuals and students. They were read widely, but today I think practically all the important writers are writing for the average middle class, and, of course, that sometimes dissatisfies the intellectual class. They think the themes they take up are not of higher mental type, but of the everyday affair.

In this country, these private novels have been very popular for the last 10 years. Sometimes it can hardly be called fiction. It has no theme or no development. The writer just takes up the daily life and sort of gives the account of what goes on in his mind and what he does every day, and it is a sort of flat account of the writer's life.

NISHIKAWA: A kind of essay.

SAKANISHI: A family essay.

FAULKNER: How much of that takes place in Japan? Is there a great deal of that?

SAKANISHI: A great deal of what I call "I" novels, and they were very popular, but now I think the public is getting rather tired, because, after all, what is the use of washing your linen in dirty water, so to speak. They demand a little more substance in fiction.

FAULKNER: Is there a class in Japan that, I might say, might dictate literary taste?

SAKANISHI: I don't think so. Of course, before the war the ruling class, the militarists, for example, dictated a certain amount so that if a writer took up a rather fashionable society the militarists or army would object to it and they thought this had bad influence and unless you stopped this you just had to stop writing. But it is perfectly free now. Everybody can write according to his own fashion. There is no force that influences the writer to do one way or the other. It is left pretty much to the writer.

FAULKNER: The young writer is free? There is no pressure that says that you must write like this or you don't get printed?

SAKANISHI: Well, in this country usually a young writer attaches himself to a well established writer as his master and teacher, and if the master sponsors him he succeeds much faster. Otherwise he may have a long lean period before he can appear in the magazines.

Now, for example, Mr. Kawabata, whom you met yesterday, has always been good to his young disciples. That more or less semi-feudalistic tendency is good in a way and easier for younger writers but, on the other hand, unless a man is very strong and has a real talent of his own, his tendency is more or less to imitate the master's work. Probably that is the reason that the master sponsors him. That is a sort of vicious cycle.

NISHIKAWA: I think it is partly because our publishing companies have no "readers" in your sense and young writers don't know how to get their manuscripts published.

FAULKNER: What would you say the young Japanese writer is mainly concerned with? What material is he trying to write? The record of Japan after the war, or is he trying to ape his master? What is the general tone of his work?

NISHIKAWA: Some of them are writing about their experiences during and after the war, but others are writing about customs and manners after the war. They are writing in a sort of comedial manner.

SAKANISHI: Among the younger writers—younger in the sense of from 30 to 40—we have a very strong intelligent group who are writing war records—their experiences, their life in the army, their experience as prisoners of war in foreign countries, like Ooka—the young man whom you met yesterday—who came out on the scene first with his publication of *Furyoki*, the record of a war prisoner, which made a tremendous impression.

But, on the whole, no matter if he writes his experiences as a prisoner of war or in an army camp and how badly he was treated or imprisoned in Japan by the thought police, they have not come to digest their experiences deeply. It is not integrated so they cannot write about it, and it still remains pretty much on the surface, and what we would like to hear is how the whole thing is integrated not only in his own mind but also in the spirit or in the events of the time. Probably I think we need a little more time to accomplish that because the whole change is so revolutionary that we have not got hold of ourselves yet.

SAKANISHI: I think the Japanese would very much like to hear what Western reading matter you would recommend.

FAULKNER: To the young Japanese?

SAKANISHI: Yes.

FAULKNER: Nothing, because I think he has read what I would recommend. I would recommend the French and pre-revolutionary Russian writings and our Bible and Shakespeare, and I would recommend the French literature by Flaubert.

SAKANISHI: Flaubert has been read rather widely.

FAULKNER: I imagine the young Japanese has read just about everything, hasn't he?

SAKANISHI: The Japanese have never learned to read the Bible as literature. When they become Christians they read it.

FAULKNER: Then he has missed something I should say. That is one of the best writings.

SAKANISHI: Fortunately the early translation of the Bible based on King James' version is very good, a beautiful translation.

NISHIKAWA: About your method of writing stories, why do you use such a complicated method of telling your stories?

FAULKNER: It is ignorance. I have had no education. I never did like school and wouldn't go and I have had to teach myself my trade, I suppose, and I haven't got rid of a certain amount of trash in me.

NISHIKAWA: Did you read James Joyce's *Ulysses* before you began to write your own?

FAULKNER: No, I began to write before I read *Ulysses*. I read *Ulysses* in the middle 20's and I had been scribbling for several years.

SAKANISHI: Thank you very much.

Notes

1. Faulkner may have said "avatar."
2. Faulkner may have said "weakness."

3. Faulkner may have said "inequality."
4. Faulkner may have said "would be satisfied" or "it would be said."
5. Presumably Anderson's "A Meeting South."
6. Faulkner may have said "simple."
7. The two essays are obviously "On Privacy" (*Harper's*, July 1955) and "On Fear," published in *Harper's* the following year (June 1956).
8. Apparently the essay "Impressions of Japan" (*Faulkner at Nagano*, 1956), to which further reference is made in this section.
9. Faulkner presumably said "all our."

Faulkner in
MANILA

From Japan and the Nagano Seminars Faulkner went on to the Philippines, where he was interviewed on several occasions, over a period of three days, by Philippine newspapermen, writers, and teachers. Several of these sessions were tape-recorded, and excerpts from them were brought together in a pamphlet, Faulkner on Truth and Freedom, *published in 1956 by the Philippine Writers Association. The contents of the pamphlet are here reproduced in full.*

ALL MEN ARE BORN with the equal right to attain freedom, not to be given freedom, but the equal right to earn freedom and keep it as they are responsible and are strong and are truthful. People should not be given anything as a free gift because that's bad for man, but all men should have the right to attain freedom if they are responsible and will work to deserve it and then defend it and keep it.

•

I would say that the urgent question—truth—is freedom; that people—man—shall be free. And it seems to me that in the world today are not two ideologies facing one another that keep everybody else in fear and trembling. I would say that it is one ideology against a simple natural desire of people to be free, and that I would choose to be free, and I don't believe that man can be free under a monolithic form of government. I think that he has got to have the liberty to make mistakes, to blunder, and to find his way, but primarily he must be free to say what he wants, to behave as he wants within the verities of universal truth which are that the weak shall be protected, that children shall be defended, that women shall be defended, that people shall not lie to each other, that no man shall be compelled to do what his conscience tells him is wrong to do, that he must have complete freedom within a government which allows him the right to be a check on that government, that when he does not like that government, he can say it: I don't like this and I will try to change it.

MAN SHALL ENDURE through fitness of character and intellect. It will be because man has a soul. He has a capacity to invent, he has created machinery to be his slave; but his danger is that he will become the slave of that machine he has created. He will have to conquer that slavery, he will have to conquer and control his machinery because he has a soul. Through his intellect, he has capacity to believe that all men should be free, that all men are responsible to all other men, not to the machinery but to all races, to the family of mankind.

*

One who becomes a writer, if he is going to be a good writer, must have absolute integrity; he must have a sense of responsibility; he must believe in man; he must believe that man is worth knowing, worth dealing with; and he must believe that man will continue to endure and prevail.

It is only man that can settle his problems; it can't be done by ideologies, by government, by politics, but by man himself; he has got to do it and he has got to do it by believing in man. And the way of the artist is to believe in man. And to be a writer is to learn to believe most in man, that man will prevail, will endure as a soul.

THE WRITER has a very great responsibility. The writer is the person that will record man's endeavor, the course over the years, the centuries by which man has improved his lot to get rid of suffering, injustice. The writer's responsibility is to tell the truth—to tell the truth in such a way that it will be memorable, that people will read it, will remember it because it was told in some memorable way. Just to report facts, to report injustice sometimes is not enough. That doesn't move people. The writer's got to add the gift of his talent; he has got to take the truth and set it on fire so that people will remember it. That's his responsibility.

He has a responsibility of his talent which is to tell the truth about man, about man's problems and his capacity for courage; to be braver than he might; to be more compassionate than he might; to be less selfish than he wants to be. He does not have any particular message to change people or to teach people. I think that's propaganda.

If that writer had integrity to tell what he believed to be true, he could write for entertainment, yes. But if just for the sake of entertainment, he was forced. He did not have the integrity of responsibility. Then he would be a second rate writer. But he could write for entertainment, in my opinion, if he is holding to the verities of his responsibility which is to never disguise, to tell the truth as he sees it.

*

To endure, all nations have had faith in many things. One of these has always been faith in its written word, its own legend, its own folklore. The duty, the job of a writer, is to record that history and to hold out to man a promise of his future as a measure against his past. And that is true always of any nation which is a living nation, and to be alive it must progress because the only alternative to that is . . . death.

*

The Filipinos have their own traditions of poetry in their

folklore, in their language, in their dialects. This must be recorded, that is the job of the Filipino writer, to do this. In doing that he gives a pattern of hope and aspiration for the nation, for the people, to advance not merely as a nation of people but as a member of a family of nations, of the human family.

*

The writer must believe always in people, in freedom; he must believe that man must be free in order to create the art; and art is in my opinion one of the most important factors in human life because it has been art, literature, folklore, music, painting, which have been the record of man's rise from his beginnings. It is the writer's duty to show that man has an immortal soul. The writer, the artist, the musician is the one factor which can show him the shape of his hope and aspirations of the future by reminding him of what he has accomplished in the past.

*

A writer's job is not simply to get books printed but to find the truth, the fundamental truth which man needs in order to endure the truth of responsibility, of courage, of honor, pride, compassion; which will have to be the pattern for our behavior since that has been the record of our past, not Filipino past nor American past but the past of all people that have endured and prevailed.

I THINK that the setting of a novel is just incidental, that the novelist is writing about truth; I mean by truth, the things that are true to all people, which are love, friendship, courage, fear, greed; that he writes in the tongue which he knows, which happens to be the tongue of his own native land. I doubt if environment or country can be enough inspiration to write a book about, that the writer is simply using the tool which he knows. I write about American Mississippi simply because that is what I know best.

The Filipino would write about his country because it is what he knows best. The Chinese about his country because that's what he knows best.

The fact that one speaks Spanish, another Japanese, another English, is only incidental; that what they are talking about are the primary basic truths which everyone recognizes.

*

So far the only Asian books that people in my country ever saw were the classics—the old ones, the old Chinese, the old Indian legends and poems, but now the writing of young Asiatics has been translated into my country's (language).

You see their stories in magazines. A few years ago you never saw that and I think there will be more and more because young people are beginning at last to speak a universal language.

I THINK that local color is part of the environment and no part of the environment can be more or less important than any universal truth. We assume that when we speak of a writer we are speaking of someone who has some universal truth to talk about, and that he is willing to accept the responsibility and integrity, to do so. And so to say that local color is merely cute . . . I can't agree with that. But the local color is incidental and of supreme importance when local color is needed. Though someone who makes a craft of writing about local color is in the same fix as he or she who makes a craft of writing in a particular style. That the style is incidental is a part of the method just as local color is a part of the method, a part of the environment which the writer uses.

*

By environment I don't mean the world he lives in, the floor, the ground he walks on, or the city, I mean his tradition, the air he breathes, his heredity, everything which surrounds him. And his past is certainly a very immediate

part of anyone's present. If he is writing with the responsibility of integrity about a universal truth which are the
problems of man in conflict with himself, his base nature,
his fellow man, or his surroundings, his environment . . .
then he is a sincere and true writer, an artist. And he is
entitled to be cute, if cuteness is going to follow the truth
he tells.

I BELIEVE that what drives anyone to write is the discovery
of some truth that had been in existence all the time, but he
discovered it. It seems so moving to him, so necessary that
it be told to everyone else in such a way that it would move
them to the same extent that it moved him. He is trying
to tell that truth in the best way he can. He may know that
he will probably fail, that he cannot tell that truth in a
way that will seem as true, as moving, as beautiful, as
passionate, as terrible to anyone else as it seemed to him,
but he will try. He will try through methods, through
style, because simply he is not trying to be difficult, to be
obscure, he is not trying to be stylish, he is not trying for
method, he is simply trying to tell a truth, that which
troubled him so much he had to tell it in some way that
it will seem troubling or true enough or beautiful or tragic
enough to whoever reads it. And that is the reason for the
obscurity; that the writer is trying to tell the truth which
seems so important to him in the best, most moving way
he can. Now maybe if he could tell that same truth ten
years later, by that time he might realize that that was a
bad way that he told it before; it was obscure, and he would
do better, but by that time it is too late and he has told
that truth and he has got to tell another truth. And that,
I think, is the reason for the obscurity; there is nothing
deliberate in it because no writer has got time to be too
interested in style or method. The story, the truth he is
telling, invents its own style, its own method.

*

I think that if the writer has got something that moves him enough to say it, then he is going to say it in spite of everything. That if he has got to go out and dig ditches to earn enough money to buy the paper and the pencil to say what he wants to say, he will do that.

*

I think the reason that any writer continues to write is that the job, the story, the poem, book, which he has just finished, did not tell the truth that he was moved by in such a manner as suited the dream, the aspiration to tell that dream. So he writes another book, a poem or story. So, as long as he lives he will continue to write to match that dream but he will continue to write because once he matches that dream and he has set that truth to light as he dreamed that he had hoped he would, then nothing remains but to stop. The Nobel Prize did not change my own belief that what I have done was not what I could do or might do some-day. If anything should make a writer think that possibly he has come close to the shape of the vision, it will be some-thing like this: when he can see these many people, some of them young people, coming to hear him because they believe that he knows something of the truth. That is better than the Nobel Prize.

*

The writer should be controlled by good taste, but he shouldn't be inhibited by any fear of censorship. If he knows it to be true and it is worth telling, then he should tell it. If he can do it with good taste, then he owes that to the simple fact that men must live together in one family of men. But he should not be inhibited from telling what he believes to be true. What I mean by truth is the uni-versal truth of compassion, honor, pride, courage, law; he should not be inhibited from telling that truth.

THE RUSSIAN AUTHORS that I have read today are propa-
gandists—yes. But I am convinced that in Russia the same
talent that produced Tolstoy or Dostoevsky is somewhere
writing the books; but they hide it, they have to, they can't
print it, but that someday that will come to light because
I do not believe that people are that different, that people
can be under the control of a government which does not
give them freedom, but it doesn't change the people. And I
am convinced that Tolstoys and Dostoevskys in Russia right
now are writing but they can't print it. They hide it from
the law, then bury it, and someday I think it will appear.

*

He (the individual) must be completely free in spirit. But
freedom, true freedom, extends only to where the next individual's freedom stops. That is, to be completely free is
not to be completely ruthless, completely heedless. He must
be free within a pattern of responsibility always. But he
must be free to say what he believes to be the truth.

A country with a government in which one cannot say
what one believes to be true is a bad government and for
that very reason, it will not last very long.

But there is a responsibility that goes with the privilege
of saying what one thinks. One must have integrity to know
the truth, to believe the truth, to speak the truth, for the
sake of truth, not for the sake of aggrandizement or for
profit or policy, but the truth because it is true.

WHEN I HAVE USED degradation and violence (in my writing)
it has never been for the sake of degradation and violence.
I have used them as tools with which I was trying to show
what man must combat, and specific instances in which he
has been strangled by degradation and violence, when he
has hated the violence he participated in, when he has
resisted the violence, when he believed in something like

honor and pride and compassion, even in degradation. To write just about the violence and degradation for the sake of violence and degradation is a failure of integrity. It is a matter of using the tool which seems to the writer the best tool to make what he is trying to make; that is, he is trying to tell people that degradation and violence must be cured, and men can cure it.

Sex is one of the most important forces in mankind and if literature is to deal truly with mankind, the human heart, then sex will have a very important part in it. I would say that just as death is a very important factor in human life, greed is a very important factor in human life, and they would be very important in fiction which deals with man's problems, or the conflict of man with himself or his fellow men or his environment.

But sex just for the sake of sex is like what I spoke of about violence and degradation. Just for the sake of violence or degradation, that's not good enough to write about. It's got to be sex as a force in man, in human relations, assuming that what man wants to do is to make a better world to live in in which all people can be free of fear, of poverty, of war.

I THINK that there is a great deal of beauty in any national language, national literature. But that tradition of literature must still be furthered more so that it can meet and can give and take from other national literary traditions. But by all means develop one's own because there is a certain portrait[1] in the legends, the customs of any people, that are valuable, and the best way to get them into a universal literature is to bring them first into a national literature. I think that nobody should turn his back on his own tradition, his own language, his own culture, to assume a foreign one. Let him go into the foreign one. Let his own and the foreign meet and produce a universal one. Each gives something to the other, takes something from the other. That is, it would be foolish for me, for instance, to undertake to write literature in the literary tradition of the Philippine Islands; it would

be foolish for a Filipino to start off to write in the tradition
of my country. Let us both follow and exploit and explore
our own traditions to get what we can out of that, and then
merge them together.

*

I would say that it would not matter really what language
that child was taught to write in. If his tradition, his background is Filipino, he would still write in the tradition of
his nativity whether he wrote in English or not. When I said
to turn to a foreign tradition, I did not mean to a foreign
language, particularly. I meant to say that my tradition is
not the one I want. I will go to a foreign land; I will teach
myself that tradition. Now, that can be done.

I can name you one man that did it—Joseph Conrad—
but then that is a phenomenon; that is an exception. I do
not think that simply because the Filipino child is taught
English in school, he is going to escape his own tradition.
He would have to make a deliberate attempt. He would
have to leave the Philippines to go to another country to
escape his tradition, the legend, the folklore of his people.
The language is not too important because he will speak
English with the Philippine flavor, to put it that way. He
will speak of things that the American would not know
about simply because things are in the Filipino child's tradition though he spoke of them in English.

*

The writer has got to be read too, and so the best language
for a writer to write in for his readers would be the language
that most readers know. It means that the language of a
people will have some of the poetry, the folklore, some of
the very important traditions in the past of the people. And
the writer must be familiar with that. It is difficult to tell
a Filipino that he should know his own language and then
write in English a novel but maybe that is the true answer,
that if he is to be read he must write in a language which
the greatest number of people can read. If he wrote in

Tagalog, for instance, it will have to be translated. Very few people can read it.

*

It may be that the writer should protect himself to write in English, to know Tagalog, to know his own language, but to write in English for the reason that it would not have to be translated. And then in the translation something is always lost. A good translator can give something to a work that was not there before, but something in that original work is lost in the transition from language to language. And that is probably a decision that the writer himself will have to make, that if he feels that there is a rhythm, or a cadence to his language which he cannot get into English then he'd better stick to his own language and depend on the translator to do the best of his ability.

WAR OR DISASTER gives a release to the impulse to write. I think young people, after trouble, they think: What shall I believe in? What shall I hold to? And that seems to take the form of writing—they are either trying to explain, although baffled by frustration, or they may try to invent for themselves something to hold to, something to comfort. Yes, I would say that a great national disaster has some influence, some effect on the resurgence of writing.

*

All literature, since it is, in a way, the same thing, is after the same thing, is after the same aim and end. It thus influences the literature of other nations and other people, especially after something like the last war when people moved and got to know each other. All the literature of countries will react back and forth.

Philippine literature will influence American literature; American literature will influence Philippine literature; Japanese literature will have its impact on all of the writing done by the young men that have gone through a pretty bad experience like a world war is.

＊

I think that the disaster that the Philippines suffered will have the same effect, and I think, too, that because it was one of great disaster that all people suffered, whether they won or lost, there will be a commonality in writing; that somehow the cultures will be closer together so that it will be a little difficult to say this is Philippine writing, this is Japanese writing, this is American writing; that the young people will have something in common, and they will understand one another. They will write about the same things in the same terms.

＊

Yes, I believe that quite often a disaster has a good effect on the literature of a people. I read one translation of a Japanese novel which to me was understandable. The translations of Japanese that I read when I was a young man, I could believe that the people did what the book said but I couldn't understand why they did. In this book for the first time people behaved as I in my own experience said that people should behave. I expect that there will be a resurgence of Japanese writing after their disaster, just as there was in my country, the South of America, after our civil war when we were defeated and occupied.

＊

. . . Since the war Western people have come to know more about the East and we have all realized how important this part of the world is; that is, it is important not to itself, but to the Western part of the world, too. And so many things of a dramatic nature have happened in this part of the world. That's one reason there has been a lot of writing by Westerners about the East, that suddenly the East became important and it became a part of Western environment. I mean by environment, not just the field, the house, the town you live in, but all the memory, all the tradition, is a part of environment, just like the air you breathe.

I would say that with communication and the fact that people, because of war or whatever, have traveled, have gotten to know one another as they didn't fifty years ago, all the world has become everyone's environment.

IT MIGHT BE well if a government could support the writer, but there you are. That gets into a controlled quality in the writer, in a way that the writer's freedom has been abrogated when he must accept money from a governmental source. Now I don't say it's bad, I don't say it won't work, but I do say that there is that risk, that if there were a bureau in government of men wise enough to realize that the writer's freedom is a precious quality—if he is to be valid as a writer, and to be of value to his country—that would be one thing.

But where does that bureau exist? Can that bureau exist? But I am convinced that the writer if he has got something to say, he will not need that. He will write no better for having a million dollars; he will write no worse for having a million dollars. And if he is poor and has to work, even if he works eight hours a day for rice and bread and a little meat occasionally, he will still find time to do the writing. And the writing will be no worse and no better. The writer, in my opinion, the artist, is extremely lucky, because the first-rate one who is so wrapped up, who has dedicated himself, his life, to make him something which was not here before, like a book, a poem, or picture, or music, doesn't mind starving a little. He is not interested in whether his belly is full or not full. He is interested in getting something on paper, on canvas.

IN A NATION, economy is, to an extent, based on a certain amount of selfishness; that is, it is the desire of one indi-

vidual to be successful in business for his own personal
reasons. It may be for glory, for renown; it may be for
money. But in order to be successful he has got to furnish
work, jobs, a certain amount of ease and comfort for other
people on whom he depends for his own success.

*

I think that in my country, since we have a culture of
success, of production, that we are little prone to save for
tomorrow; for, we will consider, what might be said the finer
things of life. That is, we might consider man's soul tomorrow. Today, we are too busy with our physical well-being,
but I do believe that all people want to be braver, kinder,
more generous than they are. And that when they are brought
to remember that they are not quite as generous as they might
be, not as brave, that they have done not quite enough, that
there shall be no hunger, no anguish, no suffering, that they
change. And that is the writer's position, his job: to remind
people that people must be braver than they were, that they
must be more generous, that they must have compassion.

That is the problem that the writer faces in my country,
which is not really a problem, it is only that he must remind
the people who are in command and in charge of our economy, our culture of success, that there is more to being a
member of the family of man than just success. And I think
my people in the United States respond to that. And for
that reason, we, the American writers, the American artists,
have a very valid position in our economy, in our culture.

NEVER IN all human relations have people and nations been
able to do without friends. Never in all human relations
have nations lived with friends more than now. I have
always believed since I have been in your country that the
people of the Republic of the Philippines are the best
friends which my country has, because you ask nothing of us
save mutual dignity and respect. When I go back to my
country it will be my duty and my privilege to tell my people

that, that when I came to your university (the University of the Philippines) to speak I saw more people listening to me than I ever saw before in my life. And I do hope that what little I may give you, tell you, you will remember after I am gone. They say that to part is to die a little, or not to die so much as to leave something behind, so that when I leave your country I will leave something of me behind, that someday I will be forced to come back here to recover it.

*

The young people wanted to ask questions of me and they asked the questions which they would ask of someone they respected but also felt kinship with. The questions that have been asked of me are not the courteous polite questions that one asks a simple guest. And that is one of the nicest things that has happened to me since I have been here.

*

We, in my country, know that the Filipino is a friend; we know that there is a mutual dependence between our two nations, our two peoples. We do know that the Filipino is our friend and that we will defend that friend. We will even go to the length of what might be mistakes. But we would defend that friend—all people—who believe as we believe.

I HAVE BEEN lucky, I think. I have written because I like to write. I like to make something that was not in the world before me, I hope to believe, and I write when I feel like it, when I want to. Once a job is started, there is an urge to finish it, but in my own nature I never felt that any sort of a schedule or set time to write did me much good. I write until I get tired, and then quit. And then when I am rested I write again—sometimes eight and ten hours a day, sometimes ten minutes a day, sometimes no time at all during the day. That works best with me. Probably every man will have his own method that suits him. Some people, writers I have known, write better when they have a rigid schedule to follow; that they will put in so many hours a day over the paper whether they put anything down or not. That works best with them. That is a matter of temperament.

Note

1. Faulkner may have said "portion."

Interview with

CYNTHIA GRENIER

In September 1955 Faulkner was interviewed in Paris on his way back to America after the Nagano Seminars. The text of the interview given here follows that of the first publication in English, in Accent, *XVI (Summer 1956); an earlier version in French appeared in* La Table Ronde, *January 1956.*

By the time he arrived in Paris Faulkner had been talking almost continuously for two months; the experience seems to have made him considerably more relaxed with interviewers, given reasonably favorable circumstances. On this occasion a combination of pleasant company and a pleasant setting in his favorite city apparently drew Faulkner on to speak more freely and easily than usual.

SCENE: The broad green lawn at the back of the U.S. Information Service building in Paris on a warm Indian summer morning in late September. William Faulkner, stretched out on the grass in his Brooks Brothers blue shirtsleeves, nurses his pipe. On the grass beside him the interviewer. Faulkner is a handsome man with a well-brushed head of white hair, tanned face, very alert black-brown eyes under epicanthic lids. His chin juts up and out meeting the world directly and defiantly. His bearing and appearance belie his fifty-eight years. He speaks in a soft, slow voice with what could be called an educated Southern accent. Sometimes his sentences are short—" 'cause I do"—and other times when he is speaking of his craft or his beliefs fine long involved rhetorical sentences roll out, as they do in his prose. He seldom takes the initiative in conversation, waiting without seeming to wait for the other person to talk. He has a distaste for journalists and official interviews, but shows a genuine enthusiasm and interest in responding to, as he terms them, "young folks' questions." At a press conference held a few days earlier, when faced with detailed questions from newspapermen on his philosophy and works, he had replied repeatedly, "I'm not a literary man; I'm just a farmer." But being a "literary" man and being a writer are two different things to him, and Faulkner does admit to being a writer and will, sometimes, talk about his craft. His manner, which is a combination of shyness and defensiveness, places an interviewer on his honor not to probe the forbidden areas— "literary" analysis of his works, symbolic content—but to seek rather to make contact on a human level. While talking or listening, Faulkner smokes his pipe, from time to time filling it almost automatically from a yellow oilskin pouch. He gives a sense of unity and great internal reserve about his person. In spite of this reserve, Faulkner emanates throughout the interview a very considerably engaging quiet charm which succeeds in being courtly and puckish at the same time.

Q: How do you feel about being in Paris now?

FAULKNER: Why, I like it fine. France and Italy are two of my favorite countries. I feel Paris is a kind of home for me. It's a part of everyone's cultural background. There's the liberty here to be an artist. It's in the air.

Q: How about you—have you ever thought of writing here?

FAULKNER: Oh, I couldn't. I'd have too much fun here to ever work. (With little side grin to interviewer.)

Q: Do you keep up with any of the writing being done today by your contemporaries or younger writers?

FAULKNER: No, I don't. Haven't read any new writing in the last ten or fifteen years. But I've been doing more reading lately than I used to, having more time, and I expect to do even more once I get back home. I want to read the new books being written today. I'm having a whole load of books

shipped home for me from Japan. And another from Italy
from the young Italian writers. I expect to do the same for
the French. (Pausing thoughtfully, drawing on his pipe.)
Books I do read are the ones I've known for years. The Old
Testament, Dickens, Flaubert, Balzac, Dostoevski, Tolstoi,
Shakespeare. But they're old friends. Don't read them straight
through any more. I can just dip in anywhere when I want
to. *Moby Dick, Don Quixote, Huck Finn, Madame Bovary,
Brothers Karamazov,* they're all old friends of mine.

Q: Just to take one of those authors you mentioned at
random, what is it about Balzac that you like?

FAULKNER: I like the fact that in Balzac there is an intact
world of his own. His people don't just move from page one
to page 320 of one book. There is continuity between them
all like a blood-stream which flows from page one through
to page 20,000 of one book. The same blood, muscle and
tissue binds the characters together.

Q: How about poetry? Do you read much poetry?

FAULKNER: Yes. But no new poets. I have my old friends
which I still read over. Keats, Shelley, Byron, the Elizabethans,
Marlowe, Thomas Campion; the French poets, Verlaine and
Laforgue. I think that every novelist is a failed poet. I think
he tries to write poetry first, then finds he can't. Then he
tries the short story, which is the most demanding form after
poetry. And failing at that, only then does he take up novel-
writing.

Q: Do you have any writer in mind when you say this?

FAULKNER (looking at interviewer): I'm a failed poet. I
tried writing poetry when I was a young man, but I soon
found I wasn't a poet. So I turned to the novel.

Q: I'd like to ask one more question on your reading, if
I may, do you read detective stories?

FAULKNER: Well, I like a good one like *Brothers Karamazov.*

Q (a little hesitant): Well, I was thinking of *Knight's
Gambit.*

FAULKNER: Oh. I think you can learn a lot from Simenon's
stories. They're so much like Chekhov's.

Q: I guess maybe I'd better read Chekhov again.

(Faulkner and Interviewer eye each other a minute.)

Q (starting up again): You've often said that primarily you were a farmer (Faulkner nods), but you did quite a few other things before you settled to being a writer-farmer, didn't you?

FAULKNER: That's right. I was a house-painter, a pilot, a bootlegger, and did a lot of other odd jobs. When my father died the responsibility for the family fell on me. Until then, I worked at any job which would bring me money when I wanted or needed money. For instance, after the First World War, aviation was new. People were willing to pay up to $100 to go up in a plane. You didn't need any license to practice this activity. As flying got more regimented and as there got to be more planes, it got less interesting and you earned less money at it, so I left it.

Q: You've mentioned several times before that you were a house-painter. Does that particular profession have any special importance for you?

FAULKNER: It was a terrible one for me, 'cause I couldn't stand the smell of paint. It made me sick, but it paid well. (Long pause, Faulkner drawing on pipe.) I used to be a bootlegger running raw liquor on a power boat from Cuba into New Orleans when I met Sherwood Anderson. We used to sit around every afternoon with two or three bottles of whiskey, laughing and talking about people. Next morning Sherwood would be in seclusion for about four hours, and next afternoon we'd sit around talking and drinking again. And next morning Sherwood would be in seclusion again. So I thought to myself that was as pleasant a life as was possible to lead. I'd found I liked to write already, so one day I sat down and started writing. After about a week, Anderson came over to my place, which was pretty nice of him, as he'd never done that before. He asked "What's wrong? You mad at me?" I said I was writing a novel. He said, "My God!" and walked off. A few weeks later, I met Mrs. Anderson, who said, "Sherwood has a message for you. He says if you won't make him read the book, he'll send it to his publishers with his recommendation." And when I had it finished in three months, he sent it off.

Q: That was *Soldiers' Pay?*

FAULKNER: Yes, that's right. . . . After I'd sent it off, I decided to go to Europe, shipping out of New Orleans as a deckhand on a freighter. When I arrived in Paris a month later, I found a check from my publishers for $200. And do you know, I didn't have a cent then, but I couldn't get that check cashed for more than three months. I just had to carry it around with me, and look at it sometimes.

Q: What do you think about the position of the young writer today, and the fact that, at least for short stories, he has fairly limited outlets?

FAULKNER: A young writer shouldn't ought to think too much about success. Shouldn't really think about it at all. (Sitting up, emphatically.) Success is feminine. It's like a woman. You treat her with contempt and she'll come after you, all fawning and eager, but chase after her and she'll scorn you. (Pauses, filling pipe.) You know, I wish I were a big foundation or was like one of those Renaissance princes. I'd like to take over a big house for young writers and painters. The painters, they'd each one get one canvas and enough paints and brushes to paint on it, and the writers'd get a ream of paper and a typewriter. Or pencils or a pen, whatever they'd think best with. And when they'd filled that canvas or that paper, why then they could come and get some more. They'd get their room and board, and a little extra money for cigarettes, liquor and maybe a new dress once in a while for the girls to keep morale up, you know. But every year they'd have to turn out a novel or a painting. Maybe more than one, but at least one every year. (Lighting pipe.) Yes, too bad I'm not a foundation.

Q: Do you think also that it would be profitable for their work to have all these writers and painters living together so that they might share ideas, and exchange criticism?

FAULKNER: No, I don't. An artist shouldn't talk too much. If he talks then he works that much less. This way, with them all living together in the same house all the time, they'd get themselves talked out pretty fast, and then they'd spend all their time working.

Q: Don't you ever, or didn't you ever, want to or feel the need to discuss your writing with anyone?

FAULKNER: No. No one but me knew what I was writing about or writing from. I always knew whether what I'd done was right and good or not. There wasn't anyone who could tell me that. If I thought it was right, then it didn't make any difference to me what anyone else thought.

Q: In view of your feeling on this matter, how do you feel when you hear or read about various critics and writers discussing your unconscious meanings, your symbolic content, and so forth?

FAULKNER (emphatically): Never read 'em. . . . But it does sort of amuse me when I hear 'em talking about the socio-logical picture that I present in something like *As I Lay Dying*, for instance.

Q: This is a rather big order question, but how do your ideas come to you? How do you shape your novels?

FAULKNER: There's always a moment in experience—a thought—an incident—that's there. Then all I do is work up to that moment. I figure what must have happened before to lead people to that particular moment, and I work away from it, finding out how people act after that moment. That's how all my books and stories come. I don't believe in inspiration. I always write out of my personal experience, out of events I've been present at, out of stories I've heard from people. (Pausing.) I think people try to find more in my work than I've put there. I like to tell stories, to create people and situations. But that's all. I doubt if an author knows what he puts in a story. All he is trying to do is to tell what he knows about his environment and the people around him in the most moving way possible. He writes like a carpenter uses his tools. . . . Like violence. Violence is just a tool I use to tell something the best way I am capable of telling it. If I could I would write all my books again, and I think I could do them better. But I don't think I'd be satisfied with them. I don't think any author can be satisfied with his work. If he were, there'd be nothing left for him to do but cut his throat. (Draws finger across throat.) Being a writer is having the worst vocation. You're demon-run, under compulsion, always being driven. It's a lonely frustrating work which is never as good as you want it to be. You have to keep on trying, but still it's not good enough. It's never good enough. What the reward is for a writer, I don't know.

Q: You said just now, that you're only concerned with telling a story. Still, it is possible to read in philosophical content in your works. There is a unity, a kind of purpose or theme binding your works together, don't you think?

FAULKNER (flatly): There isn't any theme in my work, or maybe if there is, you can call it a certain faith in man and his ability to always prevail and endure over circumstances and over his own destiny.

Q: But in many of your books, it seems as if the majority of your characters are trapped by fate.

FAULKNER: But (gesturing with pipe) there is always some one person who survives, who triumphs over his fate.

Q: Still, so many more go down than survive.

FAULKNER: That's all right. That they go down doesn't matter. It's *how* they go under.

Q: And what is the way to go under?

FAULKNER: It's to go under when trying to do more than you know how to do. It's trying to defy defeat even if it's inevitable.

Q: You say that man will endure and prevail. Would you care to comment on just how he will prevail today in this atomic age?

FAULKNER: Why, yes. Man has many more ways to destroy himself physically, but perhaps he has no more ways for destroying himself spiritually than he had hundreds of years ago. Man's environment is the only thing that changes. He must change with it. He will cope with it. The problems he faces today are the same ones he faced when he came out of the mud and first stood on two legs. Man wants to be braver than he is. He wants to have more compassion than he has. Suddenly, sometimes, he finds to his surprise he *is* more brave and more honest. He does stand up and say that this injustice shall no longer prevail, and then he does something so that it shall no longer prevail. Man does things at times that make it seem that he is not worthy of surviving. But he redeems himself at other times. He shall prevail.

(Faulkner holds interviewer with long firm look, then tamps down pipe.)

Q: Tell me, how do you feel yourself toward your own work? Do you have a favorite book, is there one you especially care for?

FAULKNER: Well, I judge my books by how much work and agony went into 'em. Something like *As I Lay Dying* was easy, real easy. A *tour de force*. It took me just about six weeks. (With a grin.) I could write a book like that with both hands tied behind my back. It just came all of a piece with no work on my part. Just came like that. I just thought of all the natural catastrophes that could happen to a family and let them all happen. . . . The book which took the most agony was *The Sound and the Fury*. Took me five years of re-working and re-writing. Never did finish it.

Q: How did you come to write *The Sound and the Fury?*

FAULKNER: It started out as a short story about two children being sent out to play in the yard during their grandmother's funeral. Only one of the little girls was big enough to climb a tree to look in the window to see what was going on. It was going to be a story of blood gone bad. The story told wasn't all. The idiot child had started out as a simple prop at first as a bid for extra sympathy. Then I thought what would the story be told like as he saw it. So I had him look at it. When I'd finished I had a quarter of the book written, but it still wasn't all. It still wasn't enough. So then Quentin told the story as he saw it and it still wasn't enough. Then Jason told the story and it still wasn't enough. Then I tried to tell the story and it still was not enough, and so I wrote the appendix and it wasn't enough. It's the book I feel tenderest towards. I couldn't leave it alone, and I never could tell it right, though I tried hard and would like to try again though I'd probably fail again. It's the tragedy of two lost women: Caddy and her daughter.

Q: This is something I've often wondered about. You know that in some of your writing, as in the short story, "That Evening Sun Go Down," you tell it simply, directly, beautifully. But in some of your novels, it's very difficult for the reader to grasp the thread and sometimes even the plot without a second or third reading. Is this intentional or is it maybe the fault of the reader?

FAULKNER: No, it's not the reader's fault. I try as every artist should to tell my story simply and clearly. If sometimes I don't succeed it is my fault.

Q: Does the fact that you now have a much greater reading public than you used to influence you in any way when you write?

FAULKNER (emphatically): No. . . . I never think about people reading my books when I'm writing them. When I was younger, never gave any thought to folks reading my books at all. Now that I'm—well—somewhat slower (with a little smile) it pleases me to think my books are read, but it still doesn't affect my writing of 'em any.

Q: You say that writing for a larger public doesn't affect you in any way. What about writing for the movies? Does this require any special attitude or adjustment on your part?

FAULKNER: Well (slow smile), you know, I don't really take American movies very seriously. I've got a friend who's a director out in Hollywood and we have an agreement. When I need money I call him, and when he wants a script he calls me.[1] But I don't take writing for the movies seriously.

Q: How do you feel about your books being read and discussed all over the world?

FAULKNER: I like it. (Little nod of approval.) I like the idea of the world I created being a kind of keystone in the universe. Feel that if I ever took it away the universe around that keystone would crumble away. . . . If they believed in my world in America the way they do abroad, I could probably run one of my characters for President . . . (studiously tamping his pipe) maybe Lem Snopes.[2] (With a quick look up at the interviewer.)

Q: I see you've got some of us Greniers living in a shack as half-wits down in Yoknapatawpha County.

FAULKNER (looking with interest at interviewer): Why sure. Grenier was one of the first three settlers in my county. There was Habersham, Holston, and the Frenchman Grenier. The last of the Habershams was Miss Habersham—remember her in *Intruder in the Dust*?

(Nod from the interviewer followed by a silence. One of the most agreeable qualities about Faulkner is his capacity for being silent in a natural, easy way.)

Q: I was reading over "The Bear" the other night, and though I don't know much about hunting or anything like that, I liked the feelings in the story. I thought it was a very good story.

FAULKNER: (Appraising look, and almost a smile. Waits.)

Q: Tell me, was there a real Big Ben[3] and a Lion?

FAULKNER: Yes. There used to be a bear like Big Ben in our county when I was a boy. He'd gotten one paw caught in a trap, and 'cause of that, folks used to call him Reel Foot, 'cause of the way he walked. He got killed too, though not so spectacularly as I killed him in the story of course. . . . (Drawing on pipe reflectively.) I took Hogganbeck from a fella that worked for my father. He was about thirty, but had the mind of a fourteen-year-old. I was about eight or nine. 'Course, me being the boss's son, we always did what I wanted to do. It's a wonder we survived, some of the things we got into. It's a wonder.

Q: I imagine from what you've said, and from what's known from your writing and life, that you've taken quite a lot from your own experience to put into your books. Like the parts in your books on aviation for instance. Did those come out of your own experience?

FAULKNER: No. They came from the imagination and experience of anyone who had much to do with airplanes at that time.

Q: Who are your favorite literary characters in your own work?

FAULKNER: Dilsey and Ratliff, the sewing-machine agent.

Q: Why?

FAULKNER: Well, Dilsey is brave, courageous, generous, gentle and honest. She's much more brave and honest and generous than I am. . . . Ratliff is wonderful. He's done more things than any man I know. Why, I couldn't tell some of the things that man has done. . . . (Pause. Sudden and direct.) And who are *your* favorite characters?

Q (startled): Isaac McCaslin in "The Bear."

FAULKNER (smiling a little, very quick and direct): Why?

Q: Because he underwent the baptism in the forest, because he rejected his inheritance.

FAULKNER: And do you think it's a good thing for a man to reject an inheritance?

Q: Yes, in McCaslin's case. He wanted to reject a tainted inheritance. You don't think it's a good thing for him to have done so?

FAULKNER: Well, I think a man ought to do more than just repudiate. He should have been more affirmative instead of shunning people.

Q: Do you think that any of your characters succeed in being more affirmative?

FAULKNER: Yes, I do. There was Gavin Stevens. He was a good man but he didn't succeed in living up to his ideal. But his nephew, the boy, I think he may grow up to be a better man than his uncle. I think he may succeed as a human being.

Q: And who is your unfavorite character?

FAULKNER: Jason. Jason Compson.

Q: I noticed that a few months ago you were quoted as having listed five American authors in order of their excellence—Wolfe, yourself, Dos Passos, Caldwell, and Hemingway—was that correct?

FAULKNER: No. It was not. I was misquoted. I listed those writers according to what they had tried to do and to what measure they had succeeded in their attempt. I put Tom Wolfe first because he tried to do the most. He tried to put the whole universe into his books and failed. His was the most glorious failure. And then myself. I tried the most after Wolfe and failed the most after him. Then Dos Passos, Caldwell and Hemingway in order of what they aimed at. Hemingway was taught to know his limitations, and he had enough sense to stay within them, instead of trying to put all the world on the head of a pin.

Q: How do you feel your books would have to be in order for you to feel you had to some measure succeeded?

FAULKNER: I'd have to feel the way I do when I read the *Tentation de Saint Antoine,* or the plays of Marlowe, or the

Old Testament. (Looking down at his pipe.) A fiction writer is a failed poet, a factual recorder of the past. A writer believes in man and life and tries to record the triumph of the human heart, as best and as honestly as he can.

Q: How do you feel towards your latest work?[4]

FAULKNER: It's a *tour de force.*

Q: I thought you spent many years writing it.

FAULKNER: That's right, but it's still a *tour de force.* I knew exactly what I wanted to do, but it took me nine years to find how to do it. But I knew what I wanted to do.

(Chestnut falls from tree, bouncing near Faulkner.)

FAULKNER: You have to watch out for those things. I was sitting in the park across the way yesterday, reading my newspaper and one of those things came right down—bang—through the paper. Just like that.

Q: I hear you went to a fashion show yesterday. What did you think of it?

FAULKNER (grinning reminiscently): I liked it fine. Seemed all sort of foolish. All those women sitting around watching those tall cold girls walking around in fancy clothes. There was one woman there who must have weighed at least 180 pounds. How she thought she was going to get into any of those dresses, I don't know. I'll bet you could remove all those people who were there yesterday from the face of the earth, and nobody'd say anything. Or maybe somebody one day would say, "I wonder what happened to Madame Jones, we haven't seen her lately." You know, there's some lines of verse. Let's see. How'd it go now? I haven't thought of it in years. "Women in their silks and fineries . . . ." No, that's not it. Mmm. . . . (Shakes head.)

(Interviewer waits while Faulkner thinks, samples out lines of verse and rejects them.)

Q: Look, I hope I'm not keeping you here. Maybe you have an appointment.

FAULKNER: Well, as a matter of fact, I do, over on the Left Bank. If I left now I could walk over. I like walking in Paris. It's always a beautiful city. Especially the rooftops. I like looking out my hotel window across the rooftops of Paris.

(Faulkner sits, pulls on his tan tweed jacket with its dark leather patches on the elbows, stretches a little. Stands looking about.)

FAULKNER: Looks like only the Government can afford to have places like this today.

(Interviewer and Faulkner start walking through garden out into parking lot.)

Q: Do you have any special advice for young writers?

FAULKNER: Yes, I do. The most important thing is for them to write. They shouldn't ought to care about the public. They should just get the words out of themselves and down onto paper. What matters is at the end of life, when you're about to pass into oblivion, that you've at least scratched "Kilroy was here," on the last wall of the universe. Nothing else matters. Don't pay attention to success. She's, like I told you, feminine. Don't chase her. Like a woman, she'll come fawning after. What counts is that you've done *something*.

(Faulkner looks up at the sky, takes a deep breath.)

FAULKNER: The French don't have any word for Indian summer, do they? They should.

Notes

1. Apparently a reference to Howard Hawks.
2. Faulkner has no such character; presumably Flem Snopes was intended.
3. Presumably Old Ben was intended.
4. *A Fable,* published August 1954.

"A LION IN THE GARDEN"

While in Paris in September 1955 Faulkner was guest of honor at a party given by his French publishers, Gallimard. The following account of the proceedings, by Madeleine Chapsal, a French journalist and author of several books, was published in The Reporter *(November 3, 1955). Though not itself an interview, it is perhaps the best account of Faulkner interviewed that has ever been written.*

WHEN WILLIAM FAULKNER came to Paris on a State Department mission, he might have known what he was letting himself in for. But anyone who took a good look at him at cocktail parties, receptions, and press conferences could have no doubt that Faulkner was in worse trouble than he had anticipated.

His most grueling ordeal was the Gallimard cocktail party. The publishing house is on the Rue de l'Université, and its large paneled rooms open onto a lawn with three trees—one of the famous secret gardens of Paris. Behind this eighteenth-century elegance the firm runs a greedy monopoly over most of the best French authors of the day.

When Faulkner arrived at precisely six o'clock, there was no one to greet him. The Gallimards—there is a whole family of them—were still upstairs. He found himself with three journalists and a photographer who, like the guest of honor, happened to come on time. They were lucky; in a few minutes four hundred people would be there. For the moment they had the hero to themselves.

At first sight the man is not impressive. But there is something unbending and strong, peasantlike, in the way he holds himself. He speaks very quietly, and he makes no sudden gestures. He looks like the kind of man who gets along well with animals and children.

The newspaper people approached him reverently: "Mr. Faulkner," they would begin. And immediately they would run into a wall, that famous wall about which Paris had been talking for days but in which no one really believed until he faced it. It is built of the most exquisite but the most obdurate politeness—the special politeness we in France think of as the attribute of certain Americans brought up in the South. When you come up against it you find yourself gently pushed back to an immense distance from William Faulkner.

Try it yourself. Ask him a question. He leans toward you, he listens to you, he answers "Yes" or "No," and then he takes a step backward. It is that step backward which seems so tragic. After forcing him to retreat—each question a step—even the hardiest newspapermen give up.

Yet the three reporters tried it one after the other. They were there to bring back a story, after all, but when they reached the wall, they gave up.

"To think that I have the sound truck outside, and all for nothing!" the radio man said, as if he were saying, "I have the Cross and the nails outside." The reporters were sorry for the radio man. Back in the office they could always cook up something to write.

The photographer took a last shot. Faulkner was left with a young woman. He asked for a bourbon. He is different with women, probably because he likes them and is not afraid of them. Women do not attack him with mechanical or intellectual gadgets; women, like Faulkner, are more inclined to feel like displaced persons. Also he had his bourbon. He is very fond of bourbon.

The performance began. The entire Gallimard clan descended upon him with one smile and a half dozen tentacles. The society women trooped in. The hunt was on. After an hour of it, Faulkner had retreated as far as he could go. He was standing at the far end of the garden, beneath the tree with the heaviest foliage, backed up against the wrought-iron barrier.

From time to time in the brilliantly lighted reception rooms, someone would put down a glass, refuse a sandwich, and plunge out into the darkness of the garden. Two minutes later he would be back again, in dismay: "It's appalling! I can't watch it; it's like seeing someone being tortured."

A lady who arrived late took a few sips and then set her drink down, proclaiming, "And now I am going out to put a few questions to our dear, our great Faulkner." The others watched her proceed down the graveled path of the garden. Half a minute later she returned: "It's cold out there beneath the trees." Her voice was not the same.

Yes, it was chilly out there for those accustomed to being enthusiastically greeted as soon as they say they are on a newspaper and smiled at as soon as they mention the author's work—for those who thrive on interminable literary chatter among people belonging to the same world even though they have never read a word written by the genius.

There is no use looking at Faulkner. You must read him. To someone who has read him, Faulkner has given all that he has, and he knows it. Then one can understand that when he keeps saying "I am a farmer," or "I wrote that book so that I could buy a good horse," it is only another way of putting first things first—what Faulkner wants one to be interested in are his books.

Faulkner does not seem to be reconciled to this persistent attempt to take from him what still belongs to him. After all, it's so little. The expression on his face, for instance, or the gestures of his hands. Nothing is more pathetic than the tired indifference with which he lets people stare at him so that they can go home and say, "What a head! What wonderful hair!"

At last the party was over. "I would like to go," Faulkner said to someone. "I would like to say good-by to a Gallimard." They fetched him one, a fat Gallimard: "No," said Faulkner, "not that one." They went into the crowd and fetched him

another, a long, thin Gallimard: "It's not that one, either,"
said Faulkner. "Which one do you want?" they asked him.
"The one who looks a little sad," said Faulkner. "The bald
one." "Ah, that one has gone to bed," they told him. "It
doesn't matter," said Faulkner, going out into the Paris streets,
tired, a little shaky, but free.

---❈ 1955 ❈---

Interview with
ANNIE BRIERRE

This interview, originally published under the title "Faulkner Parle" in Les Nouvelles Littéraires, *October 6, 1955, was another of those which Faulkner gave when he was in Paris in the fall of 1955. In deciding to allow this Paris interview by a Frenchwoman to remain in French, the editors had in mind the importance which Faulkner had so long for the French reader, and the French reader for Faulkner. Mlle. Brierre drew partly on this material in the article, "Dernière rencontre avec Faulkner," which was occasioned by Faulkner's death and published in* Les Nouvelles Littéraires *on July 12, 1962.*

MINCE, DE PETITE TAILLE, cheveux blancs, yeux bruns éclairés d'une flamme ardente, Faulkner s'incline avec la raideur courtoise d'un gentilhomme du sud pour nous accueillir.

Le romancier qui eut sans doute le plus d'influence sur sa génération est moins un homme de lettres qu'un fermier. La solitude, le calme qu'il trouve dans ses terres du Mississippi lui sont indispensables, aussi se dérobe-t-il aux interviews.

Appartenant à une grande famille aristocratique ruinée par la guerre de Sécession, il me donne quelques précisions sur ses ancêtres:

—Ils sont venus des Highlands d'Ecosse pour s'installer en Amérique et, lors de la guerre d'Indépendance, ils ont combattu contre le roi anglais.

Que Faulkner le silencieux ait spontanément prononcé

cette phrase me fait croire à un miracle et je lui pose aussitôt
une question sur les séjours qu'il vient de faire au Japon
et en Italie:

—Ce voyage a pour objet de montrer qu'il n'y a pas unique-
ment, en Amérique, des politiciens et des hommes d'affaires.

—Quant à Paris, depuis cinq ans, j'ai été gâté, j'y suis venu
chaque année. Déjà en 1923[1] j'y avais vécu un an. Il y avait
là Gertrude Stein, Hemingway, James Joyce . . . Paris n'a
changé que dans la mesure où tout doit changer. On y rencontre encore des jeunes gens et des jeunes filles qui, la
nuit, au coin des rues, se disent sans doute la même chose.
Les pigeons de Paris sont toujours là. Le Palais-Royal, la
Seine ont le même charme. La cuisine et le vin sont aussi
bons, le Louvre et la *Victoire de Samothrace* aussi beaux
. . . Mais, vivre à Paris, non. J'y trouverais trop de plaisir.
Je ne travaillerais plus, et ma conscience me le reprocherait.
Pour travailler il me faut ma ferme, la solitude, quelques
amis—éleveurs, fermiers, chasseurs—qui se doutent à peine que
j'écris.

—Votre arrière-grand-père qui fut colonel durant la guerre
de Sécession est l'auteur d'un livre qui s'est vendu à cent
cinquante mille exemplaires. Est-ce cela qui vous a incité
à écrire?

—Non. C'est un mauvais livre. Il avait fait un peu de tout
dans la vie et il fallait bien qu'il s'essayât aussi à écrire.

—Et vous, quand avez-vous commencé?

—Dès que j'ai su épeler. C'est Sherwood Anderson qui
porte la responsabilité de ma première oeuvre: au temps
de la prohibition, je m'étais fait embaucher sur un bateau
qui faisait la contrebande de l'alcool entre Mexico et La
Nouvelle-Orléans où habitait Anderson. Il m'a conseillé
d'écrire, me promettant de présenter mon manuscrit à son
éditeur, à la condition de n'avoir pas à le lire d'abord.

Ainsi naquit *Monnaie de singe.* Faulkner avait cependant
auparavant publié, sans succès, un recueil de poèmes: *The
Marble Faun.*

—C'était très mauvais. J'écris encore des vers; j'en écris
souvent. Ils sont toujours aussi mauvais et je les détruis
aussitôt.

—Ceux qui ont lu *Rameau vert,* qui vient de paraître chez Gallimard, ont une autre opinion.

—Ce qui importe, c'est ce que j'en pense.

—Y a-t-il eu un événement qui ait exercé une influence dominante sur votre vie?

Il ne répond pas de façon précise aux questions dont on le persécute. Non qu'il s'y dérobe délibérément. Mais il préfère s'abandonner à une idée, un souvenir, une impression que cette question fait naître. Ses lectures?

—Dans ma jeunesse j'ai lu *Moby Dick, Les Frères Karamazoff,* presque tout Dickens, *Madame Bovary,* l'Ancien Testament (pas le Nouveau qui est de la philosophie. L'Ancien parle des hommes), Shakespeare, Conrad. Depuis, je ne lis plus. Parfois je relis Shelley, Keats, Verlaine, Laforgue.

Il a cependant lu *La Condition humaine* de Malraux, qui fut son traducteur.[2]

—C'est bon. Mais pas tout à fait assez bon.

Pour ses propres oeuvres, il sera tout aussi sévère:

—Si un seul de mes livres répondait à ce que j'ai tenté de faire, ce serait fini, je n'écrirais plus. Le flot serait interrompu. Mais on n'atteint jamais ce que l'on cherche. L'objet se transforme, à mesure qu'il devient plus proche: comme la fiancée que convoite le jeune homme et qui, devenue femme, n'est plus la vierge qu'il aimait.

—Travaillez-vous volontiers?

—Non. Je n'aime pas travailler, jamais. Je suis fermier, j'ai exercé bien des métiers dans ma jeunesse et je pourrais aujourd'hui aussi bien être homme d'affaires ou peintre en bâtiment. Mais je n'aime pas travailler, absolument pas. Eleveur de chevaux, j'aimerais assez cela, cependant.

—Quand écrivez-vous?

—Je n'obéis à aucune règle. J'écris quand j'en éprouve le besoin intense. Je dors peu; alors, parfois, je me relève à deux heures du matin pour écrire. Parfois aussi je reste des mois sans le faire.

—Les journalistes vous laissent-ils en paix dans votre ferme?

—Non. Mais quand ils entrent par la grande porte, je me sauve par la porte de derrière.

Ici, hélas! dans ce salon, il est bel et bien coincé.

—L'humanité échappera-t-elle au chaos actuel?

—Oui. Elle survivra. Elle est actuellement victime du machinisme qu'elle a créé. Il faut qu'elle aille au-delà.

—Alors que votre oeuvre exalte les sentiments qui unissent deux frères, qui unissent un père et un fils, elle parle rarement d'amour.

—C'est un sujet trop important pour être évoqué dans un livre. Il lui faut le secret.

—Depuis que vous avez obtenu le prix Nobel, votre oeuvre est, paraît-il, très lue en Russie. Peut-être y voit-on une preuve de la dégénérescence de l'Amérique?

—On peut faire dire tout ce qu'on veut à un livre. Même à l'annuaire du téléphone.

—Aimez-vous le théâtre?

—J'y suis allé cinq fois dans ma vie pour *Ben-Hur, Hamlet,* que j'ai vu trois fois, et pour *Le Songe d'une nuit d'été.*

—Votre roman *L'Intrus* a été porté à l'écran.

—C'est un bon film, qui a très peu de rapport avec le livre. Je voudrais discuter avec lui des opinions de Sartre, Malraux, Malcolm Cowley sur son oeuvre. Là, il se dérobe:

—Les idées ne m'intéressent pas. Seuls les hommes m'intéressent. Et ces paroles reviennent dans la conversation comme un leitmotiv.

—Certains de vos livres, comme *Le Bruit et la Fureur, Tandis que j'agonise,* sont imprégnés de violence. De plus récents, comme *L'Intrus, Le Gambit du cavalier,* laissent percer une certaine espérance; peut-on considérer qu'ils appartiennent à un Faulkner seconde manière?

—Non.

—Pourquoi tant de haine, si souvent?

—J'habite dans un pays où il y a beaucoup de violence. Le devoir d'un écrivain est de refléter ce qu'il a vécu, d'apporter la somme de son passé, le récit de ce qu'il a enduré, de ce que Dieu a voulu faire de lui.

—Vos personnages sont-ils parfois inspirés par des personnages réels?

—Non. Jamais. Dieu a créé les êtres du mieux qu'il a pu.

J'essaie de faire un peu mieux que lui sans jamais atteindre ce que je poursuis. Dès l'instant où je l'aurais atteint, tout serait fini, répète-t-il.

—Après ce tour du monde que vous terminez, comment jugez-vous les Américains?

—Ils aiment réussir, ils aiment donner. Ils ne le font pas toujours très sagement. Mais leurs intentions sont bonnes.

—Cette région du Mississippi qui a inspiré presque toute votre oeuvre, c'est là sans doute que vous aimez le mieux vivre?

—Non. Il y fait trop chaud. Je déclare chaque année qu'on ne m'y reprendra plus. Et, l'année suivante, je m'y retrouve. Ce que je voudrais, c'est être à Paris quand des marronniers sont en fleurs; en Ecosse au mois d'août, en Angleterre en juin, à Rome en mars et avril.

Notes

1. Faulkner, in later years, almost never got this date right. He was abroad for most of the last five months of 1925.
2. Malraux translated no Faulkner, though he wrote a preface for the French version of *Sanctuary*.

Interview with
JEAN STEIN VANDEN HEUVEL

*Most of this interview took place in New York early in 1956.
It was first published as the twelfth in the series, "The Art
of Fiction," in* The Paris Review, *Spring 1956, and it is that
text—with the exception of two paragraphs (see p. 250 and
note)—which is followed here. The interview was accompanied
by a reproduction of the first page of the manuscript of* As
I Lay Dying *and a pen-and-ink self-portrait by Faulkner. A
slightly enlarged version was included in Malcolm Cowley,
ed.,* Writers at Work: The Paris Review Interviews *(New York,
1958).*

*This is in many ways the most important and most influ-
ential of all Faulkner's interviews; it also gives the impression
of being the most carefully considered, in terms both of what
is said and the way it is expressed. Since it has been the custom
in* The Paris Review *interviews to give the author an opportunity to go over the copy before publication, Faulkner may
have had a hand in revising or polishing the final text.*

Q: Mr. Faulkner, you were saying a while ago that you
don't like interviews.

FAULKNER: The reason I don't like interviews is that I
seem to react violently to personal questions. If the questions
are about the work, I try to answer them. When they are
about me, I may answer or I may not, but even if I do, if
the same question is asked tomorrow, the answer may be
different.

Q: How about yourself as a writer?

FAULKNER: If I had not existed, someone else would have written me, Hemingway, Dostoevsky, all of us. Proof of that is that there are about three candidates for the authorship of Shakespeare's plays. But what is important is *Hamlet* and *Midsummer Night's Dream*, not who wrote them, but that somebody did. The artist is of no importance. Only what he creates is important, since there is nothing new to be said. Shakespeare, Balzac, Homer have all written about the same things and if they had lived 1,000 or 2,000 years longer, the publishers wouldn't have needed anyone since.

Q: But even if there seems nothing more to be said, isn't perhaps the individuality of the writer important?

FAULKNER: Very important to himself. Everybody else should be too busy with the work to care about the individuality.

Q: And your contemporaries?

FAULKNER: All of us failed to match our dream of perfection. So I rate us on the basis of our splendid failure to do the impossible. In my opinion, if I could write all my work again, I am convinced that I would do it better, which is the healthiest condition for an artist. That's why he keeps on working, trying again; he believes each time and this time he will do it, bring it off. Of course he won't, which is why this condition is healthy. Once he did it, once he matched the work to the image, the dream, nothing would remain but to cut his throat, jump off the other side of that pinnacle of cut perfection into suicide. I'm a failed poet. Maybe every novelist wants to write poetry first, finds he can't and then tries the short story which is the most demanding form after poetry. And failing at that, only then does he take up novel writing.

Q: Is there any possible formula to follow in order to be a good novelist?

FAULKNER: 99% talent . . . 99% discipline . . . 99% work. He must never be satisfied with what he does. It never is as good as it can be done. Always dream and shoot higher than you know you can do. Don't bother just to be better than your contemporaries or predecessors. Try to be better than

yourself. An artist is a creature driven by demons. He don't
know why they choose him and he's usually too busy to
wonder why. He is completely amoral in that he will rob,
borrow, beg, or steal from anybody and everybody to get
the work done.

Q: Do you mean the writer should be completely ruthless?

FAULKNER: The writer's only responsibility is to his art.
He will be completely ruthless if he is a good one. He has
a dream. It anguishes him so much he must get rid of it.
He has no peace until then. Everything goes by the board:
honor, pride, decency, security, happiness, all, to get the book
written. If a writer has to rob his mother, he will not hesitate;
the *Ode on a Grecian Urn* is worth any number of old ladies.

Q: Then could the *lack* of security, happiness, honor, be
an important factor in the artist's creativity?

FAULKNER: No. They are important only to his peace and
contentment, and art has no concern with peace and contentment.

Q: Then what would be the best environment for a writer?

FAULKNER: Art is not concerned with environment either;
it doesn't care where it is. If you mean me, the best job
that was ever offered to me was to become a landlord in a
brothel.[1] In my opinion it's the perfect milieu for an artist
to work in. It gives him perfect economic freedom; he's free
of fear and hunger; he has a roof over his head and nothing
whatever to do except keep a few simple accounts and to go
once every month and pay off the local police. The place is
quiet during the morning hours which is the best time of the
day to work. There's enough social life in the evening, if he
wishes to participate, to keep him from being bored; it gives
him a certain standing in his society; he has nothing to do
because the madam keeps the books; all the inmates of the
house are females and would defer to him and call him
"Sir." All the bootleggers in the neighborhood would call
him "Sir." And he could call the police by their first names.

So the only environment the artist needs is whatever peace,
whatever solitude, and whatever pleasure he can get at not
too high a cost. All the wrong environment will do is run his
blood-pressure up; he will spend more time being frustrated

or outraged. My own experience has been that the tools I need for my trade are paper, tobacco, food and a little whisky.

Q: Bourbon, you mean?

FAULKNER: No, I ain't that particular. Between scotch and nothing, I'll take scotch.

Q: You mentioned economic freedom. Does the writer need it?

FAULKNER: No. The writer doesn't need economic freedom. All he needs is a pencil, and some paper. I've never known anything good in writing to come from having accepted any free gift of money. The good writer never applies to a foundation. He's too busy writing something. If he isn't first rate he fools himself by saying he hasn't got time or economic freedom. Good art can come out of thieves, bootleggers or horse swipes. People really are afraid to find out just how much hardship and poverty they can stand. They are afraid to find out how tough they are. Nothing can destroy the good writer. The only thing that can alter the good writer is death. Good ones don't have time to bother with success or getting rich. Success is feminine and like a woman, if you cringe before her, she will override you. So the way to treat her is to show her the back of your hand. Then maybe she will do the crawling.

Q: Can working for the movies hurt your own writing?

FAULKNER: Nothing can injure a man's writing if he's a first rate writer. If a man is not a first rate writer, there's not anything can help it much. The problem does not apply if he is not first rate, because he has already sold his soul for a swimming pool.

Q: Does a writer compromise in writing for the movies?

FAULKNER: Always, because a moving picture is by its nature a collaboration and any collaboration is compromise because that is what the word means—to give and to take.

Q: Which actors do you like to work with most?

FAULKNER: Humphrey Bogart is the one I've worked with best. He and I worked together in *To Have and to Have Not* and *The Big Sleep*.

Q: Would you like to make another movie?

FAULKNER: Yes, I would like to make one of George Orwell's *1984*. I have an idea for an ending which would prove the thesis which I'm always hammering at: that man is indestructible because of his simple will to freedom.

Q: How do you get the best results in working for the movies?

FAULKNER: The moving picture work of my own which seemed best to me was done by the actors and the writer throwing the script away and inventing the scene in actual rehearsal just before the camera turned. If I didn't take, or felt I was capable of taking, motion picture work seriously, out of simple honesty to motion pictures and myself too, I would not have tried. But I know now that I will never be a good motion picture writer; so that work will never have the urgency for me which my own medium has.

Q: Would you comment on that legendary Hollywood experience you were involved in?

FAULKNER: I had just completed a contract at M.G.M. and was about to return home. The director I had worked with said, "If you would like another job here, just let me know and I will speak to the studio about a new contract." I thanked him and came home. About six months later I wired my director friend that I would like another job. Shortly after that I received a letter from my Hollywood agent enclosing my first week's paycheck. I was surprised because I had expected first to get an official notice or recall and a contract from the studio. I thought to myself the contract is delayed and will arrive in the next mail. Instead, a week later I got another letter from the agent enclosing my second week's paycheck. That began in November 1932 and continued until May 1933. Then I received a telegram from the studio. It said: *William Faulkner, Oxford, Miss. Where are you? M.G.M. Studio.*

I wrote out a telegram *M.G.M. Studio, Culver City, California. William Faulkner.*

The young lady operator said: "Where is the message, Mr. Faulkner?" I said, "That's it." She said: "The rule book says that I can't send it without a message, you have to say something." So we went through her samples and selected I forget which one—one of the canned anniversary greeting messages. I sent that. Next was a long distance telephone call from the studio directing me to get on the first airplane, go to New Orleans and report to Director Browning. I could have got on a train in Oxford and been in New Orleans eight hours later. But I obeyed the studio and went to Memphis where an airplane did occasionally go to New Orleans. Three days later one did.

I arrived at Mr. Browning's hotel about six P.M. and reported to him. A party was going on. He told me to get a good night's sleep and be ready for an early start in the morning. I asked him about the story. He said, "Oh, yes. Go to room so and so. That's the continuity writer. He'll tell you what the story is."

I went to the room as directed. The continuity writer was sitting in there alone. I told him who I was and asked him about the story. He said: "When you have written the dialogue I'll let you see the story." I went back to Browning's room and told him what had happened. "Go back," he said, "and tell that so and so—never mind, you get a good night's sleep so we can get an early start in the morning."

So the next morning in a very smart rented launch, all of us except the continuity writer sailed down to Grand Isle, about a hundred miles away where the picture was to be shot, reaching there just in time to eat lunch and have time to run the hundred miles back to New Orleans before dark.

That went on for three weeks. Now and then I would worry a little about the story but Browning always said, "Stop worrying. Get a good night's sleep so we can get an early start tomorrow morning."

One evening on our return I had barely entered my room when the telephone rang. It was Browning. He told me to come to his room at once. I did so. He had a telegram. It said: *Faulkner is fired. MGM Studio.* "Don't worry," Browning said. "I'll call that so and so up this minute and not only make him put you back on the payroll but send you a written apology." There was a knock on the door. It was a page with another telegram. This one said: *Browning is fired. MGM Studio.* So I came back home. I presume Browning went somewhere too. I imagine that continuity writer is still sitting in a room somewhere with his weekly salary check clutched tightly in his hand. They never did finish the film. But they did build a shrimp village—a long platform on piles in the water with sheds built on it something like a wharf. The studio could have bought dozens of them for forty or fifty dollars a piece. Instead, they built one of their own, a false one. That is, a platform with a single wall on it, so that when you opened the door and stepped through it, you stepped right on off to the ocean itself. As they built it, on the first day, the Cajun fisherman paddled up in his narrow tricky pirogue made out of a hollow log. He would sit in it all day long in the broiling sun watching the strange white folks building this strange imitation platform. The next day he was back in the pirogue with his whole family, his wife nursing the baby, the other children, and the mother-in-law, all to sit all that day in the broiling sun to watch this foolish and incomprehensible activity. I was in New Orleans two or three years later and heard that the Cajun people were still coming in for miles to look at that imitation shrimp platform which a lot of white people had rushed in and built and then abandoned.

Q: You say that the writer must compromise in working for the motion pictures. How about his writing? Is he under any obligation to his reader?

FAULKNER: His obligation is to get the work done the best he can do it; whatever obligation he has left over after that he can spend any way he likes. I myself am too busy to care about the public. I have no time to wonder who is reading me. I don't care about John Doe's opinion on mine or anyone else's work. Mine is the standard which has to be met, which is when the work makes me feel the way I do when I read *La Tentation de Saint Antoine,* or the Old Testament. They make me feel good. So does watching a bird make me feel good . . . you know that if I were reincarnated, I'd want to come back a buzzard. Nothing hates him or envies him or wants him or needs him. He is never bothered or in danger, and he can eat anything.

Q: What technique do you use to arrive at your standard?

FAULKNER: Let the writer take up surgery or bricklaying if he is interested in technique. There is no mechanical way to get the writing done, no short cut. The young writer would be a fool to follow a theory. Teach yourself by your own mistakes; people learn only by error. The good artist believes that nobody is good enough to give him advice. He has supreme vanity. No matter how much he admires the old writer, he wants to beat him.

Q: Then would you deny the validity of technique?

FAULKNER: By no means. Sometimes technique charges in and takes command of the dream before the writer himself can get his hands on it. That is *tour de force* and the finished work is simply a matter of fitting bricks neatly together, since the writer knows probably every single word right to the end before he puts the first one down. This happened with *As I Lay Dying*. It was not easy. No honest work is. It was simple in that all the material was already at hand. It took me just about six weeks in the spare time from a 12 hour a day job at manual labor. I simply imagined a group of people and subjected them to the simple universal natural catastrophes which are flood and fire with a simple natural motive to give direction to their progress. But then, when technique does not intervene, in another sense writing is easier too. Because with me there is always a point in the book where the characters themselves rise up and take charge and finish the job—say somewhere about page 275. Of course, I don't know what would happen if I finished the book on page 274. The quality an artist must have is objectivity in judging his work, plus the honesty and courage not to kid himself about it. Since none of my work has met my own standards, I must judge it on the basis of that one which caused me the most grief and anguish, as the mother loves the child who became the thief or murderer more than the one who became the priest.

Q: What work is that?

FAULKNER: *The Sound and the Fury*. I wrote it five separate times trying to tell the story, to rid myself of the dream which would continue to anguish me until I did. It's a tragedy of two lost women: Caddy and her daughter. Dilsey is one of my own favorite characters because she is brave, courageous,

generous, gentle and honest. She's much more brave and
honest and generous than me.

Q: How did *The Sound and the Fury* begin?

FAULKNER: It began with a mental picture. I didn't realize
at the time it was symbolical. The picture was of the muddy
seat of a little girl's drawers in a pear tree where she could see
through a window where her grandmother's funeral was taking
place and report what was happening to her brothers on the
ground below. By the time I explained who they were and
what they were doing and how her pants got muddy, I realized
it would be impossible to get all of it into a short story and
that it would have to be a book. And then I realized the
symbolism of the soiled pants, and that image was replaced
by the one of the fatherless and motherless girl climbing
down the rainpipe to escape from the only home she had,
where she had never been offered love or affection or understanding. I had already begun to tell it through the eyes
of the idiot child since I felt that it would be more effective
as told by someone capable only of knowing what happened,
but not why. I saw that I had not told the story that time.
I tried to tell it again, the same story through the eyes of
another brother. That was still not it. I told it for the third
time through the eyes of the third brother. That was still
not it. I tried to gather the pieces together and fill in the
gaps by making myself the spokesman. It was still not complete, not until 15 years after the book was published when
I wrote as an appendix to another book the final effort to
get the story told and off my mind, so that I myself could
have some peace from it. It's the book I feel tenderest towards.
I couldn't leave it alone, and I never could tell it right,
though I tried hard and would like to try again, though I'd
probably fail again.

Q: What emotion does Benjy arouse in you?

FAULKNER: The only emotion I can have for Benjy is grief
and pity for all mankind. You can't feel anything for Benjy
because he doesn't feel anything. The only thing I can feel
about him personally is concern as to whether he is believable
as I created him. He was a prologue like the gravedigger in
the Elizabethan dramas. He serves his purpose and is gone.

Benjy is incapable of good and evil because he had no knowledge of good and evil.

Q: Could Benjy feel love?

FAULKNER: Benjy wasn't rational enough even to be selfish. He was an animal. He recognized tenderness and love though he could not have named them, and it was the threat to tenderness and love that caused him to bellow when he felt the change in Caddy. He no longer had Caddy; being an idiot he was not even aware that Caddy was missing. He knew only that something was wrong, which left a vacuum in which he grieved. He tried to fill that vacuum. The only thing was he had one of Caddy's discarded slippers. The slipper was his tenderness and love which he could not have named, but he knew only that it was missing. He was dirty because he couldn't coordinate and because dirt meant nothing to him. He could no more distinguish between dirt and cleanliness than between good and evil. The slipper gave him comfort even though he no longer remembered the person to whom it had once belonged, any more than he could remember why he grieved. If Caddy had reappeared he probably would not have known her.

Q: Does the narcissus given to Benjy have some significance?

FAULKNER: The narcissus was given to Benjy to distract his attention. It was simply a flower which happened to be handy that 5th of April.[2] It was not deliberate.

Q: Are there any artistic advantages in casting the novel in the form of an allegory, as the Christian allegory you used in *A Fable*.

FAULKNER: Same advantage the carpenter finds in building square corners in order to build a square house. In *A Fable* the Christian allegory was the right allegory to use in that particular story, like an oblong square corner is the right corner with which to build an oblong rectangular house.

Q: Does that mean an artist can use Christianity simply as just another tool, like a carpenter would borrow a hammer?

FAULKNER: The carpenter we are speaking of never lacks that hammer. No one is without Christianity, if we agree on what we mean by the word. It is every individual's individual

code of behavior by means of which he makes himself a better
human being than his nature wants to be, if he followed his
nature only. Whatever its symbol—cross or crescent or whatever—that symbol is man's reminder of his duty inside the
human race. Its various allegories are the charts against which
he measures himself and learns to know what he is. It cannot
teach man to be good as the text book teaches him mathematics. It shows him how to discover himself, evolve for
himself a moral code and standard within his capacities and
aspirations, by giving him a matchless example of suffering
and sacrifice and the promise of hope. Writers have always
drawn, and always will, on the allegories of moral consciousness, for the reason that the allegories are matchless—the three
men in *Moby Dick,* who represent the trinity of conscience:
knowing nothing, knowing but not caring, knowing and
caring. The same trinity is represented in *A Fable* by the
young Jewish pilot officer who said 'This is terrible. I refuse
to accept it, even if I must refuse life to do so,' the old French
Quartermaster General who said, 'This is terrible, but we
can weep and bear it,' and the English battalion runner
who said, 'This is terrible, I'm going to do something about
it.'

Q: Are the two unrelated themes in *The Wild Palms*
brought together in one book for any symbolic purpose?
Is it as certain critics intimate a kind of esthetic counterpoint, or is it merely haphazard?

Faulkner: No, no. That was one story—the story of Charlotte Rittenmeyer and Harry Wilbourne, who sacrificed everything for love, and then lost that. I did not know it would be
two separate stories until after I had started the book. When I
reached the end of what is now the first section of *The Wild
Palms,* I realized suddenly that something was missing, it
needed emphasis, something to lift it like counterpoint in
music. So I wrote on the "Old Man" story until the "Wild
Palms" story rose back to pitch. Then I stopped the "Old
Man" story at what is now its first section, and took up the
"Wild Palms" story until it began to sag. Then I raised
it to pitch again with another section of its antithesis, which
is the story of a man who got his love and spent the rest of

the book fleeing from it, even to the extent of voluntarily going back to jail where he would be safe. They are only two stories by chance, perhaps necessity. The story is that of Charlotte and Wilbourne.

Q: How much of your writing is based on personal experience?

FAULKNER: I can't say. I never counted up. Because 'how much' is not important. A writer needs 3 things: experience, observation, imagination, any two of which, at times any one of which, can supply the lack of the others. With me, a story usually begins with a single idea or memory or mental picture. The writing of the story is simply a matter of working up to that moment, to explain why it happened or what it caused to follow. A writer is trying to create believable people in credible moving situations in the most moving way he can. Obviously he must use as one of his tools the environment which he knows. I would say that music is the easiest means in which to express, since it came first in man's experience and history. But since words are my talent, I must try to express clumsily in words what the pure music would have done better. That is, music would express better and simpler, but I prefer to use words as I prefer to read rather than listen. I prefer silence to sound, and the image produced by words occurs in silence. That is, the thunder and the music of the prose take place in silence.

Q: You mentioned experience, observation, and imagination as being important for the writer. Would you include inspiration?

FAULKNER: I don't know anything about inspiration because I don't know what inspiration is—I've heard about it, but I never saw it.

Q: As a writer you are said to be obsessed with violence.

FAULKNER: That's like saying the carpenter is obsessed with his hammer. Violence is simply one of the carpenter's tools. The writer can no more build with one tool than the carpenter can.

Q: Can you say how you started as a writer?

FAULKNER: I was living in New Orleans, doing whatever kind of work was necessary to earn a little money now and then. I met Sherwood Anderson. We would walk about the city in the afternoon and talk to people. In the evenings we would meet again and sit over a bottle or two while he talked and I listened. In the forenoon I would never see him. He was secluded, working. The next day we would repeat. I decided that if that was the life of a writer, then becoming a writer was the thing for me. So I began to write my first book. At once I found that writing was fun. I even forgot that I hadn't seen Mr. Anderson for three weeks until he walked in my door, the first time he ever came to see me, and said "What's wrong? Are you mad at me?" I told him I was writing a book. He said "My God" and walked out. When I finished the book—it was *Soldiers' Pay*—I met Mrs. Anderson on the street. She asked how the book was going and I said I finished it. She said, "Sherwood says that he will make a trade with you. If he doesn't have to read your manuscript he will tell his publisher to accept it." I said "Done" and that's how I became a writer.

Q: What were the kinds of work you were doing to earn that "little money now and then"?

FAULKNER: Whatever came up. I could do a little of almost anything—run boats, paint houses, fly aeroplanes. I never needed much money because living was cheap in New Orleans then, and all I wanted was a place to sleep, a little food, tobacco, and whisky. There were many things I could do for two or three days and earn enough money to live on for the rest of the month. By temperament I'm a vagabond and a tramp. I don't want money badly enough to work for it. In my opinion it's a shame that there is so much work in the world. One of the saddest things is that the only thing a man can do for eight hours a day, day after day, is work. You can't eat eight hours a day nor drink for eight hours a day nor make love for eight hours—all you can do for eight hours is work. Which is the reason why man makes himself and everybody else so miserable and unhappy.

Q: You must feel indebted to Sherwood Anderson, but how do you regard him as a writer?

FAULKNER: He was the father of my generation of American writers and the tradition of American writing which our successors will carry on. He has never received his proper evaluation. Dreiser is his older brother and Mark Twain the father of them both.

Q: What about the European writers of that period?

FAULKNER: The two great men in my time were Mann and Joyce. You should approach Joyce's *Ulysses* as the illiterate Baptist preacher approaches the Old Testament: with faith.

Q: How did you get your background in the Bible?[3]

FAULKNER: My Great-Grandfather Murry was a kind and gentle man, to us children anyway. That is, although he was a Scot, he was (to us) neither especially pious nor stern either: he was simply a man of inflexible principles. One of them was, everybody, children on up through all adults present, had to have a verse from the Bible ready and glib at tongue-tip when we gathered at the table for breakfast each morning; if you didn't have your scripture verse ready, you didn't have any breakfast; you would be excused long enough to leave the room and swot one up (there was a maiden aunt, a kind of sergeant-major for this duty, who retired with the culprit and gave him a brisk breezing which carried him over the jump next time).

It had to be an authentic, correct verse. While we were little, it could be the same one, once you had it down good, morning after morning, until you got a little older and bigger, when one morning (by this time you would be pretty glib at it, galloping through without even listening to yourself since you were already five or ten minutes ahead, already among the ham and steak and fried chicken and grits and sweet potatoes and two or three kinds of hot bread) you would suddenly find his eyes on you—very blue, very kind and gentle, and even now not stern so much as inflexible; and next morning you had a new verse. In a way, that was when you discovered that your childhood was over; you had outgrown it and entered the world.

Q: Some people say they can't understand your writing, even after they read it two or three times. What approach would you suggest for them?

FAULKNER: Read it four times.

Q: Do you read your contemporaries?

FAULKNER: No, the books I read are the ones I knew and
loved when I was a young man and to which I return as you
do to old friends: the Old Testament, Dickens, Conrad,
Cervantes—*Don Quixote*. I read that every year, as some
do the Bible. Flaubert, Balzac—he created an intact world
of his own, a bloodstream running through twenty books
—Dostoevsky, Tolstoi, Shakespeare. I read Melville occasionally, and of the poets: Marlowe, Campion, Jonson, Herrick,
Donne, Keats and Shelley. I still read Housman. I've read
these books so often that I don't always begin at page 1
and read on to the end. I just read one scene, or about one
character, just as you'd meet and talk to a friend for a few
minutes.

Q: And Freud?

FAULKNER: Everybody talked about Freud when I lived
in New Orleans, but I have never read him. Neither did
Shakespeare. I doubt if Melville did either, and I'm sure
Moby Dick didn't.

Q: Do you ever read mystery stories?

FAULKNER: I read Simenon because he reminds me something of Chekhov.

Q: What about your favorite characters?

FAULKNER: My favorite characters are Sarah Gamp—a cruel,
ruthless woman, a drunkard, opportunist, unreliable, most of
her character was bad, but at least it was character; Mrs.
Harris, Falstaff, Prince Hal, Don Quixote and Sancho, of
course. Lady Macbeth I always admire. And Bottom, Ophelia,
and Mercutio—both he and Mrs. Gamp coped with life,
didn't ask any favors, never whined. Huck Finn, of course,
and Jim. Tom Sawyer I never liked much—an awful prig.
And then I like Sut Lovingood from a book written by George
Harris about 1840 or '50 in the Tennessee mountains. He had
no illusions about himself, did the best he could; at certain
times he was a coward and knew it and wasn't ashamed;
he never blamed his misfortunes on anyone and never cursed
God for them.

Q: Would you comment on the future of the novel?

FAULKNER: I imagine as long as people will continue to
read novels, people will continue to write them, or vice versa;

unless of course the pictorial magazines and comic strips finally atrophy man's capacity to read, and literature really is on its way back to the picture writing in the Neanderthal cave.

Q: And how about the function of the critics?

FAULKNER: The artist doesn't have time to listen to the critics. The ones who want to be writers read the reviews, the ones who want to write don't have the time to read reviews. The critic too is trying to say "Kilroy was here." His function is not directed towards the artist himself. The artist is a cut above the critic, for the artist is writing something which will move the critic. The critic is writing something which will move everybody but the artist.

Q: So you never feel the need to discuss your work with anyone?

FAULKNER: No, I am too busy writing it. It has got to please me and if it does, I don't need to talk about it. If it doesn't please me, talking about it won't improve it, since the only thing to improve it is to work on it some more. I am not a literary man but only a writer. I don't get any pleasure from talking shop.

Q: Critics claim that blood relationships are central in your novels.

FAULKNER: That is an opinion and as I have said I don't read critics. I doubt that if a man trying to write about people is any more interested in blood relationships than in the shape of their noses, unless they are necessary to help the story move. If the writer concentrates on what he does need to be interested in, which is the truth and the human heart, he won't have much time left for anything else, such as ideas and facts like the shape of noses or blood relationships, since in my opinion ideas and facts have very little connection with truth.

Q: Critics also suggest that your characters never consciously choose between good and evil.

FAULKNER: Life is not interested in good and evil. Don Quixote was constantly choosing between good and evil, but then he was choosing in his dream state. He was mad. He entered reality only when he was so busy trying to cope with people, that he had no time to distinguish between good and evil. Since people exist only in life, they must devote their time simply to being alive. Life is motion and motion is concerned with what makes man move—which are ambition, power, pleasure. What time man can devote to morality, he must take by force from the motion of which he is a part. He is compelled to make choices between good and evil sooner or later. Because that moral conscience demands that from him in order that he can live with himself to-morrow. His moral conscience is the curse he had to accept from the Gods in order to gain from them the right to dream.

Q: Could you explain more what you mean by motion in relation to the artist?

FAULKNER: The aim of every artist is to arrest motion, which is life, by artificial means and hold it fixed so that 100 years later when a stranger looks at it, it moves again since it is life. Since man is mortal, the only immortality possible for him is to leave something behind him that is immortal since it will always move. This is the artist's way of scribbling "Kilroy was here" on the wall of the final and irrevocable oblivion through which he must someday pass.

Q: It has been said by Malcolm Cowley that your characters carry a sense of submission to their fate.

FAULKNER: That is his opinion. I would say that some of them do and some of them don't, like everybody else's characters. I would say that Lena Grove in *Light in August* coped pretty well with hers. It didn't really matter to her in her destiny whether her man was Lucas Burch or not. It was her destiny to have a husband and children and she knew it, and so she went out and attended to it without asking help from anyone. She was the captain of her soul. One of the calmest, sanest speeches I ever heard was when she said to Byron Bunch at the very instant of repulsing his final desperate and despairing attempt at rape, "Ain't you ashamed? You might have woke the baby." She was never for one moment confused, frightened, alarmed. She did not even know that she didn't need pity. Her last speech for example:

"Here I ain't been traveling but a month, and I'm already in Tennessee. My, my, a body does get around."

The Bundren family in *As I Lay Dying* pretty well coped with theirs. The Father having lost his wife would naturally need another one, so he got one. At one blow he not only replaced the family cook, he acquired a gramophone to give them all pleasure while they were resting. The pregnant daughter failed this time to undo her condition, but she was not discouraged. She intended to try again and even if they all failed right up to the last, it wasn't anything but just another baby.

Q: And Mr. Cowley says you find it hard to create characters between the ages of 20 and 40 who are sympathetic.

FAULKNER: People between 20 and 40 are not sympathetic. The child has the capacity to do but it can't know. It only knows when it is no longer able to do—after 40. Between 20 and 40 the will of the child to do gets stronger, more dangerous, but it has not begun to learn to know yet. Since his capacity to do is forced into channels of evil through environment and pressures, man is strong before he is moral. The world's anguish is caused by people between 20 and 40. The people around my home who have caused all the interracial tension—the Milams and the Bryants (in the Emmett Till murder) and the gangs of Negroes who grab a white woman and rape her in revenge, the Hitlers, Napoleons, Lenins—all these people are symbols of human suffering and anguish, all of them between 20 and 40.

Q: You gave a statement to the papers at the time of the Emmett Till killing. Have you anything to add to it here?

FAULKNER: No, only to repeat what I said before: that if we Americans are to survive it will have to be because we choose and elect and defend to be first of all Americans; to present to the world one homogeneous and unbroken front whether of white Americans or black ones or purple or blue or green. Maybe the purpose of this sorry and tragic error committed in my native Mississippi by two white adults on an afflicted Negro child is to prove to us whether or not we deserve to survive. Because if we in America have reached that point in our desperate culture when we must murder children, no matter for what reason or what color, we don't deserve to survive, and probably won't.

Q: What happened to you between *Soldiers' Pay* and *Sartoris*—that is what caused you to begin the Yoknapatawpha saga?

FAULKNER: With *Soldiers' Pay* I found out writing was fun. But I found out after that not only each book had to have a design but the whole output or sum of an artist's work had to have a design. With *Soldiers' Pay* and *Mosquitoes* I wrote for the sake of writing because it was fun. Beginning with *Sartoris* I discovered that my own little postage stamp of native soil was worth writing about and that I would never live long enough to exhaust it, and by sublimating the actual into apocryphal I would have complete liberty to use whatever talent I might have to its absolute top. It opened up a gold mine of other peoples, so I created a cosmos of my own. I can move these people around like God, not only in space but in time too. The fact that I have moved my characters around in time successfully, at least in my own estimation, proves to me my own theory that time is a fluid condition which has no existence except in the momentary avatars of individual people. There is no such thing as *was* —only *is*. If *was* existed there would be no grief or sorrow. I like to think of the world I created as being a kind of keystone in the Universe; that, as small as that keystone is, if it were ever taken away, the universe itself would collapse. My last book will be the Doomsday Book, the Golden Book, of Yoknapatawpha County. Then I shall break the pencil and I'll have to stop.

Notes

1. According to *Time* (May 28, 1956) Faulkner responded to a question as to whether he meant this literally by saying: "I am a fiction writer and I am not responsible for any construction made on any interview I have ever given."

2. The fourth section of *The Sound and the Fury* is actually dated April 8.

3. This question and its answer first appeared in the *Writers at Work* text and was apparently not part of the original interview. Malcolm Cowley, in a letter to one of the editors, recalled that he expressed to the interviewer a wish that Faulkner had said more about his familiarity with the Bible, and that she asked the additional question of Faulkner on a subsequent occasion.

⸙ 1956 ⸙

Interview with

RUSSELL HOWE

On February 21, 1956, at the New York offices of his publishers, Faulkner was interviewed by Russell Warren Howe,
then New York correspondent for the London Sunday Times.
The interview was published on March 4 in the Sunday Times,
and a longer and somewhat different version appeared in The
Reporter on March 22.

Excerpts from the Reporter version received wide circu-
lation in the American press within the next few weeks, and
one sentence, quoted out of context, soon became notorious.
This statement was inconsistent with the rest of the interview
and with the stand Faulkner had elsewhere taken upon the
racial problem, and he went to some pains to repudiate it. In
similar letters to the editors of The Reporter and of Time,
Faulkner declared that parts of the interview were incorrect,
and offered to share with the interviewer the blame for this
situation by saying that "statements which no sober man would
make, nor, it seems to me, any sane man believe," had been
imputed to him.

With Faulkner's letter in The Reporter (April 19, 1956) was
printed a rejoinder by Howe in which he affirmed the accuracy
of the interview, which had been "directly transcribed," he
said, "from verbatim shorthand notes." However, it is clear
that the interview must be treated with considerable caution,
not only because Faulkner repudiated parts of it, but also
because the two published versions differ from one another.

The text printed here is that from The Reporter, and
Faulkner's letter, with Howe's rejoinder, is also supplied.

"MY POSITION IS THIS," said Mr. Faulkner. "My people owned slaves and the very obligation we have to take care of these people is morally bad. It is a position which is completely untenable. But I would wish now that the liberals would stop—they should let us sweat in our own fears for a little while. If we are pushed by the government we shall become an underdog people fighting back because we can do nothing else. Our position is wrong and untenable but it is not wise to keep an emotional people off balance.

"The Negroes have had ninety years of that sort of life and now that they are winning it would take a lot of wisdom to say 'Go slow.' Perhaps it is too much to ask of them, but it is for their own sake. I have known Negroes all my life and Negroes work my land for me. I know how they feel. But now I have people who say they are Negroes writing to me and saying, 'You mean well for us but please hush. You mean good but you do harm.' "

Q: Wouldn't a "go slow" strategy lose some of the ground already gained?

FAULKNER: I don't know. I try to think of this in the long-term view. Now, I grant you that it is bad that there should be a minority people who because of their color don't have a right to social equality or to justice. But it is bad that Americans should be fighting Americans. That is what will happen because the Southern whites are back in the spirit of 1860. There could easily be another Civil War and the South will be whipped again.

In the long view, the Negro race will vanish in three hundred years by intermarriage. It has happened to every racial minority everywhere, and it will happen here.

Q: What would be the best strategy for the liberals?

FAULKNER: Let the people stop awhile. If that girl Autherine Lucy goes back to Alabama University . . . she will be killed. The N.A.A.C.P. should forget about Alabama University. It should send people now to the Universities of Georgia, Mississippi, and South Carolina and let them be thrown out of each of those places, too, until the white people of the South get so sick and tired of being harassed and worried they will have to do something about it. . . .

Q: Have you heard reports of arms buying in Tuscaloosa?

FAULKNER: Yes. If that girl dies, two or three white men will be killed, then eight or nine Negroes. Then the troops will come in. You know, we've never had race riots in the South before. They've had race riots in the North but in the South we just have persecution.

The South is armed for revolt. After the Supreme Court decision [of May 17, 1954, on school integration] you couldn't get as much as a few rounds for a deer rifle in Mississippi. The gunsmiths were sold out. These white people will accept another Civil War knowing they're going to lose. If the North knew the South they would know that this is not a theory or a moral convention which they are up against but a simple fact. I know people who've never fired a gun in their lives but who've bought rifles and ammunition.

Q: How long do you think it will be before the concrete aspects of discrimination—in housing, employment, enfranchisement, education, social contacts—will have disappeared?

FAULKNER: In the Deep South, I don't know. As it was, in fifteen years the Negroes would have had good schools. Then came the decision of the Supreme Court and that will mean probably twenty years of trouble. I think that decision put the position of the Negro in the South back five years.

Q: Does that mean that you disapprove of the Court decree?

FAULKNER: I don't disapprove it. It had to be promulgated and it just repeated what was said in January, 1863. If white folks had given Negroes proper schools there would have been no need for the Court's decision.

The Negro in the Deep South doesn't want to mix with the white man. He likes his own school, his own church. Segregation doesn't have to imply inferiority.

Q: How would you re-educate the Southern white to a different way of thinking?

FAULKNER: First of all, take off the pressure. Let him see just how untenable his position is. Let him see that people laugh at him. Just let him see how silly and foolish he looks. Give him time—don't force us. If that girl goes back to

Tuscaloosa she will die. Then the top will blow off. The government will send in its troops and we shall be back at 1860. They must stop pushing these people. The trouble is the North doesn't know that country. They don't know the South will go to war.

Things have been getting better slowly for a long time. Only six Negroes were killed by whites in Mississippi last year, according to the police figures. The Supreme Court decree came ninety years too late. In 1863 it was a victory. In 1954 it was a tragedy. The same thing is happening in South Africa, in Algeria. People were too ignorant of their fellow man and they realized his equality too late. This whole thing is not a confrontation of ideologies but of white folks against folks not white. It is world-wide. We must win the Indians, the Malayans, the sixteen million Negro Americans and the rest to the white camp, make it worth their while.

Q: Apart from your advice to promising Southerners, white and black, to get their education out of the South, what would your advice to an ambitious Negro be—to get out of the South altogether?

FAULKNER: No, he should stay in the South, where we need promising people, and be patient. Now is a time for calm, but that time will pass. The Negro has a right to equality. His equality is inevitable, an irresistible force, but as I see it you've got to take into consideration human nature, which at times has nothing to do with moral truths. Truth says this and the fact says that. A wise person says 'Let's use this fact. Let's obliterate this fact first.' To oppose a material fact with a moral truth is silly.

Q: The Negroes of Montgomery, the capital of Alabama, have been boycotting the city's busses since December 5. Do you think this sort of passive resistance is a good idea?

FAULKNER: Yes, anything they do is good as long as they don't carry it too far. Today the white women of Montgomery have to go and fetch their Negro cooks by car. It is a good step, to let the white folks see that the world is looking on and laughing at them.

But I don't like enforced integration any more than I like enforced segregation. If I have to choose between the

United States government and Mississippi, then I'll choose
Mississippi. What I'm trying to do now is not have to make
that decision. As long as there's a middle road, all right, I'll
be on it. But if it came to fighting I'd fight for Mississippi
against the United States even if it meant going out into
the street and shooting Negroes. After all, I'm not going
out to shoot Mississippians.

Q: You mean white Mississippians?

FAULKNER: No, I said Mississippians—in Mississippi the
problem isn't racial. Ninety per cent of the Negroes are on
one side with the whites, against a handful like me who believe
that equality is important.

Q: Some of your remarks could be interpreted as dis-
approval of the existence of militant Negro defense organiza-
tions. How do you feel about the N.A.A.C.P.?

FAULKNER: That organization is necessary, but it must
know when to let the opponent make the next move. Ninety
years of oppression and injustice are there, but it is a lot
for the white man to have to admit. It takes an extremely
intelligent man to stop dead after ninety years of wrong-
doing, and the Southerner isn't that intelligent. He has to
feel that what he is doing (when he reforms) is not being
forced on him but is spontaneous. We have to make it so
that he feels that he is being not just honest but generous.
Give him time—right now it's emotional and he'll fight
because the country's against him.

Q: In the European press, "go slow" is criticized on the
grounds that the susceptibilities of the persecuted deserve
more consideration than the susceptibilities of the persecutor.
How would you answer that criticism?

FAULKNER: The European critics are right, morally, but
there is something stronger in man than a moral condition.
Man will do certain things whether they be right or wrong.
We know that racial discrimination is morally bad, that it
stinks, that it shouldn't exist, but it does. Should we obliterate
the persecutor by acting in a way that we know will send
him to his guns, or should we compromise and let it work
out in time and save whatever good remains in those white
people?

Q: If the position in the South was reversed and the Negroes formed a majority which had been persecuting and murdering a white minority for ninety years, would you still say "go slow" on reform?

FAULKNER: Yes. Yes, I would. But the way we see it in the South, the way I see it, is that the Negro is in a majority, because he has the country behind him. He could have the support of the Federal army.

Q: Then you don't advise delays as an expedient because the Negro is outnumbered by over two to one in the South?

FAULKNER: No. Take the case of Autherine Lucy. I say she shouldn't go back to Tuscaloosa not because she'll be one against a mob of two thousand—there'll be a hundred million Americans behind her—but because she'll be killed.

The Negroes are right—make sure you've got that—they're right. But March 1 at Tuscaloosa is not a moral condition, it's a question of fact. I've always been on their [the Negroes'] side, but if there's no middle ground, if people like me have got to choose, then I'm on the side of Mississippi.

I will go on saying that the Southerners are wrong and that their position is untenable, but if I have to make the same choice Robert E. Lee made then I'll make it. My grandfather had slaves and he must have known that it was wrong, but he fought in one of the first regiments raised by the Confederate Army, not in defense of his ethical position but to protect his native land from being invaded.

Q: Do you believe regional loyalty is a good quality?

FAULKNER: Well, you must believe in something.

Q: What about your belief in the principles expressed in your books?

FAULKNER: I shouldn't be betraying them. My Negro boys down on the plantation would fight against the North with me. If I say to them "Go get your shotguns, boys," they'll come.

Q: The churches are segregated in the South. Don't you think the churches could do much to improve the South by sticking to Christian principles?

FAULKNER: They could do much more but they are afraid to open their mouths. The Catholics have made a few moves. . . .

Q: Is the basic cause of race prejudice economic, in your opinion?

FAULKNER: Absolutely. To produce cotton we have to have a system of peonage. That is absolutely what is at the bottom of the situation.

Q: Are the psychological rationalizations for prejudice something grafted onto the economic root?

FAULKNER: Yes. I would say that a planter who has a thousand acres wants to keep the Negro in a position of debt peonage and in order to do it he is going to tell the poor class of white folks that the Negro is going to violate his daughter. But all he wants at the back of it is a system of peonage to produce his cotton at the highest rate of profit.

Q: Do you see the basic problem as one of re-education?

FAULKNER: Yes, whites and Negroes must be re-educated to the issue. The most important thing is good schools. The trouble is that Southern white people are not interested in schools. Only the Negro cares about education. If we had good schools we could get good teachers.

Q: Isn't it Utopian to hope for a high standard of schools in a rural community?

FAULKNER: Yes, it's a Utopian dream, but it must be a good dream because there's always been someone to dream it.

Q: Do you agree that the ambition spur provided by persecution has made the Negro potentially the more capable of the two "races" in the South?

FAULKNER: Certainly. He's calmer, wiser, more stable than the white man. To have put up with this situation so long with so little violence shows a sort of greatness. Suppose two Negroes had murdered a white Emmett Till—there would have been a flood of emotionalism. The Negro rose above his anger. He knows that the problem [of his equality] will be solved because it must be. But these ignorant white people have got to be let alone so that they can think that they are changing on their own initiative.

The poor white man knows that although the Negro can only buy the worst land, has bad tools and inferior livestock, he can make a living better than white men could.

With a little more social, economic, and educational equality the Negro will often be the landlord and the white man will be working for him. And the Negro won't come out on top because of anything to do with the race but because he has always gotten by without scope—when they are given scope they use it fully. The Negro is trained to do more than a white man can with the same limitations.

The vices that the Negro has have been created in him by the white man, by the system. He will make his own contribution to our society. Already his music and poetry have passed to the white man, and what the white man has done with them is not Negro any more but something else.

There is no such thing as an "Anglo-Saxon" heritage and an African heritage. There is the heritage of man. Nothing is extinct in any race, only dormant. You are brave and tough when you have to be. You are intelligent when the age demands it. There are all things in like degree in all races.

Q: How is it for a man like you to live in Mississippi?

FAULKNER: I get a lot of insulting and threatening letters and telephone calls since I established my position. The tragic thing is that some of them come from Negroes. At least they say they're Negroes. It isn't just a solidarity of race—you get doctors and lawyers and preachers and newspaper editors and some Negroes too, all grouped against a few liberals like me. People phone me up to threaten my life at three or four in the morning—they're usually drunk by then.

Q: Do you carry a gun?

FAULKNER: No. My friends say I ought to carry a pistol. But I don't think anyone will shoot me, it would cause too much of a stink. But the other liberals in my part of the country carry guns all the time.

Faulkner's Letter to the Editor
of THE REPORTER

FROM LETTERS I have received, and from quotations from it I have seen in *Time* and *Newsweek*, I think that some parts of the interview with me which I gave to the London *Sunday Times* interviewer and which, after notifying me, he made available to you, are not correct; needless to say, I did not read the interview before it went to print, nor have I seen it yet as printed.

If I had seen it before it went to print, these statements, which are not correct, could never have been imputed to me. They are statements which no sober man would make, nor, it seems to me, any sane man believe.

The South is not armed to resist the United States that I know of, because the United States is neither going to force the South nor permit the South to resist or secede either.

The statement that I or anyone else would choose any one state against the whole remaining Union of States, down to the ultimate price of shooting other human beings in the streets, is not only foolish but dangerous. Foolish because no sane man is going to choose one state against the Union today. A hundred years ago, yes. But not in 1956. And dangerous because the idea can further inflame those few people in the South who might still believe such a situation possible.

Oxford, Mississippi

WILLIAM FAULKNER

Howe's Reply

ALL THE STATEMENTS attributed to Mr. Faulkner were directly transcribed by me from verbatim shorthand notes of the interview. If the more Dixiecrat remarks misconstrue his thoughts, I, as an admirer of Mr. Faulkner's, am glad to know it. But what I set down is what he said.

—◀ 1957 ▶—

Interview with

BETTY BEALE

*Published on June 12, 1957, this interview—like Miss Beale's
earlier interview with Faulkner (see pp. 77–79 above)—appeared
in the Washington Evening* Star. *In a letter to one of the
editors Miss Beale said that she wished she had never seen
Faulkner on this second occasion because she had been "so
enchanted with him" at their first meeting.*

WILLIAM FAULKNER, considered by many to be the greatest
living American novelist, resumed his oft-held battle with
the Fourth Estate last night.

The Nobel Prize winner said the·press has no integrity,
doesn't write the truth, and when it refrains from writing
bad things about people, it does so not from discrimination,
only from fear of libel. His excoriation included publishers
as well as reporters.

The press is not free, he said. Who is free? "A writer. I
am free. I write what I please," answered the novelist.

Reminded that he could do so because he wrote about
fictitious people, he replied, "I deal with people; you deal
with facts. Facts," said the Mississippian without explaining
whether he was talking in metaphysical terms, "bear no
relation to truth."

The small-statured, soft-spoken, gray-haired Southerner was
the honor guest at the big outdoor supper given by Mr. and

Mrs. Burks Summers and Mr. Paul Summers at the former's Rockville home, Holly Oaks.

The black tie gathering was also in honor of the former Virginia Summers and her husband, Col. Nathaniel Macon Martin, and the former Jill Faulkner, daughter of the novelist, and her husband, Paul Summers, Jr.

The latter received his law degree on Monday from the University of Virginia where his father-in-law has been visiting professor of literature for the last four months.

Paul and Jill liked Charlottesville so much they plan to stay on there for his practice of law. There are lots of lawyers already there, but it's the richest community in the country per capita, said Paul. His pretty blond wife corrected him. It has the biggest bank deposits per capita of any other community in the country, said Jill.

Her mother was the only member of the family to miss the party. Mr. Faulkner said his wife was ill with a kidney infection, so remained in Charlottesville. Three years ago, just before their daughter's wedding, they both attended a similar outdoor party at Holly Oaks. At that time the famous chronicler of the Snopes family was so agreeably forthright and witty he charmed this reporter right off her typewriter.

Last evening the great man was neither in a gay nor talkative mood. After standing in line to receive the 200 guests, he came out on the porch of the white stone house, where he was approached by three or four admirers.

What did he think of a particular criticism of his newest book, *The Town*? "I never read criticisms," he replied. . . . Among his contemporaries, who was his favorite author? "I don't read them," he said. "I only like to read the books I read when I was a child."

"How about Thomas Wolfe?" "He bores me," was William Faulkner's reply. Reminded he had gone on record in praise of Wolfe, he said he had read some of his works but never finished them. . . . One had the feeling that it was not the real Faulkner talking, simply the mood he was in. Or perhaps deep down inside he was tickled, but his expression was too deadpan to tell.

The University of Virginia has asked him to return for another semester. Would he do so?

He replied in a negative vein.

He thought they ought to get someone else. He doubted if one had more to give after four months or if there was really a need for someone like him.

His next remark was greeted with chuckles. He had sat in his office, he said, and answered questions of the students —questions that either a priest or a veterinarian could have answered.

But when Mrs. James Kem's daughter, who lives in Charlottesville asked Mr. Faulkner if he would return there, he very pleasantly indicated he would.

Why the discrepancy between the two replies?

"I never tell the truth to reporters," said the novelist. Alas! To the best of these reportorial ears, all the above is true.

Interview with

SIMON CLAXTON

Mr. Claxton, an English boy studying at the Cate School in California, interviewed Faulkner in Oxford on March 23, 1962; the interview was published in The Cate Review, *June 1962. It is interesting to watch Faulkner's immediate hostility to an intruder gradually melting under the influence of the young interviewer's pleasant manners and, no doubt, his own Anglophilia, which seems to come out quite strongly in the closing paragraphs.*

YOU GO INTO OXFORD, MISSISSIPPI, and ask, and more or less anybody can tell you. However, though they may know where he lives, it is with no great friendliness that they speak of him: rather, it is with something between awe and fear. One man in a filling station pointed up the road and wished me luck in a threatening chuckle, as if he never expected to see me come out alive. All of this was not particularly encouraging, as I'd heard that Faulkner was a man who hated all strangers, especially interviewers, and who rarely lets them leave with anything valuable anyway. Still the worst that he could do was throw me out, and I had written a long and (I thought) beautiful letter, explaining who I was and why I wanted to talk to him. So it was with a good deal of trepidation, but also with a sense of amused audacity, that I set off down the road.

Faulkner's house is in a particularly attractive residential area on the outskirts of Oxford. Though his drive is only two or three minutes down a side road from a busy highway, it is beautifully peaceful. Oxford was enjoying the first signs of Spring that morning—the sky was blue, the flowers were out and the grass was a brilliant green. Faulkner, it appeared, had a few neighbors, who live in attractive houses with well-kept gardens down the side of the road. Apart from these—and one is never actually conscious of them—there is little to stop you thinking you're not in the depths of the country.

This impression is strengthened when you come to the entrance to Faulkner's house, a gateless gap in the fence, from which an overgrown and ragged drive meanders through the trees and up to the front door. The house is one of the white-painted, wooden, porticoed variety that are so numerous in the South. One glance at it, however, was enough to make my excitement vanish and my high spirits sink; for it was blatantly obvious that nobody lived in the house—all the windows were closed, the front door, I discovered, was locked and everything was very, very quiet. There was, though, something about the place that told me it was occupied, in spite of the dead quiet, which gave it the atmosphere of a house that had been deserted in the Civil War and not entered since. For instance, there was a cow tied to a tree in the drive, and a horse in a paddock nearby. I knew that Faulkner rode, but how did a horse make sense with a house that was so deserted? He must be out, I decided in disappointed resignation. Yet further investigation revealed a bright orange Fiat by the back door, which was open. Mystery . . . I had, however, already given up hope when I realized there was still one side of the house I had not checked on. So, more or less as a matter of form, a final hopeless check, I wandered to the other end of the verandah and peered round.

The first thing I saw was a man 100 yards away in the trees, working with an axe: here, at least, was somebody to ask. Then, just as I was about to move forward, I noticed an old man in a wicker chair, about 25 yards down the verandah in the shade. It was Faulkner. I shot back round the corner, and swallowed hard. He had just been sitting there, looking out towards the trees, completely and utterly still—just as if he'd been sitting there for weeks. What could I do? I had already rung the doorbell many times and nothing had happened. Should I look round the corner again and discreetly cough in the hope that it would attract his attention? Something told me it wouldn't. There was something about the figure and the legend surrounding it that prompted me to get out while the going was good, but I didn't have the heart to, having come so far. In the end I walked firmly but cautiously round the side of the building and straight up to him. He didn't hear me coming till I was within a few yards of him. He then stood up very sedately, and stared at me. (Courage, man) I flung out a hand:

"My name is Claxton, sir. Did you get my letter?"

"No." My heart sank.

But everything was O.K. I said that if possible I'd like a few minutes with him because I had some questions to ask and I'd be extremely honored if he would etc. etc. I had, however, only to say a few words before he said, "Certainly . . . be delighted to answer any questions you have," and started looking around for a chair for me. I was overwhelmed by this reception, for I had half been expecting a fire-breathing ogre, incensed even more by somebody prowling about in his garden. I had consequently prepared a little speech all about author's reports and exchange students and England and all the other things I thought might make him reconsider throwing me out, if he at any time was prepared to do so. And to have the man shake my hand the moment I introduced myself, which he had done, and produce a seat and sit down with me as if we were old friends . . . was incredible! In fact, so disappointed was I that I wasn't going to be able to give my last ditch speech, I gave it there and then. It served as a useful introduction, but I got the impression that he couldn't really have cared who I was (for he had asked me to sit down even before I said I was English), and that he would have done the same with anybody.

Anyway, by the time I had had my say, he had dug a chair

up from the back of the verandah and we sat down. As can
be expected after so promising a start, all my fears were
waived aside, though I still couldn't quite believe I was there.
Thus, already with a sense of achievement at having pene-
trated the lair of the old man himself, I got out my dirty
bit of paper on which I had written the questions I had
thought of to ask him, in the unlikely event of my ever
seeing him. Perhaps, before starting the interview, I should
say something about Faulkner himself.

Faulkner is a short, small man, with, for instance, tiny
feet. However, though he may not be very big physically,
he radiates enormous strength as a character. His face has a
set, serious expression, which many would call hard and cruel.
He rarely smiles. His whole person is centered on the face,
and especially on the eyes which are steady and small and
black, but terribly strong and, one feels, all-seeing. It is a
lined face with a hard mouth and small moustache. He,
even at 64, has a lot of white hair. The whole body is very
still. He rarely moves: throughout the interview he sat cross-
legged, looking from me to the trees with the same penetrating
stare. Everything about the way he holds himself is stately
and sedate, composed and motionless—almost to an inhuman
extent. He is very dignified and strong, you can feel it in
the air. His voice is not particularly impressive, and, though
I wasn't looking for one at the time, I don't remember a strong
Southern accent. He is not a great talker, in fact he is not a
talker at all: he will speak only to answer your questions. He
will just sit there as if he wasn't ever going to move; you can
ask him anything you like, he will give you an answer straight
away, he may add to it after a few moments of silence, but
then he shuts up again like a clam. He is a very passive man.
As for his personal appearance, never have I seen anybody
so scruffily dressed in what were basically good clothes. He
was wearing a dirty, old, patched tweed jacket, a patched
green shirt, a tattered tie, a pair of khaki pants which left
about four inches of bony ankle showing, white socks and a
pair of dirty old farm boots. This is not to say that he himself was not clean or shaven: that is the funny part about it.

Somehow it suited him: he is really very photogenic, but when you look at him, you can't escape from those eyes. In a way they are friendly smiling eyes, in another they are cruel. One gets a different impression every time. A withered old face . . . glittering hooded eyes.

As I say, he gives you the impression of having sat there for weeks, just the way he was when I arrived, fondling the empty pipe he always has in his hand. So you take your time. I asked his permission to take notes, and he readily gave it. I looked at my questions and cursed myself for not thinking of any better ones, and for not arranging the ones I'd got in a better connected order. Then I took a deep breath and started. The atmosphere was almost sleepy.

"I'd first like to compliment you on your house and town, both of which I think are very attractive."

"Oh yes," he said, looking out over the trees. It was astonishingly still. "They are very nice. It changes, you know. More cars—more people than there were 30 years ago."

"That brings me on to my first question, sir. Has there been much change between the Mississippi you were portraying in *Light in August* and *Sanctuary,* and the Mississippi of today?"

"Of course there has. Any place changes, doesn't it? Any place at all."

Stupid question deserves a stupid answer, I suppose. I think he missed my point though, as I really wanted to know whether the problems were very different: I hadn't made myself clear though. Off to a bad start, however, I assumed that the problems were as great, and passed on before I should lose courage. Of course it took me time to decipher my writing, so between questions there were long pauses, in which Faulkner just sat there, looking out at the trees, moving his pipe about in his hand. When I asked another question, he would turn and look at me. I took my time, and fortunately was completely unruffled. You see, if you speak to him firmly and sensibly, he will be kind. He doesn't like people that dither. So I worked out the questions as coherently as I could before asking them.

"Sir, can you tell me a little about the French Quarter in New Orleans, where you spent six months of your youth?"

"Depends what you want to know about it."

"Well, for a start, where did you live?"

"Quite near St. Louis Cathedral—on Royal Street." (Poking with his foot on the floor: the only time he moved throughout.)

"Would you think that New Orleans has changed very much since you were there?"

"I really don't know."

"Did there use to be artists as well as literary figures in those days?"

"Oh yes. Many."

"One notices them—the artists—of course, but it is hard to tell whether there are many authors still about. Would you think there would be?"

"I should think so."

"Sir, I notice that you have a short story coming out in the *Saturday Evening Post* next week?"

"Yes. The 31st." (Then, noticing that I wasn't sure if he meant the 31st story in the *Post* or what—) "The edition of the 31st."

It was obviously time to get him to say something. I felt rather put off by the conversation to date. He wasn't exactly being unfriendly, but I was not getting on very well.

"Can you tell me a little about the story?"

"It is part of a novel I have been writing. A couple of chapters from the novel . . . (the voice trailing away).

"When will the novel be ready?"

"In June."

"How long has it taken you to write it?"

"A few weeks. About six weeks. Two months maybe."

"Sir, in the summer and fall, you go to the University of Virginia, don't you?"

"Not to the University really. My position there is very small and easy. I don't really do a thing. I really go there for the fox-hunting."

"Do you do any work while you're over there?"

"Not really. I go, as I say, for the fox-hunting."

"Do you find that you need the change?"

"Not particularly."

"Then you could stay here and work consistently for a whole novel without being tired or needing a change of situation or anything?"

"Yes, writing is all sweat—a question of sticking it out."

"But presumably enjoyable sweat?"

"Yes. Enjoyable sweat. Otherwise you wouldn't do it."

"While we are on the subject of writing technique, a man who interviewed you last year for *Life* quoted you as saying that you didn't work to set hours every day because 'it took the fun out of it.'[1] Would you still stick to this?"

(Chuckle) "I'm liable to say anything on these occasions, and often contradict myself. Yes, I remember talking to that man. I wouldn't necessarily say that now though. It varies. Sometimes I set myself a time limit—and sometimes not. It depends on the book and whether I want to get it finished quickly."

"So you can really write at any time? You don't have to be in the right mood or anything?"

"No. If I find I have something to say, I can go in and say it anytime."

"Would you say, sir, that a knowledge of other literature is essential for a writer?"

"Yes. A writer must read everything. We yearn to be as good as Shakespeare and the only way to get better is through studying. Just as a carpenter has to know everything about wood-cuts before he's a good carpenter, and a cathedral builder all about building before he's a good cathedral builder. Reading is part of writing."

"So we should all try to study literature as much as possible?"

"Certainly."

"Sir, you must be conscious of the fact that your novels are not at all liked by many people, because they depict such a depressing picture of the South—one which they think is untrue, and which it is at least unnecessary to talk about. Does this concern you at all?"

"No. It doesn't worry me. I don't read **reviews**. I'm not

interested. I really couldn't care what other people say about me. It wouldn't affect me anyway. I should still write. Writing is my particular cup of tea."

"What, sir, is your objective in writing? Are you trying to portray the South as you see it—as essentially an area of depravity and poverty?"

"No. I'm a story-teller. I'm telling a story, introducing comic and tragic elements as I like. I'm telling a story—to be repeated and retold. I don't claim to be truthful. Fiction is fiction—not truth; it's make-believe. Thus I stack and lie at times, all for the purposes of the story—to entertain."

"Thus, apart from the knowledge you've accumulated in your lifetime in the South, you've done no research on the problems you are dealing with?"

"No, I use materials at hand. I have no purpose to present the truth, but only a story. I may introduce comic and tragic elements, but they are to illustrate Man in his dilemma—facing his environment. As for anybody who doesn't like my stories, they don't have to read them, do they?"

"On a previous occasion, sir, you have said that a writer can never produce a perfect story, though other craftsmen can achieve 100% perfection. Is it really not possible to write a perfect story?"

"I don't think so. After all, presumably a writer goes on writing because he is not satisfied with his work, and thus wants to get it better. He will always find fault in his work, though possibly his readers may not. He will, then, always keep trying."

"Does a writer need to have experienced first-hand all he writes about?"

"Not necessarily first-hand. There are a thousand and one sources from which a writer can pick his material. He has to pick and choose always, to modify and exaggerate for his story, so that he gets what he wants. He never can do so just from one source. He may have to borrow from books, plays, films, anything."

"Even though these may not necessarily be true to life and to fact?"

"The novelist does not want truth: he wants to create a

story, with his imagination and facts helping of course."

"Sir, you haven't produced so many novels in the last few years as you did, say, before the war . . ."

". . . I wouldn't say that. I'm always writing. Perhaps not very regularly, but I don't think you can make any statement about a lapse."

"I was going to ask, sir, whether any slowdown had resulted from your becoming less satisfied or happy with life."

(Pause . . .) "I don't understand what you mean."

"Are you just as happy and contented with life as you always have been?"

"Oh yes. I'm very contented. Of course at my age, one is naturally less active: I lack the heat and fury of when I was 30. But I'm very contented. This is an easy life—I enjoy the fox-hunting, the quail-shooting, and I still write."

"Do you do any other travelling apart from your trips to Charlottesville?"

"No."

"And do you make them every year without fail?"

"Yes."

"Have you ever had trouble with writing—I mean the actual work?"

"Not really. I don't have to be in a special mood or write at a specific speed. I take my time."

"What about revisions? How many do you make to a piece of work?"

"As many as are necessary. Quite a few. One has to keep touching everything up, it's never perfect, I'm never satisfied."

"Sir, we were talking earlier about truth in the portrayal of men. Do you have any particular theories about the future of mankind?"

"No. It doesn't concern me, I don't think about it. I'm confident that he will outlive all other things, even the wheel and the A-Bomb, just as he has outlived the dinosaur."

"Sir, have you seen any of the movies made from your books?"

"No. I don't go to the movies. They come at suppertime, you see, and I would have to break up the evening to go. I prefer to stay at home, have a good supper, have a drink."

"But wouldn't you want to go to one of your own movies?"

"Least of all one of my movies, because I would know what was going to happen."

"Am I right in thinking that Oxford is the prototype for the Jefferson in your books?"

"Not really. It is, of course, more so than any other place, because I grew up here. Geographically, Jefferson is about thirty miles to the West.[2] But all these towns add to Jefferson. One can't pick from only one without wasting good material."

"William Van O'Connor says that you always work in the greatest neatness, writing each page in ink and then putting it face-down in a neat pile. The *Life* article, however, says that you type everything, and with two fingers."

"I use whichever is more convenient at any time. I have no cut and dry system of writing. I write all over the place, almost anywhere and with anything that is to hand. I am neither neat in work or in anything else. Mr. O'Connor must have been thinking of somebody else."

"Do you have any more plans for books after the June novel is completed?"

"Not at the moment."

"Can you tell me anything about the novel? What is it to be called?"

"*The Reivers*—it's an old Highland name for a robber."

"Though it's got a Highland title, it's presumably about the South?"

"Oh yes. It's about a white man, a boy and a negro, who trade an old car for a racehorse."

"Do you get to the town very often?"

"About once every day now, usually in the morning for the shopping."

"And are the people friendly to you?"

"As far as I know."

"Every morning you go riding too, don't you?"

"Most: sometimes I don't go at all, sometimes in the afternoon or evening, but usually every morning."

"Before breakfast?"

"Yes. But again, I'm not systematic about my riding times."

"Is there any fox-hunting here?"

"No, there are a lot of fences, farms, fields close together."

"Sir, this isn't the original family home, is it?"

"No. We lived outside the town. I bought this house some time ago and restored it."

"Then you also farm, I believe?"

"Yes. Not as much as I used to. But it is still a worry, even if I don't live out there any more."

"Sir, what advice would you give to a prospective young writer?"

"Read a lot, and of everything—fiction, biography, history, law. I read all the law and medical books of my father and grandfather. Because they were dealing with men, with Man in his human dilemma. Wherever man is involved, he becomes the victim of the writer's will. Secondly, don't worry about the reception given your books. Maybe one day a badly received book will be acclaimed a masterpiece."

"Is it important to know the history of the South before being able to understand it?"

"Only in so far as history is the work of men and we should thus learn all we can from it. It always has its uses. I *wanted* to learn about the South—that's why I read history. But we aren't specifically concerned with it, though it is always round us. Mankind was in the past, and is in the present and will be in the future."

"You would also tell a prospective writer, presumably, not to worry overmuch about portraying the truth?"

"Yes. Let him remember that a novel is to create pleasure for the reader. The only mistake with any novel is if it fails to create pleasure. That it is not true is irrelevant: a novel is to be enjoyed. A book that fails to create enjoyment is not a good one."

This marked the end of the interview, as I had come to the end of my questions. We sat there quite happily for a few moments in silence, until I felt I should get out. So I thanked him again, he shook my hand, smiled and walked half-way down the drive with me. We talked about Cate and the English-Speaking Union, which he appeared to be very interested in, and then he asked me questions about England, and said that he hoped I was enjoying his country as much as he had enjoyed mine. He apparently knew the Lake District.

In fact he lingered such a long time that I couldn't go for quite a while. Of course I didn't want to go, but I felt I wasn't fulfilling any useful function in my staying, as I couldn't think of any other questions, and I was sure he wouldn't start telling me about himself. Besides it was getting on for lunchtime, and I finally tore myself away and left him. He waved and wished me luck.

In retrospect, I was enormously pleased. I think the secret of Faulkner and of the frigid cloud of awe that surrounds him is that he will relax and accept anyone who has something to ask or say to him. On the other hand, a person who just asked him to speak would not get anywhere. Many have made this mistake, and hence the relative failure of the interview. Faulkner is a great man, but he hates being waited on as a kind of Delphian Oracle: on the other hand, he will be only too delighted to talk to somebody with a genuine interest, in a man-to-man discussion.

Notes

1. Elliott Chaze, "Visit to Two-Finger Typist," *Life*, July 14, 1961.
2. It is tempting to think that Faulkner may actually have said "to the East," and Mr. Claxton, in a letter to one of the editors, has accepted the possibility of a misquotation here.

Interview with

VIDA MARKOVIĆ

Professor Vida Marković, chairman of the English Department at the University of Belgrade, interviewed Faulkner in Charlottesville, Virginia, on May 6, 1962. The text here is taken from Texas Studies in Literature and Language, *Vol. V (Winter 1964).*

Q: I have wanted so much to meet you, Mr. Faulkner, and tell you how widely read you are in Yugoslavia and how people admire you. I am so happy I have been given the chance to talk to you. Your Virginia is beautiful, so bright and full of color. I think I can better understand you and your work and your characters when I imagine them as living here. You love Virginia, don't you?

FAULKNER: I like fox-hunting—(comes the brief answer in a deep Southern accent).

Q: You like animals, don't you?

FAULKNER: I like horses and dogs—

Q: You like them more than people.

FAULKNER: I like intelligent animals. Horses are intelligent, and so are dogs. Not as intelligent as rats.

Q: I don't know anything about rats, but I know that pigs are intelligent. My father was an agronomer and he thought pigs extra intelligent. You like nature. You don't like to live in the town, do you?

FAULKNER: I don't like the hustle and bustle. I like peace and quiet.

Q: Do you often go to town?

FAULKNER: No, not often.

Q: You spend all your time here, and you write here?

FAULKNER: I am not writing now. There is a lot of work in the fields. I am here in winter, and in Oxford, Mississippi, in summer. I have a farm there, a lot of work. Land has to be tilled.

Q: What do you grow?

FAULKNER: Cotton and wheat. Not much fruit—it does not pay.

Q: Don't you go to town, to theatres and cinemas?

FAULKNER: No. If I could ride into a theatre on horseback, I would go. I like riding. I don't like buses and cars. Imagine if I rode straight into a theatre and asked the attendant: "Will you park my horse, please—"

Q: I can easily understand that you cannot be bothered to go to town. But I think I could not resist curiosity. I would have to peep into towns here and there and see what is happening, what has changed in life and people. You don't like the present colorless way of life of our industrial age, you don't like the rush and hurry?

FAULKNER: People do not change. No industrialization will change them. From time out of memory people have changed very little. They live more in towns at present, they used to live in the country before. But youth is youth; it does not change. When I was young, I liked that kind of restless life. I rushed all over America and the world. I took an interest in everything. And now I prefer to be here. Have you seen how neglected the fields are here? In my time all the land was tilled. Now everybody rushes into towns and the land is decaying.

Q: So you don't write in summer, you take a hand in the field work, like a real farmer, and leave all your writing for the winter?

FAULKNER: I write when I feel like it; there is no rule about it.

Q: Your novels have revealed the genuine America to us and the life in it. We have understood the importance of the Civil War, the way of life here, the relationship between the white people and the Negroes, the deep and far-reaching problem of the Negroes, the solution of which resides in themselves. Where did you take the subjects for your novels? Did they come out of the stories you listened to in your childhood?

FAULKNER: I cannot talk about my books. I don't remember them. I remember people, I write about people. They are alive. I don't remember the books. Once I have written them they no longer belong to me. I never go back to them. I don't read them. Other people read my books; once I have written them I have nothing to do with them any longer.

Q: Where do you take the characters for your novels? Who are the models on which you build them?

FAULKNER: I write about people, real people, people I used to know; I really know them.

Q: Do you like reading? Who are your favorite authors?

FAULKNER: I have no favorite authors. I have favorite books.

Q: Do you like James Joyce, his *Portrait of the Artist* or his *Ulysses?*

FAULKNER: I have read *Ulysses* once.

Q: How do you like it?

FAULKNER: It is interesting, but I probably did not like it, for I never went back to it. One goes back to the books one likes.

Q: Which books do you like? Which are the books you go back to?

FAULKNER: Every year I read *Don Quixote,* the Bible, an hour of Dickens, *The Brothers Karamazov,* Chekhov—

Q: *The Brothers Karamazov,* do you like Dostoevsky?

FAULKNER: I know nothing about Dostoevsky. I like *The Brothers Karamazov*— Is not Abraham a fine old rascal? I like him.

Q: Do you like myths, Mr. Faulkner?

FAULKNER: I like myths because they are about people.

Q: Life used to be richer before, didn't it? Don't you regret the way of life that is gone, the life that persists in your books, do you not regret the past?

FAULKNER: I prefer nature. But I did not mind the noise and the hustle and bustle before, when I was young and wild. Youth is always wild— When one is young, life is different.

Q: Do you like writing?

FAULKNER: I used to when I was young.

Q: Do you like traveling? You were in Paris. Do you like Paris?

FAULKNER: Everybody likes Paris, especially when one is young. A few years ago I was in Japan, Italy, and Iceland. State Department sent me.

Q: Did you enjoy it?

FAULKNER: It was interesting. I liked Italy. The people. Most undependable, but charming, gay and full of life. They know how to enjoy life, they know how to live.

Q: Do you go fox-hunting in style, in those red jackets and all that, like the English?

FAULKNER: Of course we do. This is a sport. (Little William Faulkner[1] is making his way toward his grandfather. He pulls him by the arm. Faulkner bends down toward him and talks to him affectionately. He beams while addressing the little boy.)

Q: Are you firm with children?

FAULKNER: I have never been, with my own either. I am not firm with those here nor the other two in Oxford, Mississippi. (It is time to go. We have spent more than an hour and a half with Faulkner. He courteously accompanies us to the car.)

Q: Thank you very much indeed. I hope I shall see you in Yugoslavia one day.

FAULKNER: If the State Department sends me— (We shake hands.) I don't know whether you have got what you expected of this interview. I am sorry. I am not a conversationalist. I can write; I cannot talk.

Q: I remember now why your voice seemed familiar to me, Mr. Faulkner. I have listened to the recording of your Nobel Prize Address. (Faulkner smiles, and both he and his little grandson wave goodbye until our car disappears from their sight.)

Note

1. His daughter Jill's son, William Faulkner Summers.

INDEX A

Faulkner's References
to His Own Works

I. BOOKS

II. STORIES, ESSAYS, SCREENPLAYS

–◄ INDEX B ►–

Faulkner's References
to Other Authors

→⊶ INDEX C ⊷←

Thematic

I. ART AND THE ARTIST

1. Art

The permanence of art: 103, 238, 253
As the record of man's endurance: 73, 103, 177-178, 202
As the salvation of mankind: 71
And the experience of disaster: 108, 180-181, 209-210

2. The Artist

Only his work important: 137, 238
His perseverance: 20, 176-177, 203, 211, 240
His rapacity and amorality: 128, 181, 239
And economic freedom: 124, 240
And government subsidisation: 211
And success: 212, 219, 227, 240
And his critics: 175, 252, 280
The artist in America: 82, 182, 193-194, 212

The agony of creation: 71-72
Inspiration: 55, 248
His compulsion to work: 36, 55, 220, 239
His striving for perfection: 81, 106-107, 116-117, 122, 180, 204-205, 238, 244, 277
The splendor of failure: 88-89, 121-122, 179-180, 225, 238
His immortality: "Kilroy was here": 103, 106, 227, 252, 253
Influence of social and intellectual environment: 104-105, 177, 202-203, 203-204, 207-209

His responsibilities: 56, 71, 94, 124, 200-202, 212, 235, 239, 243
Must believe in man: 94, 97, 200, 202, 226
And truth: 93, 106-107, 113, 116-117, 201, 202, 204, 278-279

III. LIFE AND WORK

1. Life

Family background: 7, 9, 65, 65-66, 101, 129, 232, 233, 258, 262
Childhood: 17, 29-30, 62, 65, 66, 139, 184, 224, 250
Education: 7, 13, 108, 134, 197
World War I: 5, 7, 17, 23-24, 31-32, 57-58, 133
1920-1930: 3-4, 7-8, 11-13, 13-14, 20, 26, 218; New Orleans: 11-12, 62, 66, 117-118, 218-219, 233, 248-249, 275; Paris: 219, 233
1930-1950: 26, 33-34, 59; Hollywood: 33, 40-41, 57, 64, 75-76, 223, 240, 241-243
1950-1962: 63, 65, 74, 75, 77, 84-86, 264, 269, 275; as cultural ambassador: 82, 187-188, 233; *see also* Introduction, xiii-xv

Drinking: 13, 21, 62, 75, 149, 240
Eating: 25-26, 27, 66
Flying: 23-24, 31-32, 138-139, 218
Horses and riding: 64, 75-76, 88, 139, 149, 169, 192, 234, 279, 282, 283
Hunting: 139, 149, 275, 279, 282, 285
Reading: 17, 21, 48-49, 56, 59-60, 110-111, 119, 134-135, 217, 234, 251, 268, 280, 284
Sailing: 88, 149
Smoking: 117

His children: 139, 170-171, 285; his daughter Jill: 75-76, 162
Effects of increasing age: 278, 283, 285
His preference for silence and solitude: 8, 64, 283; *see also* Introduction, ix-xii
His relationship with the people of Oxford: 20, 24, 62, 65, 233, 279
His satisfaction with his life: 148, 213, 278
His way of speaking: 128-129
See also The South: Own attitudes

2. His Role as Writer

A farmer, not a literary man: 59, 64, 169, 191-192, 216, 234, 280, 283
A writer, not a literary man: 61, 108, 252
Interested in people not ideas: 134, 188
A storyteller: 220, 277

IV. LITERATURE

1. The Novel

2. *American Literature*

3. *Other Literatures*

4. *General Topics*

V. PLACES AND PEOPLES

◄◄ *About the Editors* ►►

JAMES B. MERIWETHER *was born in South Carolina in 1928. He received his B.A. from the University of South Carolina, his M.A. and Ph.D. from Princeton. He has taught at the University of Texas and the University of North Carolina, and is now Professor of English at the University of South Carolina. Previous publications include* The Literary Career of William Faulkner, *and he has edited books by Faulkner and by Joyce Cary.*

MICHAEL MILLGATE *was born in Southampton, England, in 1929. He studied at St. Catherine's College, Cambridge, at the University of Michigan, and at the University of Leeds, and for several years taught English and American literature at Leeds, and at York University, Toronto. He is now Professor of English at University College, University of Toronto. Previous publications include* William Faulkner, American Social Fiction: James to Cozzens, *and* The Achievement of William Faulkner, *as well as articles on various aspects of English and American literature.*